THE CONTENT SHIFT

THE CONTENT SHIFT

WHY A *SEARCH MINDSET* IS ESSENTIAL TO YOUR CONTENT MARKETING STRATEGY

Mark Hawks
Jonathan Heinl

Copyright © 2022 by Mark Hawks and Jonathan Heinl

All rights reserved. No part of this book may be reproduced or used in any manner without the prior written permission of the copyright owner, except for the use of brief quotations in a book review.

To request permissions, contact the publisher SEO Savvy at contentshift@seosavvy.com.

Paperback: ISBN 979-8-218-06235-4

First paperback edition December 2022.

Project & Development Editor: Nancy Lynée Woo
Research & Stats Editor: Auroriele Hans
Copyeditor: Sarah Cisco
Indexing: Cheryl Lenser
Book design and illustrations by Daniel Lagin

SEO Savvy
6475 E Pacific Coast Hwy, PMB 451
Long Beach, CA 90803
562-912-3493

www.ContentShift.com

Printed in the United States of America

Contents

Introduction 1
    Why You Should Read This Book 5
    Who We Are 6
    What Is the Content Shift? 8
    The Struggle Is Real, the Solution Is Strategy 9
    How to Read This Book 11

PART ONE: CONTENT 15

1. Let's Talk About Content 17
    Wait, but What Is "Content"? 18
    Content Marketing Is Added Value—First 21
    Content Marketing Is Permission Marketing 22
    Content Marketing Is Pull Marketing 24
    The Golden Rule: Provide Value, Inspire Action 26

2. Great Content Builds Trust 29
    Content Marketing Before "Content Marketing" 31
    Earn Business by Earning Trust 33
    Attract—and Keep—the Right Type of Customers ... 36

3. Strategy Starts at the Search Cycle 39
    Short vs. Long Sales Cycles 40
    Adopting a Search Mindset 42
    Position Content Strategically throughout the Search Cycle ... 44
    Goodbye Sales Funnel, Hello Complex Loop 49

4. Achieving Online Authority — 53
- What Is Online Authority? — 54
- What Is the Online Experience of Your Brand? — 56
- How Strategic Content Builds Online Authority — 58
- Brands That Connect—Win — 60

5. Why Consistency Matters — 65
- Deliver Consistent Content: A Cumulative Advantage — 66
- Give Your Audience Experiences They Want to Repeat — 68
- Think Like a Publisher — 71

6. Making the Content Shift — 75
- A Return to Open Markets — 76
- The Digital Era: A More Even Playing Field — 77
- The 7 Content Shifts — 79
- Shift Toward Your Audience, Whichever Direction They Go — 81
- That's Great, but What's My Return on Investment? — 82
- How a Content Strategy Spurs Business Growth — 84
- Why Your Business Needs Content Marketing — 86

PART TWO: AUDIENCE — 89

7. Building Relationships through Content — 91
- What Is a Meaningful Relationship? — 92
- Types of Customer Relationships — 94
- Your Audience Is Human — 96

8. Audience Grouping — 99
- Audience Grouping for Strategic Content Development — 99
- Conducting Audience Research — 105
- Audience Grouping by Motivation — 107
- Introducing: The Nursing School — 109

9. Emotional and Psychological Needs — 115
- Emotions Drive Content — 116
- Understanding New Consumer Psychology — 123

10. Using Personas — 127
Meet "Career-Change Connie" — 128
What Are Personas? — 130
Personas for Different Purposes — 131
How to Build a Persona — 135
Are Personas Really Necessary? — 138

11. Your Audience Asks Questions — 141
Applying the Search Cycle — 142
Primary vs. Secondary Topics — 150

PART THREE: SEARCH — 155

12. Understanding Search Engines — 157
Search Research Optimizes Content Production — 157
SEO and Content Marketing Go Hand in Hand — 161
Good Content: As Defined by Google Guidelines — 163

13. Speaking the Language of Search — 169
Why the Right Keywords Matter — 169
Know Which Keywords to Use — 171
Direct Traffic to Core Pages — 172
Finding Opportunities in the Long Tail — 176
Long-Tail Keywords Are Specific Questions You Can Answer — 180
Target Long-Tail Keywords FIRST — 183

14. Keyword Research to Discover Content Topics — 187
The Goals of Keyword Research for Content Marketing — 189
Content Strategy: Answer Customer Questions — 189
Using Keyword Tools — 190
How to Do Keyword Research, Step by Step — 193
Your Business Goals Direct Your Focus—Every Time — 212

15. Evaluating Keyword Questions — 215
How to Decide Which Content Questions to Answer First — 216
Content Strategies for the Search Cycle — 223
Next Step: Assigning Priorities — 231

16. **Taking Search Research Even Deeper** — 241
    Note #1: Evergreen Content Is Always Good — 242
    Note #2: Fill in the Gaps with Competitor Analysis — 244
    Note #3: Draw from Personas and Audience Research to Get Even More Specific — 247
    Note #4: Group Related Questions into Outlines with Subheadings — 248
    Note #5: Use Whatever Tools You Need—Everything and the Kitchen Sink — 249
    What About Paid Ads? — 250
    Recapping the Content Strategies We've Covered So Far — 252
    Allocating Time and Resources to the Search Research Phase — 252

PART FOUR: PRODUCTION — 255

17. **Documenting Your Content Strategy** — 257
    Align Content Strategy with Business Goals — 258
    The Importance of a Documented Content Strategy — 260
    Put Your Content Strategy into Writing — 262
    Identify Your Content Marketing Goals — 267
    Track and Schedule Every Piece of Content — 270

18. **Content Types and Optimization** — 277
    Content Types by Level of Accessibility — 278
    Determining the Best Platform for Your Content — 289
    6 Essential SEO On-Page Optimization Elements — 290

19. **Streamlining Your Content Production Process** — 297
    To Hire or Not to Hire? In-House vs. Outsourcing — 298
    Prioritize and Schedule Content Topics — 301
    Preparing Your Content Blueprint — 303
    Execute, Refine, Design, and Publish — 308

20. **Creating Quality and Style Guidelines for Your Brand** — 311
    Maintain a High Standard of Quality — 311
    Think Like a Publisher: Refer to Your Style Guide — 319

21. Measuring Success with Key Metrics — 329
    How to Ensure Your Content Strategy Is Working — 330
    Quantitative Analysis: 4 Key Performance Indicators (KPIs) to Track — 332
    Metric #1: Is Your Organic Traffic from Search Growing? — 334
    Metric #2: Are You Winning More Conversions? — 336
    Metric #3: Are Your Targeted Keywords Gaining Traction? — 341
    Metric #4: How Well Does Your Content Meet Audience Needs? — 346
    Qualitative Analysis: Listen to Feedback from Your Customers — 349
    Conduct Regular Content Audits — 351

22. Repurposing Content to Maximize Results — 355
    What You Can Learn from Strong Content — 356
    What You Can Do with Weak Content — 360

Conclusion: All Boats Rise with the Tide — 369
    Finding Your Place Online — 372
    Congratulations, and Godspeed! — 375

Glossary — 377

Acknowledgments — 381

Notes — 383

Works Cited — 391

Index — 397

About the Authors — 407

THE CONTENT SHIFT

INTRODUCTION

As marketers, we're people persons. Our job is to connect people with our products and brands and messages. What distinguishes great marketers is their unwavering focus on those people—on their needs, behaviors, intentions, wants—and an ability to avoid the shiny temptations of marketing solely to things—like devices, channels, technologies.

—Lisa Gevelber

Content, and content marketing, is not a new phenomenon. In marketing, its core function has been to provide answers to questions and solutions to problems. The Internet, however—which is a relatively new phenomenon—has opened the door for anyone to do content marketing. The online marketplace provides easy access to publishing tools and endless opportunities for connectivity like the world has never seen.

Contrary to popular belief, content marketing was not invented by the Internet revolution. It has a history. A long history. In fact, as far back as the 1800s, inventive leaders were already using content marketing to bring attention to brands and products in the quickly industrializing modern world—all before "content marketing" even had a name.

Frank Woodward was among these early pioneers. He was the visionary who elevated Jell-O to the international sensation it is today, and he achieved this through some truly brilliant content marketing.[1] A high school dropout, Woodward had the foresight to buy the rights to a strange new dessert made out of gelatin in 1899.[2]

> Anything that can be written, read, viewed, listened to, or consumed through language, visuals, or audio is content. Content marketing uses content to help you connect with your audience, engage them in conversation, and communicate an intentional message—ultimately leading to customer action, brand loyalty, and business growth.

Jell-O's creator, Peter Cooper, had had no luck convincing the American people that gelatin—a translucent, colorless, flavorless food derived from animal collagen—was a desirable addition to the dinner table. (It's not hard to imagine why!) Cooper sold the patent to Pearl and May Wait, who discovered that adding sugar (*lots of sugar*) made the gelatin palatable—perhaps even enjoyable. They named the strange dessert Jell-O before selling the patent to Woodward, who possessed the marketing and sales savvy to popularize this new concoction.[3]

With perseverance and creativity, Woodward turned Jell-O into an American staple. He recognized that people didn't know *what* gelatin was or *how* to use it—so he *created content* to teach them about the benefits of Jell-O and how it could fit into the American lifestyle.

Before Jell-O became the after-dinner hit that it is today, Woodward offered up an array of branded materials to the public, such as Jell-O cookbooks featuring celebrity recipes, live Jell-O cooking demonstrations, and promotional molds that made the product easy and fun to use. What do all of these products have in common? They're all different forms of content marketing.

Jell-O focused on providing valuable information to the public before asking anyone to buy in:

- Woodward used content to *connect* with his audience over what was important and relevant to them, introducing moms to a new and easy way to make dessert super fun and convenient for the whole family.
- He engaged his audience in *conversation* about how they could add this new dessert to their repertoire, sparking surprise, inspiration, and creativity.
- He *communicated* intentional messages about how Jell-O could improve the lives of every American family, and he provided clear, accessible ways to easily integrate this product into regular meal routines.

Woodward's innovative approach used content to break down the barriers that prevented people from trying Jell-O in the first place. Jell-O went from being an unusual dessert no one could successfully sell to one of the most popular prepackaged foods in the world. This is because Woodward understood one of the most important principles of content marketing: **People value content that is relevant to their lives,** and they'll gladly consume content that is presented to them in an engaging, useful way. While the idea of a branded cookbook may seem obvious and predictable today, that wasn't the case until Jell-O came along. There are always going to be new and innovative ideas about how you can use content to reach your customers.

The digital age we live in is rife with possibilities for content marketers. However, in order to flourish, we must integrate some very important shifts in thinking to attract more of the right customers, produce more relevant content, and ultimately develop an effective content strategy with long-term flexibility. Jell-O is still stocking shelves today because the company's visionary founder understood a fundamental content marketing principle: Connect with customers through relevant content and offer value to their lives.

Successful content provides value to your specific audience—often by delivering news, insights, or novel information; by creating an emotional connection through humor, storytelling, or entertainment; or by helping to make a decision about a purchase. Especially if your business has a long sales cycle or exists in a highly competitive online space, content is arguably an essential part of educating and engaging your potential customers.

A long sales cycle simply means you would expect your audience to do a fair amount of research before buying, such as researching different models of vehicle, different college programs, different consultants, or different appliances before coming to a purchasing decision. This sales cycle could last anywhere from a few days to a few years. Businesses with long sales cycles and serious competition know the importance of nurturing long leads, and the Internet allows plenty of room for providing helpful information for your potential customers—who may end up remembering you when it comes time to make the big decision.

That said, content marketing is not just for businesses with a long sales cycle. Practically any business that serves customers who have questions can use the strategy of customer-focused content to their advantage. The type of search-focused content marketing we'll be exploring in this book can easily apply to businesses that want to gain a competitive edge, reach new markets, or nurture their already existing customer base. It also applies to businesses that have new and innovative products or services. The value you provide to your audience through content can be expected to drive more traffic to your website, boost your brand image, and, ultimately, drive sales.

> Content marketing costs 62% less than traditional marketing and generates about three times as many leads.[4]

WHY YOU SHOULD READ THIS BOOK

So, what brings you to this book? Is it a desire to learn something new to improve your already-robust business? Is it a fear of being left behind in a world of technology you don't quite understand? Is it a mandate from higher-ups to investigate new marketing strategies to bring back to the corporate think tank?

If you're a business and you're online (which is pretty much expected), you've probably heard that content marketing is crucial to competing in cyberspace, but perhaps you've never really understood why it's so important. Or maybe you never got the tutorial on how to do content marketing right, or you're skeptical about what results you can expect. Maybe you've been producing content for a while and feel like something's missing, your results are lackluster, or it's just plain not working.

Regardless of what brings you to this book, the goal is the same: **You want to deliver your products to the right audience, raise brand awareness, increase the bottom line, and grow your company**—all while trying to keep up with changing social and technological shifts. If you're experiencing content marketing frustration, if you're feeling lost in an oversaturated digital landscape, or if you're looking for a new framework of thought to help you boost your online productivity and start seeing results in organic search and conversions, then this book is for you. Solid content creation methods and search-focused research strategies form the foundation for this book, and we'll share the tools and action steps necessary to help you make a powerful shift in your organization—one that has drastic, long-term benefits.

There are tons of ways to educate yourself online (the Internet is a vast sea of information, after all), but the goal of this book is to help you **create your own unique content strategy**, using only the most important information to get you there. We'll share our winning, step-by-step process for researching topics and creating content that revolves around what your customers are *actually searching for*—helping you to reduce overwhelm and clear a path toward success.

The intention of this book is to help you do three main things:

- **Develop and implement a content marketing strategy for organic search based on answering customer questions.**
- **Increase organic search traffic, thereby increasing leads and sales.**
- **Expand your online presence and brand over time through strategic consistency.**

Whether you're the owner of a quickly growing business, the marketing director of a mid- to large-sized company, or any other professional in a field related to search engine optimization (SEO) or content marketing, the tools presented here will help you find your direction in the online space and provide a framework for creating clear business goals—*and taking action on them*.

WHO WE ARE

We (Jon and Mark) have been doing search-focused content marketing since the dawn of the industry. We have a passion for SEO-informed content marketing, and our goal is to help you improve your content marketing strategy using search-based tools and techniques. We want to share our knowledge with anyone who's ready to take their marketing efforts to the next level.

A little about us: We formed our company, SEO Savvy, in 2007, and we like to say we were both doing SEO before SEO even had a name. Mark was an SEO specialist for various companies. Before that, he was an audio engineer, and *even before that*, he was a musician in a goth band (which achieved no less than relative obscurity). Before SEO Savvy, Jon was dominating in the fields of affiliate marketing, link building, and lead generation for finance and education companies. (He was also in a band and doing link-building for his band.)

Our special area of focus is driving *relevant* organic traffic growth for companies with a long sales cycle online, especially nationally competitive companies in the education and finance space. We've helped mid-sized businesses and Fortune 500 companies increase their organic search traffic by 150–300% year-over-year and consistently rank for competitive, relevant search terms. Sometimes dubbed "SEOs for the SEOs," we've consulted well-known industry experts, taught online marketing classes, and been featured in major industry publications.

After more than 15 years of adapting to this changing field, we wanted to distill our knowledge into a guidebook for marketing professionals to help them take their content marketing in a more focused direction with search-informed marketing strategies. We noticed that a lot of content marketing tutorials out there don't even mention search, and this is what we hope to impart: how to think about content marketing in a way that drives *visibility* and *conversions* in organic search. This is truly our passion, and we're happy to share what we know with you in these pages.

"Search marketing" is a broad term we're using to describe online marketing strategies that aim to ramp up a website's visibility in search engines and, therefore, increase search traffic to that website. There are two main umbrellas under this category: *SEO* and *SEM*. SEO refers to *search engine optimization*, which is focused on growing website traffic *organically* through non-paid advertising. We also refer to SEO as "organic search marketing."

This is the focus of the book: creating search-focused content to drive more organic traffic. The other type of search marketing—SEM—stands for *search engine marketing*. The only difference is that SEM uses paid ads—or pay-per-click (PPC) advertising—to drive traffic. We won't be going into SEM in this book.

WHAT IS THE CONTENT SHIFT?

So, it seems like everyone you know is talking about content marketing. There are a ton of books out there, and it is officially considered an entire field of marketing—complete with conferences where industry experts can gather. Content marketing is a Real Thing.

With so many different viewpoints and perspectives out there, we wanted to weigh in and provide our own. Content marketing, especially for a long sales cycle or highly competitive space, should be focused around answering the questions that people are asking about your brand, product, or industry. We bring our years of SEO experience to the realm of content marketing to help you understand a very important aspect of content marketing: how to reach people through search.

We believe just creating content is not going to get you the results you want. Rather, having a strategic approach that is centered on your audience and understanding their motivations, questions, needs, and desires is the key to any long-lasting content marketing success.

The content shift is simple in theory:

> Understand your audience and how they search for information online to create a content strategy tailored to answering their questions.

It may sound simple, but the reason why this is a shift in thinking is because people often skip researching their audience and studying search and instead jump straight into producing content—*without any evidence that it will drive traffic or sales*. Eventually, they end up feeling dazed and confused, concluding that "content marketing simply doesn't work." If this is or has been you, or anyone you know, we don't fault you. It's so easy to publish online, and you probably weren't given a rulebook on how to do content marketing. But what we *do* ask is that you keep an open mind and give the content shift a chance.

Finally, while this book is geared towards content marketing for businesses with a long sales cycle or those in highly competitive spaces, the concepts and tools can still apply to businesses with a shorter sales cycle, those in a low-competition space, or businesses that are just launching. No matter what size or type of business you are, content that answers your audience's questions builds trust. Whether your customer spends months researching different models of road bikes or just a few minutes looking for a new restaurant to try out that evening, the content you create has the power to move a potential customer either closer or further from your brand. Why not do everything in your power to present clean, clear, and helpful information?

> "Passion is not a substitute for planning."
>
> —Jeffrey Hayzlett, Author of *The Mirror Test*

THE STRUGGLE IS REAL, THE SOLUTION IS STRATEGY

Lots of companies are coming to realize they "should" do content marketing to stay competetive online, but an astounding 70% of marketers still do not have a consistent or integrated content strategy.[5] It's easy to want to jump the gun and just start producing content left and right, but this "spray and pray" method (as Mark calls it), while exciting at first, inevitably leads to lackluster results. Because producing content for the Internet has a lower cost of entry than traditional marketing campaigns, like television or radio ads, there's a common misconception that less planning is necessary. But that's not true at all!

The hard truth is this: What you don't know about content marketing *can* actually hurt you. Time and time again, we've seen companies implement content marketing that either doesn't benefit them or even ends up negatively impacting them. We've witnessed companies throw hours upon hours of labor and tons of capital into content marketing with a disconnected strategy—or worse, no strategy at all. This ends up wasting time and money that could be better spent elsewhere—or that could be directed in a more potent manner. Even worse, content marketing gone wrong can go *really* wrong. Internet users, as well as Google, have very little tolerance for shoddy, inaccurate, lazy, or offensive content—and news travels fast. Bad content can actually *hurt* your reputation and set you back in your PR efforts.

Watching well-meaning and highly skilled marketing executives throw money down the drain—or have their efforts backfire simply because they weren't yet aware of the ways to effectively construct a content strategy—is actually the very thing that inspired us to write this book. There are plenty of strategies that very capable business owners and even high-level marketing directors simply don't know. It's understandable: the Internet is vast and constantly shifting. Your company is probably most focused on doing what it does best: developing products or services for your target audience. However, with some focused effort, you can channel that energy into your content marketing efforts to enhance everything you do.

In fact, a content marketing strategy can even help inform and connect other departments in your organization. This is because a content strategy really gets at the heart of what your audience wants, which can have some unexpected additional benefits for the rest of your business! Content marketing is another necessary extension of any marketing division in the digital age.

And here's one beautiful thing about the Internet: There's so much data available online that you can really hone in on what your users are searching for and what they want. You don't necessarily need in-person focus groups and surveys to get an idea of what's working and what's not. Traditional audience research can be time-intensive and expensive, with a high barrier to entry. Internet data, on the other hand, is highly accessible, relatively inexpensive, and clearly applicable. It's a pretty quick and nimble process to test a campaign and get it out into the world, receive immediate feedback, make adjustments, and then update and refine your process. It's not uncommon for the feedback from content marketing to inspire a new product, encourage a new direction, or help you reach new markets.

HOW TO READ THIS BOOK

Here's a quick snapshot of how this book is laid out:

1. First, we'll help you understand the nature of content marketing and principles for success.

    PART ONE introduces you to some foundational principles in content marketing, including the seven *shifts in thinking* we believe are necessary to inform any content marketing strategy.

2. Next, we'll show you how to get to know your audience and listen to what they want.

    PART TWO asks you to investigate who your audience is and what kind of content they want from you online, helping you to develop an *audience mindset*.

3. After that, we'll teach you how to use search-focused research to understand how to connect online.

    PART THREE addresses the importance of how search operates within a content marketing strategy, continuing your shift in thinking toward a *search mindset*.

4. And finally, we'll help you craft a content strategy that meets your business needs.

    PART FOUR brings it all home by providing tools to actually craft your own content strategy using the concepts presented throughout the book, completing the journey of the *content shift*.

You may have noticed the strategy section comes *after* the audience and search sections, and that's because a strategy requires both audience research *and* search research. In other words, **research informs strategy.** The goal of this book is not to hyper-focus on any one tactic or fleeting trend but, rather, to build a solid foundation for thinking about content marketing that will carry you well into the future—essentially, to "future proof" your content for long-lasting results. (If you're looking for easy, overnight success, you can head over to the nearest 7-Eleven to pick up a lottery ticket.)

Most importantly, we want you to be able to put these concepts and tools into action, so we've included templates and resources throughout the chapters and a Points of Discovery section at the end of every chapter to help you apply what you've learned to your own business. At some points in the book, we'll direct you to visit our website—ContentShift.com/Resources—for downloadable templates and further reading.

As Matt Blumberg of Return Path says, "Marketing when not done well is an endless checklist of advertising and promotional to-dos that can never be completed."[6] What you *don't* need is an endless task list. However, what we assert you *do* need is a well-planned, well-informed, and well-researched creative content marketing strategy that you can apply to your unique business goals.

Feel free to read straight through for a thorough understanding of content marketing, or to skip around as needed. Like any journey, you can expect to encounter challenging new ideas and unexpected discoveries, and, by the end of it, come away with a greater understanding of the ideas and tools you can apply to your specific brand. Some concepts may already be familiar to you, while others may be brand new.

If you want to create meaningful content online that connects with your potential customers while elevating your brand online, someone (maybe it's you or your marketing director) will need to invest some time into strategy before production. As Malcom Gladwell proposes in his book *Outliers*, it takes around 10,000 hours to master any complex subject or practice, which is equivalent to about ten years. The Beatles, for example, perfected their musicianship by playing onstage for eight hours a night every night *for ten years*. Don't worry—you won't need to invest that much time to begin seeing results in your content marketing campaigns. (That's why we're writing this book for you—to share what we've learned from our 10,000 hours.)

With that in mind, we want to thank you for investing in the future of your business (which we're sure provides great value to the world), and we look forward to helping you grow your organic search traffic online to connect with customers, expand your brand, and drive sales!

> *"The key takeaway when thinking about content is that **this** is your new form of customer acquisition. The best news is that it's nowhere near as expensive as the acquisition channels of the past—specifically, TV advertising or an enterprise sales force. The worst news is that it's a new competency that you'd better solve for quickly before a smaller, faster competitor figures it out."*[7]
>
> **—Dave Walters**

PART ONE
CONTENT

Chapter 1

LET'S TALK ABOUT CONTENT

Communication is one person speaking with another. Marketing is one type of communication.

—Samuel Scott, Moz

When was the last time you saw something on the Internet that made you *actually* laugh out loud? (Like when Jon sends Mark a video clip of Dr. Steve Brule, it's a winner every time...)

How about the last time you found yourself moved or intrigued by something you saw online? Can you think of the last thing you learned online or a time when you felt inspired? Maybe you sneak in some break time scrolling through Buzzfeed lists at work or checking your email for an uplifting message from your favorite motivational writer. Perhaps you scroll Facebook, Twitter, or Instagram, and then head to Google when you need to do a quick fact check (like what year *The Big Lebowski* takes place, if you're Mark). All of these seemingly insignificant moments could be opportunities for a brand to connect with you online to give you more of what interests you.

Think about the last purchase you made online and the journey you took to get there. For example, perhaps on your lunch break you navigated over to Amazon to place an order for the new blender you've had your eye on recently. You definitely wanted to get the best deal and choose a quality product that would suit your needs, so you spent a few days comparing different brands and models, looking at product descriptions and specifications, probably reading some reviews. (It's a huge hassle, after all, to make the wrong purchase and have to return an item.) So, maybe you found one with everything you needed at a price you liked, and you saved it in your shopping cart, waiting for the moment you were ready to commit. That moment arrived two weeks later when you came across a great recipe for homemade pesto while browsing Pinterest recipes, which reinforced your decision to up your cooking game. Voila! Congratulations on your new blender.

This is a fairly typical user journey along the *path to purchase* online, and it seems fairly organic and natural, right? Now let's switch our perspective and look at the same situation through the eyes of the appliance company that successfully sold the blender. What had to happen to put the product on the customer's radar? What types of content influenced the purchasing decision? How do you make sure your product appears in the search results of your target audience? As we journey deeper into the content shift, we'll unpack some of these questions for you so you can create a content strategy tailored to answering the questions your audience is asking.

WAIT, BUT WHAT IS "CONTENT"?

Everything a business produces that can be viewed, read, heard, consumed intellectually, or shared is essentially content. That includes press releases, brochures, ad campaigns, commercials, videos, website copy, blog posts, and social media posts. Content can also be a product, like newspapers or magazines, but most *products* cannot also be content. For example, a vacuum is not content.

When referring to online content, usually we're talking about any written, visual, or auditory materials that are produced, published, and shared—anything from blog posts and podcasts to infographics, e-books, whitepapers, website copy, Facebook posts, images, videos, meta-descriptions—you name it. Content is ubiquitous.

No matter what kind of company or organization you run—and regardless of whether you're just starting or fully ramped up—you likely already have content, such as:

- Product or service descriptions
- Mission statements
- Descriptions of your company
- Bios and photos of people involved
- Photos of events or products

Content is everywhere—not just in your mailbox or on TV but across multiple platforms and devices. Content can be good or bad, useful or nonessential, exemplary or irritating, and so on. Content is a neutral term; it's how you use it that gives it any descriptive quality. Like paper or canvas, content is a blank slate upon which you can create something beautiful or mediocre. Just as there are different styles, levels of mastery, and mediums of art, so too are there infinite ways to create content.

Content has certainly evolved over the years as once-novel ideas naturally became mass-produced and technology opened new doors for expression. For example, compare TV commercials in the 1960s to the sophisticated mini-movies shown during today's Super Bowl broadcast. In the old days, the layers of marketing were fairly simple. Commercials would endlessly repeat on television and radio. Many included a jingle and catch phrase, such as "Plop plop, fizz fizz, oh what a relief it is!" Alka Seltzer. Consumers might also see print ads in magazines and newspapers that conveyed the same message. This type of direct marketing has been around for decades.

Nowadays, the competition is fierce for quickly grabbing consumer attention with a memorable moment of comedy or sentiment. The Internet did not invent content, but it has transformed it into an entity that is as omnipresent as the air we breathe. Content delivers news, information, tips, recipes, product reviews, political data and opinions, sports results—and innumerable niche-audience reports on finance, knitting, gardening, foreign real estate, and antique auto restoration. Want to learn more about the health benefits of quinoa? Google it. Thinking of sending a child to summer camp? Launch a search. Need to compare airline flights? Google has you covered.

All these technological advances have provided instant gratification for consumers. Virtually any question can be answered at any time, and with the advancement of virtual-assistant technology, it's always getting easier (Alexa! Siri! Hey, Google!). Likewise, the evolution of content marketing has made an online presence essential for the long-lasting success of any business.

> Heidi Cohen has put together a thorough list of content marketing definitions, which you can access here:
> http://heidicohen.com/content-marketing-definition/

"WHAT IS CONTENT MARKETING?" ACCORDING TO THE INTERNET

As you probably realize by now, you can find almost anything on the Internet—including lots of various, sometimes contradictory, definitions of content marketing. Just for fun, here's a short list of some different ways people are referring to content marketing:

- custom publishing
- custom media
- brand journalism
- corporate journalism
- branded content
- mission marketing
- inbound marketing

- storytelling
- native advertising
- content strategy
- digital marketing
- Internet marketing

The list could go on, but we'll stop there. If you're ever bored, you might find some amusement in reading through the heated Internet debates around what exactly content marketing *is*, but for the purposes of this book, let's skip the semantics and get straight to the good stuff—like how to *create amazing experiences* for your customers. We're calling *that* content marketing. As long as the content you're producing serves an *intentional purpose* and *propels your brand forward*, call it whatever you want!

CONTENT MARKETING IS ADDED VALUE—FIRST

You'll find an endless array of definitions of content marketing on the Internet, depending on whom you talk to—like most things online. While content marketing can't be easily placed into a box and tied up with a bow, it doesn't have to be unnecessarily complex, either.

The Content Marketing Institute is one of the foremost authorities in the industry, and we really like the way they summarize content marketing here:

> Basically, content marketing is the art of communicating with your customers and prospects without selling. It is non-interruption marketing. Instead of pitching your products or services, you are delivering information that makes your buyer more intelligent. The essence of this content strategy is the belief that if we, as businesses, deliver consistent, ongoing, valuable information to buyers, they ultimately reward us with their business and loyalty.[1]

This succinctly sums up the *shift in thinking* that is required to make the jump to outstanding content marketing: **Instead of selling or advertising, content marketing focuses on providing value for the user.**

We live in a world where about 1 in 4 people in the United States enables ad-blocking software, and this trend is expected to continue.[2] People *want* to find amazing stories, tips, reviews, and videos on the Internet, but overwhelmed Internet users are increasingly less patient with interruptive advertisements. People are out there specifically searching for the information they want, scouring for answers to questions, looking online for the solutions to their problems—the content they *want* to consume.

> Search is the number one traffic source for all blogs across all industries.[3] What's more, did you know that Google drives 8 times more traffic than all social media networks combined?[4]

CONTENT MARKETING IS PERMISSION MARKETING

The content you create is meant to be willingly and actively consumed by the people searching for it. This is the essence of permission marketing. Well-known marketer and author Seth Godin coined the term "permission marketing," and he defines it as when a customer *chooses* to engage with your brand and content. You put content out into the world for your audience to find and fall in love with. There are no sales gimmicks, flashy ads, or small print. You give away something great up front, and then continue to offer more value through your paid offerings. This is the business logic behind content marketing, and, quite frankly, it works.

Creating valuable content that speaks to and serves your target audience is the foundation of any content marketing strategy. When a user chooses to engage in a conversation with your business, they are more likely to actually be open to additional messaging. Your content can inspire people to *say yes* to continued engagement, which gives you more opportunity to share your value proposition, close the sale, and keep people wanting more. In the era of dwindling attention spans, the value of this should not be overlooked. (Regardless of whether you have an ad-driven website, it's the *content* of the ad that drives ad revenue.)

> 64% of respondents to a HubSpot survey say ads today are annoying or intrusive.[5]

In contrast, "interruption marketing" is an old form of direct marketing in which consent is not present. Billboards, ads, commercials, direct mailings: These are all examples of interruption marketing, which has been the dominant mode of marketing for the entire 20th century. There's nothing inherently wrong with interruption marketing, and there's a reason why these methods work. We're not at all telling you to immediately cease all direct marketing efforts. Content marketing and broadcast marketing can exist side-by-side, but we've got to make a shift in thinking between them.

Permission marketing is a dominant mode of commerce for the busy Internet age, and content marketers need to understand this principle. For example, if a person searching online for a specific piece of information navigates to your webpage from the search results but is interrupted constantly by pop-up ads or autoplay videos on topics they don't care about, then they're actually being *interrupted* on their journey towards their goal. You might have hooked them, but they're going to navigate away if your webpage succeeds in annoying them, and it's unlikely they will form a positive association with your brand. Instead, their response: *Ignore, ignore, ignore.*

On the other hand, when a customer gives you *permission* to engage, they are, theoretically, more open to your messaging. So, what does this look like? Well, it could be someone signing up for your email list after visiting your webpage, for example, or following your brand on a social media platform, filling out an information form, pressing the play button on a video, or any other number of permission-centric behaviors.

When the user actively makes a step forward to engage, they are opening the door a little wider to connect with you. Every time someone chooses to click a link, share something, sign up, or check out, they are saying yes (in some way) to what you have to offer. This is a marked difference in advertising that is highly influenced by the freedom of choice the Internet allows. It's your outstanding content that will keep people on your site and your brand on their radar.

CONTENT MARKETING IS PULL MARKETING

Interruption marketing can also be called *push marketing*. The strategy is to *push* your message or brand *out* to a broad audience. Think television ads, radio ads, and billboards. In the online space, push marketing may take the form of banners along a website advertising a product. The user is not actively searching for a product or service.

While push marketing can certainly be one prong within an overall marketing strategy, pull marketing takes a different approach: We want to *pull* a customer *in* to our website. In *pull marketing*, we are focused on identifying a user's intent and employing tactics to bring the customer to us.[6]

Content marketing targets users who are *actively* searching for solutions to problems that your brand offers. Instead of "pushing" products out to customers, pull marketing seeks to "pull" people in to business-driven content that is relevant, targeted, and aligned with the audience's interests and needs. Pull marketing is known as *inbound marketing*, and it relies on harnessing the power of search engines to attract a target audience through search-focused, audience-driven content that informs and educates.

Specifically, throughout this book, we will be teaching you how to discover the questions your customers are asking so you can answer them in a brand-positive way. Both authors have been working in the fields of

SEO and content marketing for more than a decade, and this is what we really want to add to the content marketing conversation: **You can use search-marketing strategies to enhance the effectiveness of all the content you produce.**

> Don't get us wrong, banner ads can still play a useful role in an online marketing strategy overall. Even if users aren't paying close attention to them, they still increase brand recognition. If those ads are related to what users have searched for—or, better yet, a brand or product ad after a user visits your website—the effectiveness is even greater. This is a segment of paid online advertising called *retargeting*. Though it's beyond the scope of this book, we are not against utilizing all methods of advertising to market a product, service, or brand. We've seen the effectiveness of all marketing channels working together (think Coke, Apple, Amazon, Tesla, and others who have a strong presence everywhere). Yet, we've also seen companies grow like wildfire by simply doing search-focused content marketing, and *that* is the focus of this book. Mastering search-focused content marketing is always beneficial for businesses that compete online.

You've heard the phrase, "Build it and they will come." In search marketing, we want to build intelligent website content that draws users in, follows through on satisfying their desires, answers their questions, and anticipates their needs. We want to build such a strong empire of brand, content, and voice that users come to us—and bring others to us as well. Like a lighthouse, we are focused on directing ships in to safe harbor; that is, lighting a path toward our website as an answer to users' questions.

We build this path by creating content that we know people are searching for. And this results in organically growing our website traffic over time—more people, more eyes, and more customers.

In order to achieve this, we must first identify the *needs* of our target audience. Then, we create online content with intention and purpose, using evidence-backed *search research* to attract the relevant audience. Finally, we continually follow through by creating quality content to increase user engagement and keep potential customers interacting as long as possible, measuring results and innovating as we go.

Instead of *pushing* advertising campaigns on unsuspecting people, the strategy is to *attract* users to us through content we know they are searching for. The rest of the book walks you through this process so *you* can be the one answering your customers' questions—and the one they turn to when they're ready to make the purchase (rather than your competitor).

THE GOLDEN RULE: PROVIDE VALUE, INSPIRE ACTION

Content marketing does not hit your customer over the head with neon signs that light up with "Buy, buy, buy." But the content you create can subtly and organically convey to users what they need to know to begin doing business with you.

The average city dweller sees 5,000 ads per day. Modern tech-savvy consumers are bombarded with advertising messages everywhere they go, so it's become a natural defense mechanism to simply tune out. How can you hope to cut through the clutter?

People are more likely to engage with content that speaks to them and clearly offers value to their lives. It's amazing to us that this might be surprising since advertising and marketing are, at their core, about communicating messages of value to customers, rather than trying to coerce a sale.

> This is the core of content marketing:
> Give people things that make their lives better.

This is what we really love about content marketing: As marketers, our job is to accurately express the benefits of a particular buying decision, way of thinking, or new consideration. And we do this through well-written, informative content that resonates with our target audience and is designed to reach them. If you can show people how you are making their lives better, you can inspire them to take action. That action may be a small step or a huge change; it may be a click on a link or a direct call.

We all want things that make our lives better. And with so much sales schmuck littering our modern world, think about what a breath of fresh air it is to simply connect authentically with other people about real things that concern us. We all want to do business with people and companies that we trust will help us solve our problems, make things easier, or generally increase our good feelings. Guess what? Your customers want the same from you. Your content can convey knowledge, inspire trust, and initiate a business relationship.

> Content marketing is conversation
> that inspires action.

And that's our short-and-sweet definition of content marketing. It really can be as simple as that.

POINTS OF DISCOVERY

Now it's time to take the concepts we've covered and apply them to your own business. Take a moment to brainstorm your answers to the following questions to start shifting into a content marketing mindset. Keep this list on hand, and continue thinking about these questions as we go.

1. What are some ways your business or brand can make your customers' lives better?

2. What questions are your customers asking?
3. What problems are your customers trying to solve?
4. What types of conversations do your customers want to have with you?
5. Make a list of topics you think your customers would be interested in.

Chapter 2

GREAT CONTENT BUILDS TRUST

If you talked to people the way advertising talked to people, they'd punch you in the face.

—Hugh MacLeod

We all use the Internet for a lot of different reasons—to be entertained, inspired, intrigued. To feel connected, relieved, encouraged. Whether it's a silly YouTube video, a cat's Instagram account, a useful how-to article, or a subreddit for moustaches, the Internet is fully stocked with content that speaks (hopefully) to someone out there in cyberspace. Stories, communication, and *content* are integral to our lives.

Content marketing is the art of crafting content that speaks to your audience online. The *content shift* is about understanding your audience so exceptionally well that you already know what they are searching for—so your content can answer their questions effectively.

While the best content seems to perform effortlessly—attracting thousands of visitors, driving sales, and increasing brand exposure—it does so because the right amount of thought went into producing a cohesive strategy. On a large scale, the digital universe we now find ourselves in is revolutionary for human communication. The content shift that is happening now, and that will persist into the future, requires businesses to prioritize *content as connection*. We are more connected than ever before, and the pace at which technology is advancing is incredible.

Understandably, if you are not hyper-focused on the digital space, it could appear exhausting and even paralyzing. We admit the digital world can sometimes seem overwhelming, especially for us Digital Immigrants—those of us who grew up before the widespread use of digital technology. (Do you remember landlines and analog? We certainly do.) Digital Natives, on the other hand—especially Millennials, who grew up in an information marketplace—have only experienced the fast-paced, ever-connected world around us.

However old you are, the profound technological changes occurring around us are, inarguably, revolutionary for everyone. U.S. consumers spend around 3½ to 4½ hours a day on their mobile phones[1] and around 11–12 hours per day consuming media.[2] That's a lot of time browsing the Internet—and a lot of reason for content marketers to get in the game.

The Internet has changed modern society so deeply that even our brains are being rewired constantly. A UCLA study conducted by neuropsychologists have found that *just five hours* on the Internet already changes the neural circuitry in the prefrontal cortex, the area of the brain that controls decision-making, working memory, and mental processing of complex information.[3] While the extent of these effects are largely unknown, it does lead us to a positive interpretation: Because our brains are so elastic, anyone can learn how to do content marketing well with a bit of concerted effort.

> "The illiterate of the 21st century will not be those who cannot read and write, but those who cannot learn, unlearn, and relearn."
>
> **—Alvin Toffler, author of *Future Shock***

When the Internet revolution first started in the 1990s, fully blowing up in the early 2000s, we (Jon and Mark) were both drawn to this new frontier. After more than a decade in Internet marketing, we're still energized by the exciting changes sweeping the field. And more than anything, we want to impress upon you, our readers, how important search is to a content strategy. Search helps you connect with the people already looking for information online.

93% of all online experiences begin with a search engine.[4] Infusing search into your content strategy could *double* your amount of incoming organic traffic.[5] It eludes us why more people aren't talking about search optimization and content together. (Well, we know SEO can seem very confusing and frustrating for people, and that's why we want to take the guesswork out for you.) That being said, one thing still remains constant: *marketing relies on human connection.*

What great content does is provide a reliable, familiar, comfortable avenue of connecting online amid the noise and confusion. Through storytelling, conversation, entertainment, and education, content is the connective thread between humans and growing technology. Simply put, despite all the changes occurring in technology, we're still people behind the screens—people who want our desires to be fulfilled and our stories to be heard.

CONTENT MARKETING BEFORE "CONTENT MARKETING"

We all want things that make our lives better. Content marketing operates on the belief that if you provide value to your customers' lives, they will reward you with their business. Content has the power to influence emotions, thoughts, behaviors, and decisions. If you show your customers that you're credible and helpful, and that you can share information that will improve their lives, a certain type of trust and recognition forms between your customers and your brand.

To illustrate, we can look to the genius of John Deere, a company that was enacting this principle of content marketing before "content marketing" had a name. Much like Woodward and Jell-O, Deere recognized content marketing as a smart business practice early on. Back in 1837, John Deere was a pioneer in the field of agricultural machinery. The company is still prominent today because the company focused on making people's lives better rather than selling a product. John Deere became the trusted and reliable source for farmers all over the world by first offering free information in the form of a regularly mailed catalogue, which focused on issues that affect farmers.

The Furrow is a free agricultural journal produced by Deere & Company that features insight, advice, tips, interviews, and more to help farmers become more successful. It's been in print for over 100 years and is still in circulation today, both online and in print. Two million people around the world still subscribe to this publication.[6] How often do you think John Deere products and services are presented? Only a handful of times. But who do you think will come to mind when a farmer is in need of farming supplies? You guessed it: John Deere. This company has positioned themselves as a thought leader in the agricultural industry.

Figure 2.1: Deere & Company catalogue, *The Furrow*, from July–August 1959.

Astoundingly, John Deere understood a primary content marketing principle, even way back in the mid-1800s: If you give valuable content to your customers, they will reward you with trust and loyalty. So, why is it so hard for some companies to make the shift from talking *at* customers to talking *with* customers?

It takes time and effort to produce content that *speaks* rather than *sells*. Empty messaging and catchy slogans are not the tools of content marketing. And here we have why so many are frustrated: Not every business was formed to operate like a publishing house, and yet this is essentially what successful content marketing asks of you. This doesn't mean you have to stop everything and start the presses on overdrive, but it does mean acknowledging the importance of crafting substantial content that your users want to see and engaging them in ways that are appropriate—using the specific resources at your disposal—and answering questions that affect your specific audience base.

Great content can:

- Show your customers that you care about their well-being and want to make a positive impact on their lives.
- Humanize your brand and form authentic emotional connections with your audience.
- Legitimize your authority as a trusted resource.
- Help customers learn something new, solve a problem, or make a decision.
- Earn trust and deepen loyalty.
- Connect your products and services with a relevant, interested audience.

EARN BUSINESS BY EARNING TRUST

"Now wait a minute," you might say. "You mean to tell me I'm just going to give my hard-earned expertise away for free? I'm spending all this time, money, and energy to publish this well-researched, thoughtful content on the Internet, just hoping that people will engage with it? How exactly is that good business?"

This is a complaint we hear often, understandably. You do have a business to run, after all. But so did John Deere, and, by offering people valuable content, that company is still thriving today as a trusted resource for agricultural products. Why not expect the same to hold true online? In fact, one Google study that surveyed around 1,600 people found that 56 percent of smartphone users ended up purchasing from an "unexpected brand" when they considered the brand helpful.[7]

> 75% of B2B marketers and 65% of B2C marketers used content marketing to build credibility and trust with their audience in 2020.[8, 9]

Still not convinced? Here are five reasons why content marketing actually makes sense as an investment:

1. **If people are already searching online for what you have to offer, there's a good chance your investment will pay off.** You can learn which search terms people are using within your industry to better tailor your content to those concerns and questions. The more you can validate your efforts through search and audience research, the clearer you will be on how to create results-oriented content. A strategic focus leads to better results.
2. **You can decide how much and what type of content to produce based on what makes sense for your business and your audience.** There's no law saying that you have to spend X amount of money to produce Y pieces of content in any given time frame. You can strategize the process of content marketing to fit your schedule, bud-

get, and workload. You can scale up or down, depending on what you need.

3. **The unfortunate and painful reality is that if people are searching and landing on your competitor's website, you'll surely feel the pinch.** It may take a while, but if your website isn't appearing in the search results for relevant key phrases because you haven't populated your web presence with amazing content that rewards both users *and* search engines, your business may lose out on opportunities to connect with new customers.

4. **In a lot of ways, your content is doing your work for you online.** You might not be able to individually teach every single potential customer what they need to know about your product or industry, or personally answer all their questions, but your online content can. Once you do the up-front work to create the content and it's fully out in the world, it takes on a life of its own. It becomes a visible, potentially long-lasting tool of communication that keeps reaching new people who are looking for that information—and, in turn, your products or services.

5. **Providing information that educates and informs your audience positions you as a *trustworthy source* that people will likely come back to again and again.** If you can establish a credible reputation with your audience, it's much more convenient for a customer to continue doing business with you than to repeat the process all over again with a new provider.

You might also ask, "Well, if I'm giving away free knowledge, aren't I pushing my company into obsolescence if people are able to just find everything they need for free on the Internet?" No. The information you provide does not (and could not) replace your products or services; rather, it serves to position your brand as a trustworthy authority in your field.

ATTRACT—AND KEEP—THE RIGHT TYPE OF CUSTOMERS

The customers you want are the ones who are intrigued, impressed, and attracted to your brand through your content. They are the ones who want more of what you have to offer; in other words, your paid services or for-sale products. To put it simply, *great content attracts leads in the form of organic traffic.* You know the rest. Leads become conversions. Conversions become sales.

For example, let's say you're a window-and-door repair company with locations all over the country. You release a video tutorial on how to accurately size and install screen doors. With this content, you're sharing your knowledge and expertise as it specifically relates to your products and services—both to help and inform anyone who might need it and to establish your company as a reputable authority.

Yes, you're giving away free knowledge, but you're also anticipating a return. Some viewers may decide to go ahead and size and install their own screen door, and it might not even be a screen door from your company. This is inevitable. But there is still value in educating your audience, no matter what. The next time that person wants to replace their windows, they could remember the content that helped them with their original task. Others will quickly realize that the task is harder than they thought, that they don't want to risk doing it incorrectly, or that it would be more convenient to hire a company to do the job, thereby saving hours of frustration.

At this moment, you're theoretically first in line for their business because they've already formed a favorable impression of your company. You know the subject so well that you made a video on how to do it! Your competitors didn't. If your customer has limited time and energy, and infinite options (as we all do in the Internet era), they may feel relieved that they can so easily find a reliable new company.

In another scenario, let's say the industrious consumer decides to replace the door on their own, but they find that they need to buy special parts. Who do you think they'll go to, the company whose tutorial they trust or another random business they find online? Naturally, you'll be at the forefront of their mind for any future needs.

The shift in thinking here is that by putting out valuable resources for people to find on the Internet, a good number of those people will end up coming back to you—sometimes in ways you could never predict. So, keep putting content out there, and keep adding value.

You earn business by earning trust.

- Your content has the potential to convey all sorts of benefits of working with you—such as your many years of expertise, your unique selling points, or your great customer service.
- Your content has the capacity to successfully establish your company as an authority in your field, and this is important in the self-publishing era of Instant Experts.
- Your content has the ability to offer useful information to your audience while also intentionally conveying that your knowledge, skills, and experience are valuable and, in some cases, irreplaceable.

Information does not replace experience.

Once information has been delivered to an audience, often your customers decide the job might be best left to the experts—you. And herein lies the fundamental goal of content marketing: **By giving your knowledge away for free, you can expect to receive the benefits of customer action, retention, loyalty, and stewardship.** In the new world of marketing, this is the ultimate win-win scenario.

In an oversaturated online marketplace, customers are selective, and your phenomenal, useful, engaging, helpful, entertaining, educational, unique content is what lifts you above the crowd and separates you from your competitors. Content marketing, like any form of marketing, is meant to deliver information and raise awareness about a business, product, or service. Rather than advertising directly, search-focused content marketing can provide value to users when they come across your helpful answers to their pressing questions online.

POINTS OF DISCOVERY

Now that you have an understanding of what great content does—and how it can work for you—ask yourself the following questions:

1. What are some of the blogs, magazines, podcasts, etc. that you regularly consume? What do you like about them? Why do you keep coming back?
2. What type of experiences do your customers want from you? What emotions do they want to feel? What do they want to learn?
3. How is your business changing lives? In other words, what is it that you *really* do?

Chapter 3

STRATEGY STARTS AT THE SEARCH CYCLE

[C]ontent marketing is channel-agnostic. That means that content marketers should be looking at ALL available channels to engage with customers . . . print, in-person, and online (including mobile).

—Joe Pulizzi

Isn't it great that we can find nearly anything we want online? Feel the itch to know what year your favorite TV show aired? Google it. Looking for the best brand of sneakers for tennis players? Start by Googling it. Want to know what The Dude said in your favorite scene of The Big Lebowski? That's right, dude, just Google it. The staggering amount of information available to every Internet-connected person is influencing every aspect of life today: communication, entertainment, business, health care, government, education, technology—and shopping.

In a very short period of time, modern users have come to expect that anything they want can be found through a series of searches. Our entire modern reality has shifted: Theoretically, the entire human world can be connected online. Communication is instantaneous and anyone can have a web presence—meaning, there's a low barrier to entry and high competition.

If you are a business, potential customers are searching for you, right now. They are searching for the service or product you provide, at the price point you've set, at the terms you offer, in the location where you offer it.

With the power of Google's advanced search engine at nearly anyone's fingertips, modern users have become accustomed to finding what they need quickly and easily. The question for your business becomes: How do you make sure potential customers land on your website (quickly and easily) rather than on your competitor's? (Then, after that, you want to ask what will keep them with you, but first thing's first: You've got to get them in the door.)

In the Information Age, it's important to be thinking about how your customers are finding you online—that is, how they search for information. When a decision comes up, whether it's which movie to see, which car to buy, or which hospital to go to, Internet users today expect their information instantly—and specific to their personal needs. Even if a purchase is made in a brick-and-mortar store, search is increasingly the starting point for consumer research. This is why the *content shift* teaches us that in order to connect with our audiences through content, we first need to know what they're searching for. Find the questions they want answered, and you'll know what content topics to produce.

Internet searches are one of the first major steps consumers take before making a purchase. A 2018 study found that a whopping 88% of buyers do online research before making major purchases.[1] While a person may well ask friends for recommendations, watch TV ads, or see advertising in print, the search engine is a powerful tool—meaning, along the path to purchase, you definitely want the right content positioned on your web pages, at the right stages, to answer those shopping questions, inviting people to sign up, share, and buy in.

This is where the *Search Cycle* comes in. The Search Cycle specifically relates to the steps a user will take online before reaching the purchase stage. We'll go in-depth with this soon.

SHORT VS. LONG SALES CYCLES

Especially for large purchases, search has become a vital tool for consumers online, creating a content marketing opportunity for businesses. For example, when a person is considering making a large or expensive purchase, search has come to augment—and even, in some cases, replace—previous methods of making purchasing decisions. Buying a car is a perfect example of a large purchase with a long sales cycle. Before the Internet, classified ads, commercials, or product brochures might have been some of the primary ways you became aware of different car options. You might scan over prices and specs, call dealerships, visit in person, pick up a printed brochure, take a few test drives, and ask for advice from friends before finally pulling the trigger on such a big purchase. Today, these options are all still available—with the added convenience of having access to endless information online. The Internet naturally helps customers in their *pre-purchase discovery* phase. The longer the Search Cycle is for your product, the more content you will want to have in place along various touch points to support the decision to choose you over a competitor.

Consider the difference between buying a pack of gum and buying a car. Gum sales generally have a very *short sales cycle* and a low price point, while purchasing a car has a *long sales cycle* and a high price point. It doesn't take much research to determine which type of gum you want to buy in the checkout line at a grocery store. There are a few immediate factors to consider: brands you already know and like, the appeal of packaging, flavor preferences, size, and cost. Probably very few people spend hours online searching for the exact right type of gum to buy. But most people would consider that level of research a necessary part of buying a car because it's such a significant investment.

Businesses with a long sales cycle should definitely be doing content marketing. People spend time researching large purchases like cars, educational institutions, homes, boats, investments, consultants, and other significant allocations of resources. These are products with high complexity, high cost, and high stakes. A wrong decision can mean a world of pain, so lots of time and resources are often dedicated to the research process. These are decisions that can tremendously impact a person's life, and, therefore, require more diligence on the part of the consumer. Gum is an impulse buy; a new car is not (for most people).

For big-ticket items, a consumer usually starts with a question or idea about what they want or need, and then they spend time investigating options. This is where content marketing really shines. Positioning content online that answers those questions at the right moments can help customers learn more about what you have to offer—in a helpful, relevant, non-salesy way. If your potential customers are looking for information, provide it. (And keep in mind, content marketing can be beneficial for most businesses, not just those with a long sales cycle. Positioning your brand to align with customer values, tell your brand story, connect emotionally, provide entertainment, or create community are some other ways that content marketing helps build trusting relationships with customers.)

Content marketing, in a large way, is all about education. Educate customers about the benefits and considerations of your product so they can make an informed decision—one which, hopefully, leads to engaging with your company. We believe that every brand and every product can be supported through content marketing. The key is to find the best ways to engage with your particular audience.

ADOPTING A SEARCH MINDSET

If content marketing is the new means of connecting with customers in the digital age, search is the bridge that unites you. Therefore, adopting a *search mindset* has become necessary in today's rapidly developing Internet culture. Businesses that adopt a search mindset are more equipped to navigate the digital space successfully because they understand how search operates, how important it is, and how to maximize their efforts.

To help your customers arrive confidently at your digital doorstep, you will first want to understand exactly *how they are trying to find you*—and how to make it easy for them. With the mushrooming glut of information constantly being added to the Internet on a daily basis, there needs to be a way of categorizing and segmenting all of it. Enter the role of the search engine. Search engines filter results based on keywords entered into a search bar, thereby providing a path through the ever-changing Internet labyrinth.

When the Internet first began to explode in the late 1990s, with it came a new wave of doing business online. *Organic search marketing*, also called search engine optimization (SEO), became a way to strategically maximize a website's placement in search engine results through a variety of methods, like HTML structure, website architecture, keyword usage, inbound links—and *content*.

Just for a bit of context, it wasn't until around 2007 that content really started to play a more essential role in search marketing. Before then, and pretty much all through the Wild Wild West of the digital 90s, a website could actually rank on Google with simple SEO techniques, like keyword stuffing, excessive cross links to pages with keywords they want to rank for, and even filling web pages with invisible text. Both the Internet and search marketers have grown up a lot since then; most of those manipulative tactics are now easily detectable by Google.

Why does this matter? Even though there was a time when these methods were widespread and fairly effective, the websites that eventually outperformed the others were focused on producing better content and engaging the reader. This trend has only continued, and we would argue that, today, SEO and content marketing are inseparable. You really need both: an understanding of SEO *and* content that is meant for people (rather than search engines). Again, you can find hours of amusement online diving into this debate, but, as search marketers writing a content marketing book, our position is strong and clear: SEO now relies so fully on content marketing that they have essentially become integrated. Likewise, you're doing content marketing ineffectively if you're not considering search.

POSITION CONTENT STRATEGICALLY THROUGHOUT THE SEARCH CYCLE

Search engines "reward" websites that show high *search relevance* and high *user engagement* with content. We achieve greater reach and engagement by creating strategic, high-quality content that answers users' questions and fulfills their needs.

So, how do you know what your audience's needs are? You can learn a lot by researching the types of searches they're making related to your business and what those searches mean along the *path to purchase*. (This is the series of steps a customer makes before committing to a purchase.) You may also hear some people call this the *consumer-decision journey* or the *buyer's journey*.

The *Search Cycle* is our unique model outlining the path to purchase online. As noted earlier, it specifically relates to the steps a user will take online before reaching the purchase stage (making a commitment). We distilled our many years of experience doing search research into five simple stages of a user's online path to purchase. This is especially useful for long sales cycles.

The Search Cycle outlines the five most common online search stages a user will cycle through before, during, and after committing to a purchase. These stages may not always occur in linear order:

1. Awareness
2. Information Gathering
3. Evaluation
4. Commitment
5. Support

The Search Cycle provides a roadmap, showing us how users are operating online and how they're finding what they want, as shown in Figure 3.1 . Not all searches perform the same function. It's important to understand at which stage a customer is meeting you online and to have content prepared for that particular customer need or question.

Understanding Search | Search Cycle and Behavior

1. Awareness	2. Information Gathering	3. Evaluation	4. Commitment	5. Support
Need	Solutions	Specifications	Decision	Use
Want	Explanation	Comparisons	Purchase	Evaluation
Problem	Options	Alternatives	Inquiry	Post-purchase
Issue	Service	X vs Y / Pro vs Con	Sign-up	Tell Others
Opportunity	Provider	Quality	Schedule	Recommend
Improve	Supplier	Reputation		Review

Figure 3.1: Understanding the Search Cycle

The Search Cycle is fairly short for products like gum, soda, food, and other impulse purchases that have a low price point. However, the Search Cycle can be hugely beneficial for companies with longer sales cycles and those in competitive spaces. In a survey of 158 business professionals by Arm Treasure Data, 71% estimate the time between first customer engagement and purchase at a month or longer.[2] One woman in a Google study spent 73 days and interacted with more than 250 touch points (searches, page views, video views, etc.) before purchasing a single pair of jeans.[3] This type of lengthy research before purchase is not unusual for modern consumers.

The Search Cycle outlines how people conduct searches online before, during, and after a purchase. If someone in your target audience is searching specifically for questions your company can answer, you'll want to have content prepared at each stage of the Search Cycle. This is a great tool for helping businesses understand how customers search for information online before purchasing.

We'll be returning to this model throughout the book in more depth.

Stage 1: Awareness

In this stage, a person is becoming aware of a need, problem, or desire. This can happen in myriad different ways, and it can be caused by internal or external stimuli. It can be a functional need, a social need, or a need for change. Awareness can happen online or offline.

Stage 2: Information Gathering

Once a need is identified, a consumer launches into information-gathering mode. This can involve talking to friends, recalling previous knowledge and experience, and turning to Internet searches—especially for significant purchases where more information is needed. This is an important stage because it provides you with the opportunity to develop content that answers your customers' questions, offering them the information they need to support their purchasing decision.

Stage 3: Evaluation

After gathering information, a consumer will embark on evaluating their different options using the criteria already set forth. This can involve comparing different brands, products, and features to determine the best fit. This is another area where content can be developed to help consumers weigh out the options to support their purchase.

Stage 4: Commitment

Once all available options have been evaluated, a consumer is ready to take the next step. This may entail making a purchase, making a call, or requesting more information via a form. Regardless of the case, they are committing to the beginning of a relationship with your brand. They are giving you permission for further engagement. Enough trust has been earned that the user is ready to make some type of commitment. This may be a small commitment to continue engaging with your company or a full purchasing decision. The Search Cycle can be repeated multiple times, resulting in deeper levels of commitment each time.

At this stage, even though purchase or commitment is more likely, the quality of the user's experience can still make or break the decision. A frustrating ecommerce experience or a rude salesperson can deter the consumer from following through with the decision, so it's important to have supportive elements in place. You can position your content to be that good salesman who speaks for your brand, is available online at all hours of the day, and is ready to help your customers find what they're looking for and guide them towards purchase.

Stage 5: Support

The commitment or purchasing stage does not need to be—and should not be—the last stage of the Search Cycle. The support stage is often overlooked, but it can actually be one of the most valuable ways to focus your content creation. After a commitment has been made, content in the support stage could involve following up with the customer to reinforce their purchasing decision and engage their feedback—for example, asking for a review or sending follow-up coupons.

Giving your customer digital versions of product manuals or quick-start guides, or even customization options, are other great ways of reinforcing the purchasing decision. For example, even though IKEA products typically come with an assembly guide, some customers might need a little more guidance. Maybe a customer needs very specific information about the dimensions of a product to determine if that bookshelf will fit in their living room. If they can quickly and easily get their questions answered online by the company that sold them the product in the first place, that will only support their satisfaction with the purchase. This could also help prevent returns and, therefore, negative reviews. IKEA could have a "how-to" video ready for that specific search inquiry, ultimately preventing the customer from feeling frustrated and regretting the purchase.

Support content shows your customers that your brand is still invested in helping them, even after the sale has been made. The goal here is to maintain customer loyalty and continue to create positive messages around the brand, inspiring people to come back and spread the word. (This stage can also act as support *before* the purchase, showing a user that you are prepared with supplementary information to help them *if* they do decide to buy.)

> The Search Cycle is vital to crafting content because it allows us to conceptualize the needs of our customers at various points in time.

Despite the technical considerations of SEO, people are always at the heart of search. The Search Cycle is one way to better understand the mindsets of people looking for you online. Keep this in mind as we continue to merge the concepts of search, audience, and content.

> Since the dawn of search engines, professionals in the industry have been categorizing search queries into three basic categories:[4]
>
> 1. **Informational**: seeking static information about a topic.
> 2. **Transactional**: shopping at, downloading from, or otherwise interacting with the result.
> 3. **Navigational**: sending users to a specific URL.
>
> Google also calls these, "Know," "Do," and "Go," respectively.[5] Each of these can occur, theoretically, at any of the five stages, but informational searches tend to occur in the beginning stages. Transactional searches usually occur leading up to the moment of purchase, and navigational searches tend to occur during the evaluation or post-purchase stages.

GOODBYE SALES FUNNEL, HELLO COMPLEX LOOP

To make matters even more interesting, each of these five stages could occur virtually anytime, on any device, and in no particular order. While the Search Cycle appears to be linear in Figure 3.1, that's mostly just for ease of conceptualization; it's not necessarily a linear progression.

Potential customers can find you at any time online, starting at any of the search stages. For example, continuing our example about IKEA specifications, what might be surprising to think about is that a customer can even *begin* the Search Cycle with a support-stage search query. Someone might decide they want to know how to assemble the product *before* making the purchase. The how-to video could solve this. Having this knowledge can better equip you to meet your customers' questions with answers at any stage of the journey. In today's digital age, the linear idea of a "sales funnel," as illustrated in Figure 3.2, is obsolete.

Today, a customer may (or may not) walk into a store, find something they like, search for it online, compare reviews, find another store, and save a bookmark on their mobile phone—only to buy it weeks later at a discounted price from an online retailer. The "funnel" is now a complex loop that can be better conceptualized outside of a linear model.

Figure 3.2: The Obsolete Sales Funnel

Because consumers can access any of these stages at any time on any device, the model now looks more accurately like the image shown in Figure 3.3.

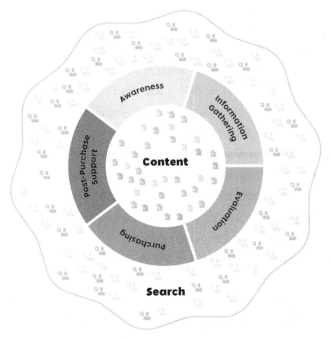

Figure 3.3: The Nonlinear Nature of the Search Cycle

Content is at the center of everything, and the five stages of the Search Cycle can occur in virtually any order. The audience, on the outer edge, may interact with any of the stages at any point in a completely nonlinear fashion. A search can start at evaluation, for example, and then move back to information gathering, and then return to evaluation again.

A search can occur on a mobile device, on a tablet, on a desktop computer—or all three at different times—and can even include voice assistance. One person could be making multiple searches across multiple devices, happening all at once or across long spans of time. A linear marketing model no longer works because of the complex nature of the Internet.

Still, content is at the center because knowing that these searches even occur at all, and in some predictable fashion, hugely informs a content strategy. If you know that this general model exists, you can begin to understand why and how people search online, what phrases they're using, and what their intent might be. This is an essential start to the content production process.

You can strategically align your messaging with the desires of your audience—based on solid, tangible search terms, or *queries*. A query is a phrase typed into a search engine, for example, "where to find discount sneakers" or "massage training class" or "clear sandals that the Dude wore in Big Lebowski." Investigating the queries around your product or industry is the essential search research that will link your content production to your audience's needs. What are the questions that users are asking online related to your business? These are the questions you want to answer with your content. We'll guide you through this process completely in Chapter 14.

The bottom line is this: If a customer is looking for your exact product or service, you want to do everything in your power to be found. Identify search terms, then answer those questions or address those topics with valuable, relevant, and useful content. We'll go into the keyword research process to identify search terms later in the book because this is the essential search research *shift* we are very excited to present to you.

POINTS OF DISCOVERY

Now that you understand the role of search in content marketing, ask yourself the following questions:

1. How long do you think your average customer spends researching or thinking about your product or service before deciding to pull the trigger? What sorts of information could help them make their decision?
2. What are some of the ways people are becoming aware of your business, either online or off?
3. What types of search phrases do you think people might be typing into Google to learn more about topics related to your business?

Chapter 4

ACHIEVING ONLINE AUTHORITY

> Today, what generates interest, persuades, engages, and creates a sense of customer loyalty is the consistent engagement and unexpected delight in the experience that people have with the brand.
>
> —Carla Johnson and Robert Rose, Experiences: The 7th Era of Marketing

There are some brands that just can't be touched. You know the ones—Kleenex, Coca-Cola, Tide, McDonald's. We all know what these brands have to offer and what they represent. They've become iconic. From Coca-Cola's memorable red cursive font to Tide's unmistakable bright orange background, the *brand identity* of these companies is clear, robust, and unmistakable.

Brands like Coke, Pepsi, and Google are the apex of *brand awareness* and *brand authority*. How many times have you said to a family member, "Do you have a Kleenex?" You were asking for a tissue, but you said Kleenex, right? The same is true when ordering a beverage at a restaurant. Do you say you'd like a sweet, carbonated cola? No, you say, "I'll have a Coke." Similarly, Google is synonymous with search. These terms are defined as proprietary eponyms.[1] These brands are so well known that the company name has replaced the generic description of the product they manufacture.

In today's constantly changing online marketplace, where new companies can crop up literally overnight, how do you compete with the brand behemoths at the top? How do you achieve recognition? Fortunately, the online playing field allows access to nearly anyone. You don't need a huge advertising budget to be found anymore. You just need a great product, a quality website, and a smart content strategy to build *online authority* for your brand so you can be known for what you do best. The content shift doesn't care how big your brand is; you just need to know your audience and what they are searching for to create content that provides solutions.

WHAT IS ONLINE AUTHORITY?

Authority is the power to influence thought, opinion, and behavior. *Online authority* occurs when a website has achieved such a high level of regard among users and search engines that the brand is considered synonymous with a certain subject matter. Brands who achieve online authority are thought to be experts in their field and at the top of the competition. In online marketing, "Become the branded search" is a common mantra. When your brand is so well known that people skip the generic search and go straight to the branded search, you've probably reached some level of online authority.

Tom's of Maine is a great example of strong brand identity with a high degree of online authority. For example, rather than searching for "natural organic deodorant," a searcher might type into Google, "Tom's deodorant." The searcher already associates the Tom's brand with the product, so they skip straight to the branded search. There's no need to research options because the brand is already trusted for this product. This is online authority.

Tom's is a company focused on natural personal care products, whose content is in alignment with both their products and their brand messaging. You'll find articles on their blog on a variety of topics—all about appreciating the natural environment, discovering alternative health remedies, inspiring awareness in others, making conscious purchasing decisions, and choosing the healthier option. (Side note: Punctuation and capitalization don't matter to Google, so "Tom's deodorant" functions the same way as "toms deodorant"—they are essentially the same query.)

Competition falls to the wayside once you hit critical mass. Who can compete with "Tom's deodorant" as a search term? Retailers, critical news, or potentially in-depth reviews may also appear for this term, but otherwise this is a pretty clear query. This shopper is close to the point of purchase—they don't even need to determine what sort of deodorant to buy; your brand is already at the forefront of their mind. What do you think of when you think "electric cars?" Is it *Tesla*? Now, while there may be others out there, Tesla is a brand that most people can easily associate with that industry.

Consider Amazon as an example of a brand that has achieved ultimate online authority. Most of us now accept Amazon as an online behemoth that controls many market sectors. The fact that a river in South America is now associated worldwide with fast, easy, convenient online shopping is the ultimate pinnacle of online authority.

How did Amazon get there? Before the website was launched, millions of dollars were spent on various media platforms (lots and lots of *content*) to announce the imminent launch of a new idea: an online bookstore. At the time of its inception, some consumers found it difficult to equate the name—which suggested one of the world's largest rivers—with books. As the store expanded to include clothing, electronics, music, food and beauty products (to name a handful of categories), the idea of an expansive Internet shopping mall began to make sense. Amazon.

The messaging Amazon created was obviously effective because the name is now an enviable concept and mega-brand—a retail force to be reckoned with. Amazon became the online authority it is today because of a *strategic plan* to create the association in users' minds between a South American river and an online shopping mall.

Companies that want to compete online absolutely need strategic content marketing to enjoy positive brand recognition. Amazon didn't start out as the go-to online store when it was founded in 1994.[2] **Repeated experiences all need initial experiences first.** Wherever you are in the evolution of your company, you can start improving your content marketing and building your online authority at any time. It's sort of parallel to the idea of compounding interest: The earlier you start, the more value you build, so beginning now is better than tomorrow. No matter how long your company has been around—whether you bought your domain yesterday or whether you've been in business for 35 years—it's never a bad time to take stock of your content strategy. Moving forward and expanding your brand online is a process best begun as soon as possible.

WHAT IS THE ONLINE EXPERIENCE OF YOUR BRAND?

More and more, savvy modern customers are invested in the entire experience of a brand, and not just the product. This is a huge shift from decades ago and arises from the age of interaction and interconnectivity. In *Experiences: The 7th Era of Marketing*, authors Carla Johnson and Robert Rose propose that we're entering (or are already in) the 7th era of marketing, in which experiences have taken the spotlight for most online customers or users.

> "The idea of providing education, delight and general usefulness (as a brand's approach to engage its customers) provides a new way to enrich interactions with customers at every stage of the buying journey."[3]
>
> —Carla Johnson and Robert Rose, *The 7th Era*

When you focus your energy on creating content that people want and connecting in an authentic way, you make it that much easier for people to feel positively about their experiences with you. The more positive experiences shared, the more your brand can grow. A crucial goal of content marketing is to create consistently positive experiences for your audience while consistently showing Google that you're an expert in your field—thereby earning exposure to a wider audience and building online authority.

Even if you're ostensibly competing against big brands like Coca-Cola or Pepsi, who are already the giants in the field of fizzy sodas, the Internet opens doors for smaller producers to thrive. Let's say you're a specialty soda selling your products solely online. Today, you very well may be successful because you can use the breadth of the Internet to find the people who don't want Pepsi but who want exactly what you have to offer—something that's *different* than what's already out there, say, cucumber soda, birch beer, or sarsaparilla.* These are all real sodas we found on the first page of Google by conducting a simple search for "specialty sodas." Pepsi doesn't produce these, but someone out there does.

Maybe your field is the world of organic pet treats. Or sustainable underwear. Or Brooklyn-style pizza with a California twist. Instead of trying to beat out Walmart, Amazon, or Coca-Cola, do what you do best. Who cares if your product isn't in every single home in America? If you can appear on the first page of Google for relevant search terms (a desired outcome of strategic content marketing), you can have the opportunity to entice an interested searcher and invite them into the experience of your brand. Your audience is not "everyone." Your audience consists of the people specifically searching for what you have to offer, so it's vitally important to reach them—and not so important to reach everyone else.

> **Brand identity:** *The image constructed by a company about itself.*
>
> To start building content to support your brand, your brand identity must be clear first. No significant progress can be made if your company's products, services, mission, vision, goals, and messaging are confused or inconsistent.

---

* These are all real sodas. A simple search for "specialty sodas" will show you what we mean about the huge variety and availability of products out there, and the effectiveness of search to connect products with customers.

Brand image: *The idea of a brand as perceived by customers or the public.*

Get solid on who you are and what you do—first! Then, when your brand identity is robust and confident, your brand identity can stand on its own and becomes perceived by the public as your brand image.

Brand awareness: *The extent to which people recognize the existence of a company's product or service. Basically, people are aware that the brand exists.*

With enough exposure, your brand can be prominent enough for people to know who you are.

Brand recognition: *The extent to which people recognize specific products or services offered by a brand, based on prior knowledge or experience. People know about the brand.*

With even more exposure, you can achieve brand recognition, where your brand is widespread enough to even reach people outside your target audience.

HOW STRATEGIC CONTENT BUILDS ONLINE AUTHORITY

To some degree, authority is an external event. It's not something you can assign yourself (unless you're Kanye West), but it is something you can work diligently toward achieving. Traditionally, brand authority was earned through consistent output and customer satisfaction over time, through delivering repeated messages and earning customer trust.

Since many top-brand products were of similar quality in the 1950s and 1960s, the only way to dominate was to perfect consumer relations: Know your customer and match the product to their needs. The same is true for content marketing today. Know your audience and deliver the content they want.

Even huge brands need to sit down with a content team and consistently check in on their content strategy. Coca-Cola, for example, has been one of the world's largest ad spenders, fronting $4 billion for ads in 2019.[4] Recently, however, the global brand has been pivoting toward more digital content and real-time content production like streaming.[5]

Content is how both users and search engines determine whether you are a source to be trusted. Search engines won't reward sites that don't provide value for the people who visit. Nobody wants to waste their time with content that is vapid, deceitful, or irrelevant. (Well, to be fair, sometimes some of us do: how else could we explain tabloids?) But even that type of content, superficial or hyperbolic as it may be, provides intentional value—entertainment value. The key is that content should be purposefully creating *some kind of value*. Killer content is the avenue towards brand recognition and authority in your field online.

> Strategic content creation connects you with your potential customers.

Here's what online authority looks like in action:

Well Developed, Trusted Content

- You're a trusted source of knowledge or expertise, and your positive online reputation precedes you.
- You have a unique, specific point of view. You are a thought leader in your industry or have an irreplaceable service, product, or position.
- You have a consistent, reliable output of content that contributes meaningfully to your customers' lives and to the industry as a whole.
- People who come across your content online have an easy time determining that you are a source they can trust.

Domination in Search Results

- Your content ranks well in search for the target subject matter of each piece of content.
- Content can be sourced and referenced online through backlinks and citations, indicators of trusted content to a search engine.
- Google awards your website higher positions in search, possibly even featuring your content in *search features*. These elements may change over time, but they show up as the featured sections from a Google search result, such as Answer Boxes and Featured Snippets.
- Search volume research shows that people conduct searches for your product or service using your brand name.

Robust Relationships with Your Audience

- People share and engage with your content online.
- You have a large, wide audience base, including brand ambassadors—people who advocate for you.
- You are in touch with influencers—people in your industry who vouch for you.
- Even people outside of your audience are aware of your existence.

BRANDS THAT CONNECT—WIN

If you want to know the simple yet complex key to building online authority, it's this: Create an emotional bond with devoted fans.[6] This impulse elevated brands to eponymous status in the 20th century and is still at the core of creating popular content today. Brands are now producers, and the savviest brands are the savviest producers—*companies that know how to connect*.

Content created for your content marketing campaigns will probably not be—and really shouldn't be—entirely focused on your brand. However, everything you create should somehow be related to your brand so that when people are excited about sharing what you've given them, the implicit tie to your company is always there.

In short, strategic content that connects with people builds brand awareness and online authority. The connection that people make with your brand today, online, has the potential to be authentic, meaningful, and long-lasting. You can provide answers, solutions, encouragement, knowledge, humor, or entertainment in nearly any form imaginable online—sparking positive emotional responses that will get your website seen, saved, and shared because people genuinely appreciate what you put out there.

Still, you might be asking, "How do I get there?" A content strategy directs the type of content you need to create to achieve this goal. Knowing what your audience wants, then going the extra mile to give it to them better than anyone else, establishes your legitimacy. You move toward online authority by producing high-quality, relevant, personalized messaging that benefits users consistently.

Authority arises through recognition by some group subset—one that you hope to influence—that you have something important to give, do, or say. It doesn't matter how large or small of an audience you might command, it's all about the right people believing in your point of view or way of doing business. While you can't control your audience's responses to you, you can control the messages you are publishing online, your interactions, your brand personality—and the quality of your content. We'll talk about this more later, but the truth is that poor-quality content can actually hurt your brand identity by creating a negative association with users.

The good news is that you are completely in the driver's seat of your content production. It's not just preferable to produce great content that people want—it's an essential part of any online brand identity.

BENEFITS OF ONLINE AUTHORITY

- **Public awareness:** When people enjoy your content, they are likely to share the link to an article or video.
- **Good neighbor status:** A willingness to provide valuable content that helps users, demonstrates that you're in it for the long run, not a fly-by-night operation.
- **Indirect sales results:** Discovery of good content may win customers who were previously unaware of your company.
- **Improved teamwork:** Quality content is a group activity. The marketing department must necessarily interact with sales people and management.
- **Traffic increase:** Excellent content created with an understanding of search engine optimization (SEO) will attract more visitors to your website.
- **Direct sales results:** With increased exposure and authority, you can expect more relevant organic traffic that leads to sales.

How do you get there? Consistent quality.

POINTS OF DISCOVERY

In this chapter, we discussed how you can expand your brand through content. Now, consider the following questions as they relate to your brand:

1. What do you have to offer your customers that no one else can?
2. How can you improve the lives of your customers?
3. What information or insight would help your customers live better lives, do their jobs better, or make progress in areas they are interested in?
4. What topics are you an expert in?
5. What problems are your customers having that you can solve?

6. Who are a few authorities in your field that you follow or admire? What do you like about what they are doing?
7. How is what you offer, or your perspective, different from or better than what already exists? In other words, how does your company uniquely add to the conversation in your field?
8. If your customers were to describe your company in one word, what are a few of the words you'd hope they'd use?

Chapter 5

WHY CONSISTENCY MATTERS

It may not seem sexy, but consistency is the secret ingredient to making customers happy.

—Alfonso Pulido, Dorian Stone, and John Strevel, McKinsey & Company

What's better, attracting 1,000 new visitors to your website and converting two of them to leads or keeping 100 customers happy? Ideally, you strive for both—consistently. The content shift can be applied to new and existing customers; both segments of your audience could be searching for answers to their questions online, providing you with opportunities to connect. You shouldn't just be producing content to reel in new customers—*but also to maintain the customers you already have*. The way to do this is by gently and consistently reminding them of the value you offer, reinforcing their decision to continue doing business with you, and providing a consistently enjoyable experience that none of your competitors can beat.

The experience of interacting with your brand should outweigh the anxieties of making a purchase, and it should do this so fully that a customer walks away feeling entirely certain they made the right choice. Interacting with your brand should easily produce a positive feeling, and the more consistent that feeling becomes, the easier and easier it is for a customer to continue choosing you. People are not only buying products and services; the market is oversaturated with competition for just about everything. People want authentic relationships and unique experiences.

Another shift in thinking to adopt is this: You're essentially building a community online around your brand, so it should serve those in the community as well as welcome newcomers. Brands that support specific lifestyles or community values can foster community and engagement through interactive approaches, like allowing comments on blog posts, hosting a webinar, or holding giveaway contests on social media. These are some of the ways brands are providing value outside of their direct products or services while maintaining a close connection to core values. For example, an online vegan food vendor might find great success by hosting an online forum for community members to trade vegan recipes. They could also send out an email newsletter featuring curated recipes that showcase the company's ingredients or begin hosting in-person events to bring people together.

Even if your company isn't starkly in favor of any particular stance or lifestyle choice, there are certainly values, ideas, and principles driving your movement forward. As leadership expert Simon Sinek says, "People don't buy what you do; they buy why you do it." Bring your "why" out to the forefront and connect with the people who resonate with what you're doing.

So, how do you build community around common values, create memorable experiences, and keep delivering value to grow your business online over time? One of the most important elements of content marketing success, especially to maintain an engaged and active audience, is consistency. This is not just a wayward hypothesis, either, but a well-researched phenomenon called *cumulative advantage*.

DELIVER CONSISTENT CONTENT: A CUMULATIVE ADVANTAGE

In today's overwhelming online marketplace, where competition is fierce and loud—and where emails you didn't sign up for appear in your inbox, sign-up forms pop up on the websites you visit, and ads follow you around—it's no wonder people are tuning out. We are constantly bombarded with information. And a lot of that information is trying to persuade us to do or buy something, which can become tiring. Often, we'd rather not do anything.

A company that keeps us happy with the least amount of effort is one we're likely to continue doing business with. You want to be the type of company that maintains customers by delivering consistent quality. A.G. Lafley and Roger L. Martin of the *Harvard Business Review* define cumulative advantage as "the layer that a company builds on its initial competitive advantage by making its product or service an ever more instinctively comfortable choice for the customer."[1]

Another, broader definition from Thomas A. DiPerete and Gregory M. Eirich of Columbia University position cumulative advantage as "the 'advantage' of one individual or group over another [that] grows (i.e., accumulates) over time, which is often taken to mean that inequality of this advantage grows over time."[2] This concept can be applied to various social systems, including economics and social mobility, but, for our purposes, it directly applies to content marketing and the cumulative benefits of producing content consistently.

In simple terms, cumulative advantage means that the more you provide someone with a good experience, the more they will want that experience, and vice versa. For example, how much do you love researching a new car insurance plan? If you're like most people, it's probably not at the top of your list of fun weekend activities. If your car insurance company is competent and smart, they'll do everything they can to keep you happy so they retain your business. Likewise, it's in your best interest to stay satisfied with your carrier so you don't have to make yet another choice.

It's mutually beneficial for both parties (the company and the customer) to keep having good experiences with each other, but the responsibility is on the company to make sure this happens. Even if your car insurance company raises their rates a little bit or changes their privacy policy (assuming these are uncomplicated updates), their method of communication can be streamlined to make the experience as painless as possible in order to retain the customer.

> Each time you choose a product, it gains advantage over those you didn't choose.

Especially in today's world, innovation isn't always the biggest selling point—*convenience* is. Can you make your customers' lives easier, better, and happier? Most of all, can you add value to their lives by keeping them satisfied with your brand so they don't have to add yet another item to their to-do list? Once you acquire a customer, maintaining their business by consistently producing reliable service, products—and **content**—is the foundation of cumulative advantage.

Even if your product or service isn't the *perfect* choice (because what choice is ever entirely perfect?), if what you offer fits well enough into your customers' emotional, logical, financial, and ideological worldview—and if it satisfies their needs—it's easier for them, in the long run, to continue choosing you over your competitors. While this may not be an entirely new concept, it's a pivotal one to master in the digital age. As the world around us is constantly changing, comfort, security, and familiarity are just as important as novelty and innovation. We're still creatures of habit, and change is not always met with enthusiasm.

GIVE YOUR AUDIENCE EXPERIENCES THEY WANT TO REPEAT

While trends are everywhere, novelty alone is not enough to keep your company thriving. Don't get us wrong, this doesn't mean you can consistently produce boring content and have that be the end of it; no, innovation, creativity, and smart messaging are still at the core of any good content. Yet, it's not quite enough. One outstanding blog post per year, while it may indeed be the best blog post you've ever written, won't be enough to sustain any serious momentum for your company. But one outstanding blog post per month or week, for example, can consistently, over time, attract the customers you want to keep.

> Innovation and creativity are necessary, but consistency is the cornerstone of content marketing success.

For example, let's say you, as a customer, are subscribed to an RSS feed (a blog that automatically emails you when there's a new post). Every Friday, the blog sends you three short paragraphs of fun, inspirational musings about a topic you're interested in, say dancing. Naturally, it would make sense for this type of post to come from a company that offers different types of dance classes. You receive the email every week and usually skim it, depending on the subject matter, but sometimes you spend the five minutes to read it fully and always end up feeling fulfilled and satisfied afterwards.

By continuing to engage with that material every week, you come to look forward to the stories and insights, and you'd probably notice if the emails suddenly stopped. (This can always be a great checkpoint for your company: Would anyone miss your content if it were gone?) So, bringing it back to cumulative advantage, we can see that a positive association is already formed in the user's mind, so when it comes time for that person to say yes to dance classes, the decision is easy. It would actually be *more difficult* to go out and research the best dance classes in your area than to simply sign up for one that's offered by your favorite weekly blog post.

In addition to cumulative advantage, there is another concept that supports the idea of brand consistency: *processing fluency*. Processing fluency is the ability of our brains to recognize repeated experiences. The more an experience occurs, the easier it is for the brain to process it.

Consider the experience of walking into your neighborhood grocery store, one that you've shopped at for years. You know where everything is, and you can run in and out for a few items quickly because your brain doesn't need to spend extra energy mapping out the aisles or trying to decode the signs. The processing fluency for this experience is high because repetition has created ease, familiarity, and efficiency. Now consider walking into the grocery store after a major redesign, and your brain is tasked with learning where everything is all over again. From a marketer's perspective, we can understand the psychological reasoning behind rearranging a grocery store. The purpose is to increase sales, for example, hoping customers will find new items they want on their way to the milk or whatever they came in for—but it's not necessarily pleasant for the existing customer.

This is a bit what it's like when a brand undergoes a design overhaul, or drastically changes their messaging or products. We can see this concept come to life in plenty of brand stories: Instagram tried a rebranding of their logo to public outcry; Coke and Pepsi faced backlash when attempting to rebrand their diet sodas; Myspace faced disintegration by adding too many features and losing the streamlined nature of the platform. While these scenarios are certainly not the end of the world for anybody, in general, chaos creates confusion, and change can bring about discomfort. It's easier for consumers to keep choosing the option they already know than to spend precious time interpreting new stimuli.

"Consistency will always trump delight."

—Jake Sorofman

In general, users want a *consistently* positive experience. We've probably all experienced that moment of logging onto Facebook, or your bank's website, or your email platform, and while you've been away, someone decided to do a layout change or website redesign! While, logically, this shouldn't be a major concern, and it probably isn't, there's probably some small part of your brain that goes, *Ouch! Change! Ack! I don't like it.* That's because, neurologically, our brains are wired to find comfort and security in familiarity, and change requires the brain to reassess a situation, which can be jarring, uncomfortable, or even distressing. Understanding processing fluency can help us align our marketing strategies with what people want.

We want it to be so easy for a customer to choose our product, service, or brand that they don't even have to think about it at all. We want every aspect of the online experience to be quick, easy, convenient, pleasing, valuable, and relevant to their lives. There are a lot of elements that go into user experience—everything from the ease of navigation on the page to the quality of images to the shopping cart experience. These are very important for a consistently positive experience, yet a discussion on user experience is outside the scope of this book. Instead, what we want to focus on is the importance of *publishing content consistently.*

THINK LIKE A PUBLISHER

Content marketing essentially requires a publishing mindset. Publishers release content regularly—and so should you. We're not all writers, videographers, or storytellers—but the beautiful thing is, *we can be*, and you probably already are. Just hop over to YouTube to see how many people are boldly stepping into their roles as storytellers, reviewers, tutorialists, artists, etc. The Internet has opened up the playing field to virtually everyone. Though we may not think about it this way initially, every DIY YouTuber or blogger or Twitter fanatic is enacting content marketing. That is, they are producing content that aims, at the very least, to be seen and, at the most, inspire action. In this way, every piece of content you create should be the beginning of a conversation with your audience.

Thinking like a publisher doesn't mean you have to stop everything else that your business is doing to start publishing a 100-page, glossy, full-color magazine every month. It means that you plan ahead and strategically outline what content you are going to publish online, at what frequency, and through which channels in order to consistently reach the audience that wants to consume your content. This means you create a publishing schedule, and you hold your content team accountable for creating and publishing relevant, search-focused, audience-driven content pieces on a regular basis.

People are creatures of habit, and with so many options to choose from, sometimes we really just want something that we already know delivered to us when we expect it. A brand that is familiar to us can activate those places in the brain associated with comfort and pleasure because repetition means safety and ease. An email that shows up regularly in our inbox every Sunday creates a sense of safety and security, even if this response is subconscious and we're not totally aware of it. A podcast that is released regularly every second Saturday of the month notifies listeners that the producers will reliably create more content every month. Same goes for whichever medium you choose—blog posts, YouTube, webinars. Because we're in the era of instant publishing, it's so easy for anyone to start a project. It's much harder, and much more valuable, to show your audience that you will *reliably* create more content on a consistent schedule. This makes it much safer for someone to buy in to whatever content stream you're offering.

Brands that can achieve both reliability and innovation are the ones that are going to ride that sweet spot well into the next phase of our technological evolution. Consistent messaging, consistent branding, consistent excellence—operate within this framework, and you'll have a strong content marketing foundation to carry you through the digital age.

Do what you do well and keep doing it.
Uphold consistent quality.
Earn trust.

POINTS OF DISCOVERY

In this chapter, we discussed the benefits of consistency in creating positive brand experiences for your customers through content. Consider the following questions:

1. Ideally, how often do you think your audience would want to engage with your content?
2. Brainstorm: What kind of consistent content schedule do you think your marketing department can realistically commit to?
3. What are some of the consistently positive brand experiences you either already provide or would like to provide?

Chapter 6

MAKING THE CONTENT SHIFT

> The reason we struggle with content marketing is because we haven't started with "Why?"... Customers don't care about your vanity metrics. Ask them, "How can I help?"
>
> —**Kristina Halvorson, CEO and Founder, Brain Traffic**

For thousands of years, "markets" were real, open-air marketplaces—or bazaars—where merchants came to trade their goods with a village or township. In the original iteration of true markets, conversation was a two-way street. These bazaars were open-air forums where merchants hawked their wares and throngs of people would stop to mingle and chat. "Apples! Apples! Get your apples here!" was not an advertising jingle but a conversation starter.

Where did these apples come from? How is this dress made? Will this pair of shoes last through long journeys? These are the types of questions a consumer could ask a producer directly, face to face. In historical marketplaces, conversation was expected as a natural part of commerce. You can easily imagine the crowded marketplace, where people milled about and socialized with each other.

So many aspects of society have evolved since this time, including "market"-ing. *The Cluetrain Manifesto*, originally published in 1999, is a landmark inquiry into the changing state of digital marketplaces, and many of the principles explored are still extremely relevant two decades later—especially to the practice of content marketing. In the book, authors Rick Levine, Christopher Locke, Doc Searls, and David Weinberger explain it this way:

"For thousands of years, we knew exactly what markets were: conversations between people who sought out others who shared the same interests. Buyers had as much to say as sellers."[1]

Massive social shifts throughout history have changed how people consume products and information, how products are produced, and how messages are conveyed. Today's malls and shopping centers aren't entirely the opposite of this original marketplace, but producers are far removed from the buyer's experience. If conversation happens, it's most likely between a customer and a clerk. These social shifts, combined with technological shifts, have produced a marketing field where we hope you will join us in making the *content shift*—refocusing on your audience's needs and search questions to produce content that can answer those questions.

Conversation has not necessarily been part of the dominant mode of commerce in the 20th century. *Push marketing* (ads, billboards, flyers) relies more on frequency of exposure than depth of interaction. Even in a real-life scenario, consider the following: How often do you go grocery shopping to strike up a conversation? The picture today probably looks more like this: You push your shopping cart down the aisles and choose from the options available. No bartering occurs at your local supermarket; you choose from the available goods presented. The numbers of items sold over a given time period signal to the merchant whether or not a product is selling well. Today's version of a marketplace is less a bazaar and more of a place for transactional orders to occur.

A RETURN TO OPEN MARKETS

Since the days of traditional bazaars, the modern world has evolved in countless ways. The general style of a merchant-customer relationship has shifted from *conversation to consumption*. And yet, at this moment in time, it's fascinating to note that innovative content marketing is actually returning to certain principles that defined ancient forms of "market"-ing—namely, the focus on customer-centric relationships and conversation. In fact, open marketplaces are reappearing now as a transformative element in the 21st century's digital landscape.

Today, a person can "stroll through"—or *scroll* through—a merchant's website, and, if the opportunity is there, ask the producer directly about "them apples." Anyone can send a Facebook message, fire off a tweet, or submit an email or comment with complaints, questions, opinions, or concerns. The Internet has made communication more convenient, and it's made companies feel more accessible to customers. This shift makes it easier for customers to actually voice their concerns and desires with the producer in a direct fashion. And if that producer wants to stay relevant, they'd be smart to listen. Truly, it seems we are returning to a state of dialogue in our current online marketplaces.

The digital market is now an all-access playing field in which "consumers" are just as vocal as "producers." The rules have changed. Customers once again have access to an "open" marketplace where they can engage in conversation with the people they're thinking about doing business with—except, this time, it might be a 24-hour, anywhere-anytime digital marketplace.

If a customer can't have a conversation with you, or doesn't like the one you're offering, they're going to go find one they do like. To keep up with this rapidly shifting marketplace, businesses need to be on their toes. Adaptability, flexibility, and innovation will be the sails that weather the storms.

THE DIGITAL ERA: A MORE EVEN PLAYING FIELD

Once the Internet began revolutionizing marketplaces, some interesting shifts started to occur. At first, the dot-com boom in the 2000s brought many advertising executives to an exciting new frontier as they enthusiastically applied their broadcast strategies to the World Wide Web. Of course, they'd be thrilled—the Internet was at first widely seen as one more platform on which to advertise, like TV or billboards. SEO (search engine optimization) arose as a specific field to maneuver certain messages to the top of the search engines where people would see them.

What not everyone predicted, however, was how truly game-changing the Internet would prove to be for modern business (as well as for a slew of other things). Rather than simply being another outlet for advertising campaigns, the Internet brought with it a remarkable shift back to what resembles the original open-air marketplaces.

> "The Internet itself is an example of an industry built by pure conversation."
>
> —Rick Levine, Christopher Locke, et al.
> *The Cluetrain Manifesto*

On the Internet, the distinction between producers and consumers becomes less important than *the conversation between them*. Consumers (implying the primary act of consumption) are once again customers (implying the primary act of a social custom, *such as conversation*). Anyone with an Internet connection can now participate in a back-and-forth exchange with nearly anyone—be it buyer, seller, consumer, company, friend, family member, or anyone else.

> "Connected, [customers] reclaim their voice in the market, but this time with more reach and wider influence than ever."
>
> —Rick Levine, Christopher Locke, et al.
> *The Cluetrain Manifesto*

Unfortunately, there is no shortage of businesses that still fail to understand how the old paradigm of the 20th century is changing. So, what do marketing professionals need to know to be competitive in the modern playing field? We've put together seven shifts in thinking that will help your business thrive in a fast-paced, complex, digital marketplace.

THE 7 CONTENT SHIFTS

We're giving you what we think are the seven major shifts in thinking for content marketing. These seven essential principles take a bird's eye view of content marketing, and we strongly believe that these concepts, when implemented consistently, can truly elevate your content marketing efforts.

Content Shift #1: Produce purposeful content.

As of December 2020, there are more than 1.8 billion websites on the Internet, and that number grows every second.[2] It's easy and quick to produce and publish content online. However, quantity does not necessarily equal quality. Focus on producing *the best* content you possibly can rather than *the most* content you can. What should all content be? Useful. Valuable. Relevant.

Content Shift #2: Listen to your audience.

How do you develop the content that your audience wants? Ask them, and then listen. With increased avenues of connection available in the digital age, you can truly stand out from the crowd by genuinely investing yourself in your audience's changing needs and desires. Ask what those are, and incorporate your findings into your content strategy for long-term adaptability. Don't assume. Validate your ideas by listening.

Content Shift #3: Join the conversation.

The Internet is an open forum for all kinds of communication to occur. We use the Internet to educate and inform us, to share our opinions, and to connect with others. It's a 24/7 non-stop conversation about everything under the sun, including your field, your industry, and your business. The chatter will go on with or without you, but a developed content strategy will help you make sure you're contributing meaningfully to the conversations that concern you and your audience.

Content Shift #4: Adopt a search mindset.

So long, encyclopedia salesmen! The Internet is an open book. A quick search on Google typically yields millions of results. Great content that no one can find is just as ineffective as content that no one wants. Adopting a search mindset means incorporating SEO into your strategy and intelligently optimizing everything you do so that the people looking for it can find it.

Content Shift #5: Offer value first.

Rather than pushing for a sale, offer free information, like answering a question. This will move the customer closer to your product. Content is more than a promise to a potential customer; it's an example of how you're already invested in making their lives better—without asking anything in return. Content is a bridge to more than the bottom line. If you can make your customers happy before asking for their money, you'll become more than a product or service, you'll become irreplaceable.

Content Shift #6: Don't blast, attract.

By producing quality, search-focused content, potential customers and search engines will organically be attracted to your website. The more people you attract, the more traffic and exposure you receive. Like a snowball effect, if you focus on fostering relevant connections with your target audience, those connections will attract even more connections, and your sphere of influence will naturally grow.

Content Shift #7: Prepare more, perform better.

"Rome wasn't built in a day." Meaningful, authentic, inspiring content that changes your customers' lives takes time to build. You want your content to appear effortlessly engaging, and, in order to do that, a strategy is essential. Content leaders prepare, plan, and execute—and then prepare, plan, and innovate. In the age of instant publishing, stand above the crowd by spending time thoughtfully preparing for success. And then, prepare some more.

SHIFT TOWARD YOUR AUDIENCE, WHICHEVER DIRECTION THEY GO

If it seems like most of the seven shifts we just mentioned center around prioritizing your audience's needs, you're reading them correctly. Mary Wallace of Marketing Land says it well:

> "Customers are the heart and soul of every successful business. It's been that way since businesses began to flourish in ancient Greek and Roman times. Technology, such as the Internet, search engines, social media and mobile devices, has brought great change. It has moved us to an always-on society where the customer is controlling the relationship."[3]

The marketplace of the World Wide Web is more like an open-air bazaar than a gated mall. People talk to each other, and the conversations flow from every direction—from companies to customers, from customers to companies, and, most importantly, from people to people.

Today, the market is everywhere. People will post reviews of a bad customer service experience right alongside praise. Ordinary citizens of the United States can now tweet at the president, at CEOs, at big companies—and these are the voices of real people having real conversations in their authentic voices.

The new marketing paradigm is this: Talk to people in your authentic brand voice, answer their questions, and form a lasting relationship with your ideal customers. The content shift is happening, and it's moving us all toward more meaningful and strategic connections—ones that we actually want.

THAT'S GREAT, BUT WHAT'S MY RETURN ON INVESTMENT?

As a business, you obviously also want to know how putting all this effort into content marketing will create a great return on investment for you. While we wish we could tell you that producing X pieces of content Y times per month will absolutely yield a Z percentage increase in sales, so much depends on individual variables within your organization. This includes the strategy and scope of your projects as well as your level of consistency, follow through, and innovation. But what we can tell you is this: By focusing on understanding your audience, researching the language they use to perform online searches, and planning ahead to streamline your content creation process, you can expect your relevant organic traffic to increase over time.

So, what's the difference between *relevant* organic traffic and *nonrelevant* organic traffic? Nonrelevant organic traffic can be anyone—meaning, they're not necessarily part of your target audience. Your target audience consists of people who are likely to already be looking for what your business offers. Some marketing campaigns are nonspecific about the target audience. However, our content marketing strategy is highly focused on attracting *relevant* traffic, or the people who are specifically searching for what you offer. Relevant traffic is more likely to convert than nonrelevant traffic, so we focus on attracting those potentially interested customers rather than just anyone.

The simple logic of content marketing ROI (return on investment) is this:

1. Content marketing increases *relevant organic traffic*.
2. A percentage of that traffic will convert to *leads*.
3. A percentage of those leads will convert to *sales*.

The more organic traffic you bring in, the more value your content provides, and the more targeted that content is to your particular audience, the greater the chances of increasing conversions and sales. Calculating ROI from content marketing is very specific to the type of strategy used, the way it was implemented, the metrics tracked, and even how the data is interpreted. Still, there are some eye-opening ROI metrics that can give us an idea of how impactful search-focused content marketing can be. Here are just a few:

- 75% of B2B marketers surveyed by The Content Marketing Institute generated demand and leads, and 51% generated sales and revenue with content marketing in 2020.[4]
- According to MarketingSherpa, the average rate of organic traffic-to-leads conversions in content marketing campaigns across seven major industries is 16%.[5]
- According to HubSpot, the average rate of leads-to-sales conversions in content marketing campaigns is 14.6%.[6]
- According to BrightEdge, 51% of all website traffic comes from organic search, and over 40% of revenue is captured by organic traffic.[7]
- In a survey conducted by Databox, 70% of respondents said that SEO is better than Pay-Per-Click for generating sales.[8]
- According to Demand Metric, 82% of consumers feel more positive about a company after reading custom content.[9]

In our work with clients, we've seen their organic traffic across the board increase by as much as 300% year-over-year. Again, these numbers will be extremely specific to each individual industry and business, and highly dependent on strategic output, but the bottom line is this: More relevant, organic traffic from strategic, search-focused content attracts more leads and sales.

HOW A CONTENT STRATEGY SPURS BUSINESS GROWTH

Content marketing as a regular marketing strategy can help your business achieve plenty of things: online expansion, audience engagement, brand awareness, sales, and more. We want to always remember to keep clear business objectives on the front burner, even as we delve into the nuances of content marketing techniques. Here are some ways that content marketing can fuel your overall business growth:

1. Increased Organic Traffic

If a successful traditional marketing campaign for a brick-and-mortar business brings a flood of people in the doors, a successful modern online campaign brings more visitors to your website. One of the greatest returns on your content marketing efforts is continued growth of your organic search traffic. There's no getting around it: Your site needs to keep growing and bringing in more relevant traffic. Increasing relevant organic search traffic is the number one goal of a successful content strategy.

2. More Sales, Conversions, or Leads

The more you invite online engagement and position your brand in front of the right audiences, the greater the probability that a percentage of those visitors to your site will make a purchase, sign up for your e-mail list, make a call, download an offer, subscribe to a feed, or visit you in person. Increasing your flow of traffic is the first step to increasing your conversions, both for leads and sales.

3. Online Authority in Your Field

Content should supply the information users are looking for. Producing relevant content for users over time could lead to establishing authority in a subject matter in your field. In the world of online content, where essentially anyone can publish anything, being recognized as a trusted source of information secures your position in a competitive arena.

4. Higher Organic Search Rankings and More Exposure Overall

Search-focused content aims to not only increase your rankings in Google for desired search phrases (getting you seen on page 1), but it also gains you more exposure overall. In other words, your entire website becomes more visible in search—many different pages across many different search terms. More exposure could also mean being featured in Google search features like Answer Boxes and Featured Snippets, and Google services like Images, Maps, etc. All of this combined serves to boost that organic traffic growth you want.

5. Heightened Brand Awareness

Compelling content creates positive associations in users' minds, and when that content is linked to a brand, your company receives the benefit of greater exposure in more places. With enough great content strategically located online for your target audience to find, your brand identity grows stronger and stronger over time.

6. Greater User Engagement

Simply put, users are potential customers. You want the content you put out into the world to stoke a reaction in your audience—to spark a feeling, an insight, or a positive response. If you want people to interact with your brand, give them content that will inspire engagement, continue the conversation, and create relationships. The Internet has unlimited potential for building community and strengthening brand loyalty—or destroying it.

7. Overall Business Growth

Greater brand awareness, increased traffic, heightened user engagement—the goals are clear. The more people who visit your site and interact with your content, the more growth and energy that gets fueled back into your site, propelling your business forward.

WHY YOUR BUSINESS NEEDS CONTENT MARKETING

If you're still not convinced (or you're trying to convince an executive why it's important to invest in high-quality content marketing), consider this parallel: How would you respond if you were invited to speak on a panel at a well-regarded industry conference on behalf of your company? Most likely, you would spend time thinking about and preparing your presentation. You might collaborate with others in your department to bounce ideas around. You might decide to use a visual aid, like an infographic or a video, to complement your presentation. Nerves aside, this sort of thoughtful preparation would likely leave you feeling pretty confident in the subject matter and capable of presenting yourself—and your company—as knowledgeable experts in the field. Why? *Because you value the importance of your presentation.*

You can easily see how excelling as a conference panelist is important to your career, your company's reputation in the industry, and your overall business objectives—all while bringing valuable insights to the audience. You probably would never even consider cramming the night before. You would never do this because you care about how your organization presents itself to the world, and there is too much at stake not to do everything in your power to achieve excellence. You want your ideas to be communicated flawlessly so you can connect with the people in the audience who are involved in the conversation. Now apply this mindset to the content you produce for the digital realm.

Getting up on stage and babbling drivel just to fill the time would never occur to you. But this is what poor content does—oftentimes, content is produced just to fill up space or because "we've heard we need a blog and should post X times a week." This presents to the world a lack of thought leadership, a disregard for your audience, and a lack of investment in whatever it is you are producing. Just because the audience is on the other side of a screen and you can't see them doesn't mean they aren't there. Content marketing is virtual rather than physical, but the same quality assurance and level of thought should apply.

This is the essence of the content shift: Content is not like a hose, spraying out word gunk to water a lawn. Content is a conversation. Your digital content is your virtual face to the world, your presentation of your company's products, values, story, and integrity. When you can integrate this idea into your content marketing strategy, your content will unfailingly improve. Having a worthwhile conversation with your audience online takes time, thought, and planning to achieve, and it's this sort of dedication and depth you want to bring to your content marketing strategy. Content shouldn't be separate from what you do; it should be an intelligent extension of your business. Every time. Otherwise, why do it at all?

POINTS OF DISCOVERY

We covered the seven major shifts in thinking we believe are essential to make when doing content marketing. Consider your relationship to these shifts in thinking with the following questions:

1. What types of questions, concerns, and comments are your customers communicating with you?

2. What kinds of content could you give away to your audience that could benefit them or solve their problems?
3. What results would you like to see from your content marketing efforts?

PART TWO
AUDIENCE

Chapter 7

BUILDING RELATIONSHIPS THROUGH CONTENT

Beyond supporting the single purchase, you can imagine the long-term customer satisfaction of buyers who are confident their favorite brand is personally vested in their happiness.

—**Dave Walters,** *Behavioral Marketing*

Today, customers want meaningful relationships and experiences online. Though attention spans and loyalties may shift as quickly as opening and closing a tab on a web browser, we tend to remember the brands that leave us feeling warm and fuzzy, as well as the brands that leave a bad taste in our mouths. Maybe we forget about the rest. We're pretty sure you know where on this spectrum you'd like your business to be.

Before moving into any kind of content production, it's essential to start by asking lots of questions about the audience who will be encountering your content. When we work with clients, the first thing we do is have a discussion about the company's target audience groups and conduct a thorough audit of their audience research. This helps us understand the type of search terms that might be relevant and what kind of content will meet their audience's needs.

If a potential customer lands on your blog, what are your words going to convey? Will your content say you have some idea about what's important to your customers and that you want to help them with their problems? Hopefully, the answer is *yes*. Knowing the types of information, services, and solutions your audience is searching for is a necessary first step to producing content that connects.

Content marketing is relationship-based.

This first step in developing a content strategy is to identify your different audience groups and understand what they're looking for. Audience research helps us strategically deduce the interests, needs, and desires of our primary audience groups. We place these at the center of our search research and content strategy.

> The American Marketing Association defines marketing as "the activity, set of institutions and process for creating, communicating, delivering, and exchanging offerings that *have value* for customers, clients, partners, and society at large."[1] [emphasis ours]

WHAT IS A MEANINGFUL RELATIONSHIP?

Though the idea of marketing based on *customer needs* rather than *company products* is not new, it's absolutely necessary for content marketing. Theodore Levitt innovatively elucidated customer-oriented marketing principles in his landmark paper "Marketing Myopia," originally published in the Harvard Business Review in 1960, which won the McKinsey award and revolutionized the way the world thinks about marketing.

Rather than start at the line of production, Levitt posits that any company's marketing strategy should begin at the point of customer engagement. He states:

> "The view that an industry is a customer-satisfying process, not a goods-producing process, is vital for all businesspeople to under-

stand. An industry begins with the customer and his or her needs, not with a patent, a raw material, or a selling skill."[2]

Without a customer, there is no product. And without relationships, there is no content marketing. Consider this definition of marketing from Paul Flanigan at Experiate.net: "Marketing is the act of developing an engaging relationship with every single human being that shows an interest in you."[3] What a great definition. Your knee-jerk reaction might be, *"But that's impossible! How do you develop an engaging relationship, let alone with everyone who shows an interest in you?"* This question is at the heart of strategic content marketing.

"Engaging relationship" can mean a lot of things, so let's unpack that phrase. You might think "an engaging relationship" must be face-to-face with a one-to-one connection. This is one way to have an engaging relationship, but not the only way. For a mid-sized to large-scale business with lots of staff and customers or clients in the hundreds or thousands, one-to-one personal communication probably won't be the primary avenue to meaningful relationships—and this is where content marketing arrives to pick up the slack. Even when you're not directly engaging a customer or client one-on-one, that relationship can still be nurtured through content.

> Your content can act as a vehicle for engaging relationships—with every single human being that shows an interest in you or your business.

You can have different types of relationships through content, from a one-time interaction to a decades-long subscription. Your content allows your company to keep in touch with your customers and followers in a direct, engaging way without needing to physically maintain every single relationship. Understanding your audience's needs and desires opens up a world of possibilities for content creators, and it provides endless opportunities to connect with the people specifically searching for you.

Get to Know Your Audience Groups

Your *target audience* is the group of people who buy your products or consume your content. Your target audience will consist of customers and potential customers, but they may also include influencers. A target audience might see your content online and then convert to a customer at any point along the search cycle, and they may also be instrumental in sharing your content and raising brand awareness. Most businesses will have multiple audience groups—different types of customers who may have slightly nuanced desires or motivations for engaging with your brand. (We'll cover this in more depth in Chapter 8.)

Let's use a sports store as an example of a business wanting to identify and reach different audience groups. The target audience may have one thing in common: They're all interested in sports. A few different audience groups might include runners, tennis players, and outdoorspeople—all of whom may expect slightly different types of content or offers that are specific and highly relevant to them. Your target audience might also include influencers, like coaches and parents, who share your content with potential customers. At its core, a target audience might buy and/or engage with content at different points along the search cycle or at different moments in their lives.[4]

TYPES OF CUSTOMER RELATIONSHIPS

If you consider *who* is likely to consume your content and *what* they want, your content can open doors to engage with customers at every turn. So, to "maintain engaging relationships with every single person who shows an interest in you," you need to first know who is showing an interest in you. Consider that every person who lands on your website or social media pages is already showing interest. You can easily identify who they are and how they got there by understanding the user journey, keywords, and analytics. (We'll discuss these search strategies more in Part 3 of the book.)

You can start with the assumption that every online relationship is a one-time connection, yet there is potential for a longer-lasting relationship. People tend to want to engage further with a brand when they're convinced of the quality it offers—and when what it offer aligns with what they want. The more you know about your audience, the more likely this will be. What type of relationship might your content spark? In other words, how is your search-focused content going to translate into a business opportunity?

- **One-time engagement** – Anytime someone comes across your content online, whether that's through a blog post or social media channel, a relationship has been initiated. Like bumping into someone on the street, the relationship may be temporary and fleeting, but it's still a mode of connection. Your content is the handshake that welcomes a potential customer (or doesn't). You want to consider every new user to your website as the potential beginning of a longer customer relationship.
- **Ongoing relationship** – There may be many different subcategories within this distinction because there are endless ways to keep a connection going. A one-time engagement may turn into an ongoing relationship when a user signs up for an e-mail newsletter, bookmarks your blog, follows you on social media, or generally opts in, giving you *permission* to communicate. In other words, your content and your audience just "click." You want to keep producing content that fosters that relationship and inspires action.
- **Influencer** – If you can connect with your audience authentically and meaningfully, you may see some of them pay it forward tenfold. People who love your company, what you stand for, and what you offer may easily move beyond the role of customer and into the highly valuable position of influencer. Influencers recommend your company to others through their platforms because they had such an amazing expe-

rience. You absolutely want to understand and serve your audience so well that they rave about you. If you change someone's life for the better, you'd better believe they will be talking about you to anyone who will listen.

Knowing your audience groups and their needs gives us the in-depth knowledge we need to target those groups more specifically and with more relevant content. Not to mention, ongoing audience research is a valuable tool for business development to help a company adapt to changing customer needs.

> "Rather than admiring brands, [consumers are] more interested in brands that admire them, know them, and serve them."
>
> **—Kit Yarrow, Decoding the New Consumer Mind**

YOUR AUDIENCE IS HUMAN

Though at first it may seem counter-intuitive that technology can actually *open* the doors for us to have more authentic connections, the digital era removes physical barriers so we can theoretically connect with our audience anytime, anywhere. While technology surely has the potential to divide and alienate, we can focus on how to use it to connect more meaningfully. What is most successful is what speaks to humanity.

Technology is not a living force; humans created all our computers and intelligent devices. Especially in our hyper-technologized world, people want to connect on a human level. It's easy to forget that **content is communication** when we can only see one side of the screen. Remember, there's always someone else on the other side. We are, after all, people behind these screens—and the best content connects on a human level. Consider that around 90% of human communication is non-verbal—

gestures, facial expressions, and body language. Video content is great because it captures both the verbal and nonverbal elements, but for every piece of content that lacks the face-to-user relationship, we need to close the gap by doing everything else possible to still create that type of authentic connection through language, images, and timing.

Think about the conversations you have with your partners, colleagues, friends, and family members. Stilted, insincere attempts at forging connections with people in your real life are probably just as effective (by which we mean, not very) as bludgeoning the Internet with sales talk and advertising jargon that isn't focused on helping your audience. A broadcast mindset needs to be combined with relational finesse.

The more humanized, candid, and sincere your message, the more real human interaction you can expect online. When we take into consideration how our content is operating in real time, we want to make sure we infuse everything we do with genuine consideration for our readers, viewers, and users on the other end.

No algorithm can replace the feeling of satisfaction and appreciation from a great customer service experience or a life-changing *aha!* moment. When the waiter at our favorite restaurant jokes with us in an authentic, good-natured way, or when the woman on the phone empathizes with our frantic call to get our car towed, we feel good. Similarly, if we come across a video that makes us cry or a blog post that enlightens us, we feel a strong connection with that experience. What if you could create more of these experiences online for your customers? You can—by knowing your audience, knowing what they are searching for, and crafting a content strategy to keep answering their questions in the way only your company can.

POINTS OF DISCOVERY

In this chapter, we discussed how content can facilitate meaningful relationships with your customers. Consider the following questions about your relationships with the people who come across your content online:

1. What kind of experience would you like your audience to have when encountering your content online? Describe it. What does it look like? What does it feel like?
2. Think about your ideal customer relationship. What does that look like?
3. Take a few moments to brainstorm some ways you could connect meaningfully with your audience online. What types of content experiences could you offer that they might enjoy?

Chapter 8

AUDIENCE GROUPING

If a producer intends something to be absolutely right for one audience, it will, by definition, be wrong for another.

—Chris Anderson, *The Long Tail*

We don't need to reach everyone. We just need to reach the people who are trying to reach us. In the 1950s, a company could market a product widely to "stay-at-home moms," one large demographic, and probably enjoy relatively easy success. Today, there are segments upon segments of different *types* of stay-at-home moms: domestic divas, natural-earth mommies, stay-at-home *dads*, PTA moms, dance moms, and on and on. Each one, theoretically, comes with its own online community, specific concerns, and nuanced questions, so just one product or marketing message won't cut it.

In today's era of content marketing, we want to group our different audiences by *important motivating factors*. This allows us to create more relevant and targeted content for specific types of people, which, in turn, helps us to drive more organic traffic and create long-lasting customer relationships.

AUDIENCE GROUPING FOR STRATEGIC CONTENT DEVELOPMENT

Doing audience research starts by listening to your audience express what makes them distinct and unique from each other. We use these differences to understand how we can tailor content towards specific audience groups.

Audience grouping (also called *segmentation*) is the process of subdividing a general audience into distinct subsets of customers who occupy similar demographics, behave similarly, or have similar needs. We personally like calling these segments "audience groups" because it sounds less technical and more down-to-earth than "audience segmentation," but it basically means the same thing. We certainly didn't invent this idea and it's a common practice in marketing. Specifically, the goal of audience grouping for content marketing is to identify your main target demographics so you can tailor content to each group more effectively.

Some content might appeal to all your audiences, while some might appeal only to one or two audience groups. You might be thinking, why does this really matter? Don't we just want all the traffic and all the customers we can possibly get? Well, yes and no. For those search nerds out there, we want to make an important distinction: You can certainly conduct keyword research, find search terms to target, and then create content around those phrases without understanding the nuances of each target audience. And sure, you can absolutely take a shortcut and start producing topics for specific search terms without doing audience research. As Jon says, "If they're searching for it, they're interested in it."

However, to make your content production process more streamlined, focused, and effective overall, having an understanding of your distinct audience groups will equip you with the knowledge to make more informed content strategy decisions the entire way through. Defining your audience groups can be applied to the content process in many different ways. To understand this better, let's take a look at the top five reasons why you want to segment your audience into smaller, specific groups.

1. Primarily, if you know roughly what percentage of your audience is from each distinct group, you can tailor content topics toward a specific audience group to attract that particular traffic. For example, if you know about 10% of your audience is a "natural-earth mommy" and 30% of your audience is a "domestic diva" (however these are defined and with whatever attributes related to your business), then you can create and distribute your content proportionally to target each group's specific needs and questions. Meaning, you might direct 10% of your content to target search terms related to the "natural-earth mommy" and 30% to the "domestic diva," or in any other strategic way you choose.

Knowing your audience groups can help you determine where to focus your content output based on the goals you want to hit. In any given month, you may decide you want to spend more energy attracting a new audience group you've identified or strengthening relationships with an existing one. It all depends on what your goals are for organic traffic growth and engagement.

2. Build trust and goodwill by speaking only to certain audience groups' needs and providing higher quality conversation. Remember how so many modern users are overloaded and frazzled, browsing the Internet with the attention span of mice? If you know your audience so well and care about them so much that you go out of your way NOT to bombard them with irrelevant marketing messages, the *absence* of annoying ads or clickbait could mean just as much as the *presence* of valuable information.

For example, a video tutorial called something like "Relaxing Prenatal Yoga" has a pretty clear audience: pregnant women wanting to relax. Reasonably so, this video would not appeal to someone looking for a high-impact cardio yoga workout—and so the content creator would have done their job by not falsely attracting the wrong audience. This may seem like a pretty obvious example, but just consider how many videos (or other forms of content) are out there with generic titles and descriptions trying to appeal to everybody—and in so doing, deter people by wasting their time.

Different audience groups want different things. The more specific and tailored you can be in your content, the more you can minimize content as a disturbance and maximize content as added value. And even though this book isn't going to go into social media or e-mail marketing, you can certainly use the audience groups you determine for every division of your online marketing plan. On social media, you can share content in groups categorized around a certain interest; in e-mail marketing, you can send e-mails with special tips or offers tailor-made for one specific group. In today's overloaded world, *more* quality and *less* distraction is the name of the game.

3. Knowing your audience groups can help you discover additional search-focused topics for content creation. If you know you have different audience groups, you can take one topic that is good to target (as validated through search research) and spin it for each different group. So, if you're a health and fitness company geared toward different types of mothers, for example, instead of just one general video on yoga, you can create specific videos for whichever audience groups you'd like to target—pregnant women, busy working moms, advanced athletes, etc.

Knowing each different group's particular needs and motivations gives you more opportunity to find even more relevant topics. For example, you could offer video reviews on yoga mats and other fitness equipment, blog posts on nutrition for different physical conditions or goals, and tips for squeezing in a workout at the office. As time goes on, and as you cover all the major general topics in your industry, crafting specific titles for specific groups will open up new doors to content topics.

4. Knowing the pain points and desires of your audience groups can help you craft titles that connect and get clicked. It might seem like a minor detail, but whether or not your titles get clicked on in the search results could be the difference of just a few words. Let's say you validate the topic of "nutrition for women" through search research. Great. Next, when determining a title, the difference between "Nutrition Tips for Women" and "Nutrition Tips for Busy Working Women" might not seem like a huge leap, but these two small adjectives tell this audience group (busy working women) that the publisher of the post (your company) already understands them. It signals to these women that your company knows they do not have time to waste and that they could reasonably expect a clear, concise, helpful article that gets straight to the point—without the fluff. These are the types of details that can help you rise above the competition, bringing together validated search research and the authentic needs of your customers for greater success.

5. Last but not least, understanding the needs and desires of your audience groups can inform the content production process. This might seem like a no-brainer, and that's because it is. How can you craft a successful message to a potential customer if you know nothing about them? Content production involves voice, tone, images, reading level, writing style, length of content, and so much more. Knowing, for example, that a corporate client is likely to respond more favorably to factual, straightforward copy and standard typography can help you resonate with that type of person more. Perhaps a creative client would respond more favorably to a casual, conversational tone and bright colors. Finding out who your audience groups are and what they need and want gives you the power to craft a message for them in a way that is more likely to garner a response. Audience research (based on factual data) can only increase your chances of reaching the right people with the right messages.

> **TOP-LEVEL AUDIENCE CONSIDERATIONS**
>
> Your audience may be a consumer buying at the level of retail (B2C), or your audience may be a business buying products or services for business development (B2B). You should definitely consider which is your primary audience, as this differentiation can influence your content marketing strategy.
>
> **B2B**
> B2B (business to business) and B2C (business to consumer) are two broad business category types that require very different content

marketing approaches. This is because their audiences are markedly different. B2B businesses may have an audience of high-level experts who are informed in the industry, and, therefore, content should be tailored to meet their level of understanding, providing assurance that their business needs will be well handled. A B2B content strategy is often most effective when the audience is approached in a way that conveys trust, integrity, and thought leadership—perhaps through longer, information-driven, research-backed reports, whitepapers, and industry news.

B2C

B2C businesses, on the other hand, usually do well when appealing to the emotional, social, and psychological needs of customers. Effective content may be shorter, more shareable, more social, and more interactive—such as videos, blogs, and infographics that promote desired feeling-states that reward engagement with the brand.[1] Of course, some companies occupy both spaces, and different strategies can be used with intention and integrity.

Length of the User Journey

Another type of top-level audience differentiation is the difference between the long and short sales cycle, which can apply to both B2B and B2C businesses. As we mentioned in Part 1, different sales cycles can affect your content marketing strategy. A longer sales cycle means a longer user journey, and most likely the need for more content along different touchpoints.

A short sales cycle could describe a product like soda produced by a brand such as Pepsi. Customers probably aren't going to care about Pepsi's thought leadership in the industry of carbonated beverages, but creating positive associations with the brand around lifestyle, emotional and psychological states, social inclusion, taste, and visual design may be effective forms of content marketing. Buying a soda is considered a short sales cycle because there isn't a lot of lead up to the purchase and the product occupies a low price point. Because of this, Pepsi's content doesn't need to belabor the details of their product's specifications and, instead, they can focus on appealing to emotions, familiarity, nostalgia, lifestyle, and taste.

Buying a car, on the other hand, has a long sales cycle. A prospective customer would likely be thinking through multiple considerations before committing to a large purchase, such as reliability of the brand, warranties, availability of parts, safety ratings, price points, features, etc. Therefore, it would be smart for a car company to produce content that answers the prospective customer's questions in their online content. A customer may take weeks or even months to conduct research before making a purchase, and they'll likely sift through lots of information and reviews. In this case, emotional appeals are certainly valuable, but they would need to be supplemented by factual information and analysis. The length of the sales cycle very much influences the type of content strategy that will be most effective.

CONDUCTING AUDIENCE RESEARCH

So, how do you know who your audience groups are and what they want? First of all, you don't guess. Making up information based on "hunches" rather than real data is not at all what we suggest, and it might even hurt your efforts. The only way to learn who your audience groups are is to ask them questions, listen, and learn.

Anyone can do audience research, and every company will benefit from it. Though it's always been a good idea to listen to what customers want and expect, in the digital era, it's essential to flip the script and sit at your customer's table. As the authors of *The Cluetrain Manifesto* articulate, the entire web of business has transformed in such a way that, on the Internet, "all participants are audience to each other."[2] Developing an audience mindset for your content strategy requires that you learn to become *the audience to your audience* and incorporate this as a regular marketing habit.

The audience research process is an entire field of study itself, so we'll go over some basic notes to get you started. However, full-scale audience research is outside the scope of this book. If you already have a lot of this audience research done, that's great. If not, there are tons of free and low-cost online tools to get you started. (Visit ContentShift.com/Resources for a handy list of some audience research tools.)

Either way, it's not a step to be skipped. All we're saying is this: You'll need to collect audience data to formulate audience groups and personas, so do whatever is relevant to gather that information. To start, anytime you receive feedback from a customer or user, think of it as highly valuable information that can help you evolve your content strategy. You may receive feedback indirectly, or you may intentionally set out to gather information. You might listen to specific, individual comments directly *and* analyze aggregate online data. Both *qualitative* and *quantitative* data is useful.

You might be surprised how illuminating it can be to simply sit down and look at customer feedback. This might entail looking through website chat logs, reading responses from people who contacted customer service by phone or email, analyzing company surveys to better understand your customers, or looking through social media comments and recent reviews.

Here are a few ways of listening in:

- **Customer surveys:** It can be very useful to collect customer survey data after the purchase. This information can help you discover the questions and pain points that your customer experienced before, during, or after the purchase. It can also help you understand how customers are finding you.
- **Customer service feedback:** Similar to customer surveys, any feedback from customer service calls or touchpoints can be useful in uncovering why someone chose to use your products and services, how useful the experience was, and what can be improved.

- **Social media:** Monitoring social channels, including messages and comments, can provide another avenue for understanding how people are talking about your brand, and what questions or comments they have.
- **Chat logs:** If your company offers chat to customers online, these logs are an especially useful place to determine where customers are having questions or problems when they try to use your service, especially if there are common questions that keep coming up.
- **Reviews:** Company reviews—such as on Yelp, Amazon, or Google—can provide insight into what customers are liking and disliking about your product or service. Pay special attention to questions they are asking.
- **Aggregate research:** Use any and all of your company's market-research data—like focus groups, census information, population data, demographic data, etc.—to get a picture of your audience groups on a macro level.

It may be easy to let this data fly by you when you're caught up in the day-to-day operations of your business. But to really do content marketing strategically, we recommend at least one person in the marketing division sit down regularly to review audience feedback and incorporate any new findings into your evolving content strategy.

After doing your initial audience research when first formulating your content strategy, keep checking in. Customer needs and concerns may change over time, so get in the habit of paying attention and adapting accordingly. You want to have a clear, evidenced idea of who makes up your audience groups and what they want—not a guess.

AUDIENCE GROUPING BY MOTIVATION

Once you've gathered some data, how do you decide what defines or describes a particular group? What if you're not sure exactly which audience groups are the most important, or you need to figure out how to allocate limited resources to only a few audiences? Not all audience groups will have the same strategic value. To characterize a segmented population as valuable to marketing efforts, the audience group must meet the requirements of the M.A.S.A. rule: Measurable, Accessible, Substantial, and Actionable.[3]

Here are some factors to consider when honing in on your most valuable target markets. These are all considerations; it's up to you to decide what makes an audience group valuable:[4]

- **Size:** Is the group large enough to be worth tailoring your marketing to? What proportion of your overall market does the segment represent?
- **Uniqueness:** Is the audience group different enough from other segments to justify customized marketing? Does the group's relationship to the product, such as how the product could meet its members' specific needs, vary enough from that of other segments? Could one marketing message be appropriate for multiple audience groups?
- **Profitability:** What are the group's purchasing habits? Would you profit from marketing specifically to this audience group?
- **Accessibility:** Do you have the marketing tools necessary to reach this group in a cost-effective manner?
- **Competitors:** Are competitors vying for the group's attention and business? What is the cost to compete? What is the likelihood that you would be successful? What differentiates your product or service?

Market research is a huge field of study on its own, and there are endless ways to use data from your audience research. For our purposes, we will be focusing on identifying search questions relevant to your audience to drive your content production.

> For content marketing, audience grouping is
> best driven primarily by purpose or motivation.

We can learn a lot about how to reach our audience emotionally and psychologically by understanding their fears, desires, and concerns. This teaches us far more than just looking at surface-level demographics.

In audience grouping for content marketing, we want to move beyond simplistic demographic considerations and into relevant categories that will help us build relationships with different types of audiences. For instance, maybe it's not important to differentiate customers by a demographic like gender but rather by a stage in life, like "Graduating High School Student." What would be important to a graduating high school student that might not be relevant to a working adult? These are the types of questions we can use to tailor our content more effectively to our primary audiences and increase relevant visibility in search.

INTRODUCING: THE NURSING SCHOOL

To bring these concepts to life and to help us form a concrete idea of how this all leads to a solid content strategy, we're going to focus on one example: a nursing school. We'll use this example through the rest of the book to show you how we'd use these elements—audience, search, and content—to arrive at a content marketing strategy that drives organic traffic growth. Although the following example is entirely fictional, the strategies and conclusions we arrive at are based on real-life success with a similar type of client.

So, first, to illustrate the process of audience grouping for content marketing, let's imagine we've been hired to do content marketing for a nursing school. For the sake of simplicity, we'll simply call them "The Nursing School." The Nursing School has a physical location in Awesometown, USA. They offer two main training programs: Registered Nursing (RN) and Licensed Practical Nursing (LPN). They want to enroll more students and grow their web presence online. (We'll get more specific about how to link specific business goals to the search research process in Chapter 14.)

The big-picture content marketing goal for The Nursing School is to attract students to their nursing training programs by producing content that's aligned with the target audiences' needs. Attracting *relevant organic traffic* should naturally lead to more potential students signing up to learn more about enrollment and, eventually, enrolling. We'll get to know this fictional nursing school really well over the next few chapters, so strap in.

As with any content strategy, we want to start by uncovering audience data. We're trying to understand who the customers or potential customers of this business are, as well as their motivating factors. The Nursing School's market researchers conducted a school-wide survey of all currently enrolled students to find out what motivated them to enroll, and they also consulted with on-site guidance counselors and teachers who had firsthand interaction with students. Here's what they discovered. There were two primary motivations for enrolling in nursing school across the board:

- A desire for job security
- A passion for helping people

This is fantastically valuable information that can be used to target content topics and attract the right audience for this business. We can already tell that producing content around job security in the nursing field and how nursing is a great career for helping people would be slam dunks. The Nursing School market researchers also discovered a few important demographic insights:

- Around 90% of attendees are female. (This means 10% are male.)
- Age ranges tend to be heavily grouped into two categories: students are either between 18 and 24 years of age (often entering the training program recently out of high school) or between 30 and 45 years old (entering the program because they want a lucrative career change).
- A sizable portion of students are single, working women with children and no higher education.

This demographic information helps us understand the nature of some valuable audience groups, which can inform our content direction. Researchers were also able to obtain some information about prior experience and career goals:

- One of The Nursing School's programs is a two-year-long RN training program. About 25% of these students enroll with some previous work experience in a hospital (or other healthcare training) and a motivation to attain a higher degree.
- The other 75% who enroll in the RN program have no prior nursing experience.

Both of these segments are valuable because, even though one segment is smaller, the smaller group is already invested in this career path, and they will most likely be highly motivated to enroll. Even though the percentages are weighted differently in size, they might be equally valuable, which could mean that the content director decides to split the amount of content produced to target each group equally.

Finally, the data shows that people outside of a 100-mile radius frequently inquire but less frequently enroll, so we can discard out-of-area students as a valuable segment. All of these insights will be helpful in crafting content that understands the pain points and motivations of each demographic.

Based on the information collected, The Nursing School's content marketers have created the following audience groups:

- High School Graduates
- Career-Seeking Moms
- Nursing Assistants

Creating audience groups should involve very little guesswork. Even though the audience groups may be general categories containing general descriptors, these distinctions arise from concrete data gathered from real customers of the business. In this example, there is clear evidence supporting the creation of these separate audience groups, and each one is significant enough and distinct enough to be labeled a target audience group.

(Notice there is no audience group for male nurses—but there could be! Even though the group was unique, The Nursing School decided not to focus energy on specifically creating content for males interested in nursing since it was such a small percentage of enrollees. This is the type of decision that every company will make on its own. However, male nurses could, later on, become its own audience group if the company decides to go in that direction. This is also an example of how a content strategy is continually evolving.)

The bottom line: Putting in energy up front to become *very clear* about who your target audience groups are will pay off down the line, particularly when sitting down to come up with content ideas and directing the production of that content. Audience research is like the sculptor's chisel—it refines your process and allows a clearly defined image (or strategy) to emerge. Without it, and without solid data to back up your hunches, you run the risk of targeting audiences that won't necessarily fuel your business or sales goals. If you know *who* you're trying to reach with your content, you can make creative calls easily and confidently about what kind of content to create.

In the next chapter, we'll dive into the emotional and psychological needs of different audience groups to discover the motivations that drive our customers to interact, and we'll also uncover the types of content they're looking for. And finally, we'll reveal how the emotional and psychological needs of our audience groups influence our content strategy.

POINTS OF DISCOVERY

In this chapter, we talked about the value of doing audience research to better align your content with the people searching for it. Consider your own audiences and how you might go about learning more about them:

1. What avenues of customer feedback do you have available to you? Collect all the relevant audience data that you can.
2. Based on the audience data you have, begin grouping characteristics together to identify specific types of customers—audience groups. Which are the most valuable audience groups? What makes them the most valuable?
3. What are the primary motivations of each of your most valuable audience groups?

Chapter 9

EMOTIONAL AND PSYCHOLOGICAL NEEDS

Brands can serve as an emotional conduit to connection.

—Kit Yarrow, *Decoding the New Consumer Mind*

What are the questions, motivations, and desires of each audience group? What would they like to learn? What information do they need to feel good about your brand or make a buying decision? To build an engaging relationship with every single person who shows an interest in your business, follow this line of questioning to really, deeply understand your multiple audience groups. Even if you already know a lot about whom you're serving, you can always learn more.

Audience research for content marketing aims to uncover the deeper, surprising questions your audience is asking and pinpoint the desires that might not be so obvious on the surface. We can keep peeling back the layers of your audience's interests to continue engaging and delighting them. The well of content ideas is endless when you ask the right questions and strategically align your content to the shifting needs of the people it's designed for. Get this habit down, and you'll never have to feel like you're shooting in the dark for content to produce. The answers will be clearly illuminated; the light always shines in the direction of your audience.

EMOTIONS DRIVE CONTENT

At the end of the day, we're all human beings who want basically similar things: food, water, sex, sleep, safety, security, family, love, friendship, self-esteem, social recognition, self-actualization, and achievement of our hopes and dreams. You may recognize these items as the elements that compose Abraham Maslow's Hierarchy of Needs, shown in Figure 9.1—a landmark psychological model for human motivation, pioneered in 1943.[1]

Figure 9.1: Maslow's Hierarchy of Needs

When thinking about the infinite number of nuanced desires any individual in any first-world country may have today, it's helpful to remember what incites people to want things, to seek information, to share with others, and, of course, to buy in. Though our technology is highly advanced, what motivates the average person to do anything probably isn't that different from any other human era. In today's digital world, we have more tools and resources at our disposal to find out precisely what our audience wants, what motivates them, and what holds them back.

Emotions can serve as a powerful tool in content marketing. Our emotional brain processes sensory information in one-fifth the time that our cognitive brain does, so emotional content can quickly engage audiences.[2] Moreover, emotions can drive desired consumer actions. Happiness, sadness, anger, fear—our human emotions affect every aspect of our lives, including our consumer choices. For example, we're more likely to share content that elicits feelings of happiness, amusement, and excitement on social media. Makes sense, right? We all want to feel good, and we feel even better when we share that happiness. Anger tends to make us more stubborn, and sadness cultivates empathy.[3]

Surprisingly, content that scares us can foster brand loyalty. A study published in the Journal of Consumer Research showed that when consumers watched a film that scared them, they felt a greater affiliation with a present brand than other consumers who watched films that sparked other emotions, like happiness, sadness, or excitement.[4] Interestingly, the theory behind this is that, when we're scared, we naturally want to connect over that experience with others—and if there aren't any people around, even a non-human brand will do![5]

Emotions drive us to make choices, and content can drive emotions. Particular motivating forces vary between individuals and groups, however, and understanding the nuances of your audience's emotional psychology can mean the difference between content that drives relevant leads and content that no one cares about. If we are creating content to meet our users' needs along the Search Cycle, we need to know what those needs are.

Content should consider the following major types of needs and desires:

1. **Emotional:** A desire to feel good, or a need to feel less bad.
2. **Intellectual:** A desire to find information, or a need to verify information. Often, this desire goes hand in hand with the need to elicit a feeling: allaying fears, supporting beliefs, etc.
3. **Social:** A desire to connect with other people, or a need to feel socially accepted.

4. **Physical:** A desire to improve some physical or material aspect in life, or a need to satisfy a physical requirement, such as eating or sleeping.

One or more of these needs will usually be driving potential customers' online search habits. We all still basically want to feel good in our lives, and our emotional desires are at the core of everything we do, including browsing the Internet, clicking links, and spending time reading articles or watching videos.

Identifying the different needs of various audience groups helps us consider both how they are searching for content online and what type of content they might be interested in. At the end of the day, the companies that can help us do better, look better, feel better, achieve more, and feel happier will ultimately earn a coveted place in our lives. The rest will be ignored, forgotten, or deleted.

Based on market research for The Nursing School, let's understand the emotional needs of our three audience groups even better. Some of the needs and desires will be similar across all groups, and some will be distinct or nuanced.

1. High School Graduates: Based on the data collected, The Nursing School found that graduating high school students who are in their target audience tend to have some similar traits. They tend to be female, non-Caucasian, and not necessarily headed to a four-year college. They may be unsure about their direction in life, but they're ambitious enough to seek out a vocational training program.
    - Their *emotional* state is excited but slightly fearful, and they want reassurance about the future. They are seeking independence, confidence, and security.
    - *Intellectual* needs include wanting a college program without the academic demands or the financial burden and time commitment of a traditional four-year university.

- *Socially*, they still want to make friends and expand their social circle.
- *Physical* needs include knowing they will be able to make a living after they finish the program, and they may need housing or a part-time job while going to school.

2. **Career-Seeking Moms:** The second primary audience group consists of 30- to 45-year-old women with children who are considering a career change. They tend to work in low-wage, unskilled jobs, and they want to go back to school to advance their career and earn a better living.
    - Their *emotional* needs primarily focus around reassurance; this would be a big life change for them. They feel uncertain and anxious about going back to school after so much time away, yet they're excited to consider the possibilities of a nursing career.
    - Their *intellectual* needs are related; they want to know what kind of study skills they need to learn and what kinds of resources are there to help them succeed.
    - *Socially*, they could benefit from a helpful and supportive atmosphere—peer group, teachers, and counselors.
    - Their *physical* needs include how to balance school while working and raising a family; essentially, they want to know how much time and energy a nursing training program would require.

3. **Nursing Assistants:** The third audience group is the most unlike the other two. While graduating high school students and career-seeking moms are both new to the field of nursing, nursing assistants are already working in the field. A nursing assistant is a lower-level job than a registered nurse, so this audience would be seeking career advancement from a position of some experience.
    - They already know they like working in a hospital, and they're primarily motivated to attain a higher level of professionalism in their career, which would translate to higher pay (a *physical* need). They

might need a flexible schedule to keep their current nursing assistant job, and they may also need evidence that they are likely to recoup their tuition expenses after they achieve a level of career advancement.
- Their considerations for seeking nursing training are focused on what the program has to offer them in terms of accreditation and preparation for tests they need to pass (*intellectual* needs). They would be comparing the teachers, campus, training modules, and quality of overall instruction across programs.
- Their *social* needs are not prominent since they already have a nursing assistant job where they socialize with others in the field, but if the school can improve their professional network, that would be an attractive quality.
- *Emotional* needs are less prominent than the other two groups, but they may revolve around the feelings of security and assurance that they are making a good decision for their career advancement.

We've synthesized the different types of needs across our different audience examples into the table shown in Figure 9.2.

Some similarities across all groups can show us how to build a strong foundation for a content strategy. The needs/desires that are similar across most or all of the audience groups include:

- An emotional and physical need for job security
- An emotional desire for personal satisfaction in their work (a passion for helping people)
- A physical need to understand the cost and return on investment
- A physical need for supportive resources, such as a flexible schedule, job placement support, quality instruction, test preparation, etc.

These needs and desires provide the starting point for discovering the questions your audience is asking when they search online.

EMOTIONAL AND PSYCHOLOGICAL NEEDS

Audience Group	Emotional Need	Intellectual Need	Social Need	Physical Need
High School Graduates	• Desire to be independent and self-sufficient • Desire for meaningful work helping people	• Need to understand academic requirements • Desire for less academic rigor than university	• Desire to make friends • Desire for college experience	• Need for financial support (part-time job, scholarships) • Possible need for housing • Need to know return on investment
Career-Seeking Moms	• Desire for personal improvement • Need for job security • Need for reassurance • Desire to feel accomplished	• Need resources like study skills, GED prep, homework help	• Desire for supportive peer group	• Need to balance school with current job and family • Need to be easy to attend • Need to be financially viable
Nursing Assistants	• Trust the school to advance career with professional accreditations	• Need quality instruction and relevant career training • Need certifications to advance career	• Desire for professional network	• Need to have flexible hours • Need to financially support career advancement

Figure 9.2: Audience Grouping by Needs

For example, knowing your audience is looking for information about the cost of nursing training, you can find out what types of phrases are being searched to fill that need. If it turns out a popular search phrase is "how much does nursing training cost," that's easily a clear winner. Absolutely produce content to answer this question in a clear and reassuring way! With your audience's needs, desires, and questions clearly identified, you can create informational content that's designed to lead them further along the search cycle toward commitment.

> Audience research informs search research, which directs strategic content production.

ONE OF OUR FAVORITE CLASSIC MARKETING CAMPAIGNS

Let's take a look back at an example from the early 1920s, during the Industrial Revolution, when marketing as we know it today was just revving up, leading to some huge, far-sweeping changes in society. When toothpaste was first invented, the American public couldn't care less about this newfangled notion of "washing your teeth," which was supposed to have some health benefits. During World War I, dental hygiene was so bad, especially among soldiers, that the Army called it a national security risk.[6]

The habit of brushing daily didn't fully enter the national American psyche until Claude Hopkins was brought in as marketing director for Pepsodent. His research led him to focusing a marketing campaign on *what people wanted*—beauty.

Hopkins achieved a radical shift in world consciousness and actually got people to start using toothpaste (not to mention, bringing business to toothpaste companies and dentists alike) by appealing to vanity. His ad campaigns focused less on health (boring!) and instead targeted the emotional need for sex appeal. One of his ads read in part:

> *"Note how many pretty teeth are seen everywhere. Millions are using a new method of teeth cleansing. Why would any woman have dingy film on her teeth? Pepsodent removes the film."*[7]

Understanding and approaching our underlying psychological motivations is exactly what Hopkins did to achieve a global shift in thought. He saw a need, created a solution, and spoke to people's innermost desires. Even though brushing teeth daily with toothpaste did improve the oral hygiene of an entire population as a nice public-health side effect, Hopkins appealed to Americans' desire for beauty, and therefore sex and social recognition. These principles can be applied to any digital marketing campaign today because the focus was on *what the customer wants* and not what the company had to sell.

UNDERSTANDING NEW CONSUMER PSYCHOLOGY

While we all still want our basic human needs fulfilled—and human emotions are pretty much universal—the Internet has actually changed the way our brains process information, altering some of the ways our nervous systems regulate emotional responses to stimuli. We need to take these neurological shifts into account when producing content so we can best align with our audience's state of mind—not overwhelm or overload them. We want to make sure we're formatting content in ways that make sense for the user.

Have a hard time believing that the human brain can be rewired in the span of only a few years? Just think about how often you check your phone daily. Some studies put the number around 50 times per day for the average American. Our cell phones have become basically part of our regular wardrobe, and our psyches have adapted to this new constant. We actually receive a dopamine rush every time we receive a notification, like the little red flag on Facebook or the blue bird on Twitter that tells us someone is interacting with us online. So, like technology addicts, we tend to keep going after the next hit, and the next, until our brains feel overwhelmed with information. Kit Yarrow, consumer behavior psychologist and author of the book *Decoding the New Consumer Mind,* reminds us that our customers "are entering the marketplace, be it online or in stores, already overloaded."[8]

The Internet has made us "neurologically different" than we were before. We're more easily distracted, less focused, and less patient. As a result of the overwhelming floods of information arriving toward us constantly, we're less willing to tolerate uncertainty and ambiguity from brand messaging and content.

The clearer you are on what your audience wants,
the clearer you can be in your communication with them.

As content producers, we absolutely need to understand not just what types of content our audience wants, but also how to deliver it in a way that creates a pleasant (rather than frustrating) experience. This encompasses how we format our content and the user's experience with it as well—for example, taking into account how a web page appears on mobile, how easily a page can be scanned, using appropriate imagery, graphics, and so on.

If it's not clear what a web page is trying to communicate after a quick scan, users are most likely going to become easily frustrated and move on. It can be exhausting trying to find what is needed on an overly complicated order form or web page. Most people navigate the web with high expectations for easy-to-read, clear, direct, honest, authentic brand messages and low tolerance for disorganized, salesy, incomplete, jargon-filled "sales talk."

Emotions are easily heightened to a point of irritation, frustration, and even anger when we feel slighted by content. None of these emotional states are the kind you want to create in your customers' increasingly impatient and overloaded psyches. The Internet allows displeased customers to be quite vocal, as we know.

When it comes to content quality, the same principles apply. A customer can easily feel deceived when a company provides misleading information to "steal" their already limited and precious attention. For example, creating "clickbait" titles—posing a question with overhyped or sensationalized messaging like "You won't believe . . . !" and then never delivering anything worthwhile in the body of the content—can immediately disappoint any reader of the article. You don't want your potential customers feeling let down or unfulfilled by lazy content that's more focused on just "getting clicks" than actually offering something interesting. These are easy types of mistakes to avoid when you constantly remember that your job as a content producer is to provide value and inspire action, not just publish for the sake of publishing. Poor quality content creates negative brand perception, and this is something to absolutely avoid.

If you can provide deep emotional and psychological security for people in our highly anxious, overloaded world of constantly shifting technology and social reorganization, your customers will likely feel a sigh of relief—and reward you with loyalty and stewardship. The more clear, direct, honest, and authentic your content can be, the more trust you will earn from your audience base. The competition is fierce, and loyalty is hard to come by.

People really *want* to find content and companies they can trust, and when they do, there's a lot more incentive to stick with that source of safety and fulfillment than to venture back out into the Wild Wild West of Internet options. Remember the concept of *cumulative advantage*? (We discussed it in Chapter 5.) You can produce relevant, exciting content to keep existing customers satisfied so they don't need to look elsewhere.

The Internet allows us to learn so much about our audience, and it's worth it to *really listen*. You need to figure out what they want if you expect to design content that interests them. Search research is one tool we'll focus on to help you design content focused around your audience's questions. Today, authentic connection, clear communication, real conversation, and trustworthy, reliable follow-through are the gateways to positive, long-lasting customer relations.

> Knowing your audience better means you can make sure to tailor your content to empathize with them.

POINTS OF DISCOVERY

In this chapter, we took a close look at the emotional and psychological factors motivating our customers to seek knowledge about what our businesses offer. Consider the following questions to get to know your audience even better:

1. Think about an audience group (in other words, a type of customer) that you figure you know pretty well. What primary need are you able to fulfill: emotional, intellectual, social, or physical? Describe the need. What do they want on a deep level that you are able to provide? Do this for as many different customer types as you can think of.
2. What offer are you making that you want your audience to say *yes* to? What kind of information or emotional reassurance might they need in order to do that?
3. Conduct a site audit of your website if you have one. Notice any places in the copy, design, or user experience that might potentially cause stress, confusion, or frustration for a user. Bookmark these to address when the time is right.
4. Brainstorm: What are some ways you can use content to build trust with your audience?

Chapter 10

USING PERSONAS

Marketers with a deeper, empathic understanding of the psychology of consumers can build high-impact, sustained strategies swiftly and with confidence.

—Kit Yarrow, *Decoding the New Consumer Mind*

When you can better understand what each of your audience groups wants, what motivates them, and what reassures them, you are on your way to crafting content that connects. The more your content can connect on a human level, the more trust you build as an authority in your field. Providing your audience groups with specific, relevant information they are looking for could be the beginning of a long-term relationship.

All of your audience groups will have some things in common, primarily because they are interested in something you have to offer, but the particular reasons why each audience group is seeking your products or services may be slightly different. The more we know about what your different audience groups are truly desiring or wondering about, the more we can craft content to provide insight and answer those questions. These essential differences between your various audience groups can be understood even better through the use of personas.

MEET "CAREER-CHANGE CONNIE"

Imagine: A 37-year-old single mother of two named Connie browses the Internet during her lunch break at the restaurant where she works. She's been feeling like she wants a change in her life. Connie has two children in high school and she's always stressed the value of an education to them, so she's proud that they're both planning to apply to four-year universities straight out of high school. Education is very important to her, but she had children at a young age and never had the chance to pursue her own educational goals.

She's always wanted to go back to school. At her restaurant where she's head waitress, she's realized that she truly loves helping people, but she wants more pay, more opportunities for career advancement, more challenge, and greater meaning in her life. Now that her kids are getting older, she's working up the courage to envision herself getting that education she's always wanted. She's always been fascinated by the medical field and wonders what a career in nursing would be like. She's nervous that if she went back to school, her attention span, energy levels, and ability to provide for her kids financially would be compromised.

She does some light research on her break, typing in searches like "what is nursing like," "how hard is nursing," and "changing careers." She is encouraged to come across an article on The Nursing School's website called "You Can Do It! Juggling Nursing School, Work, and Kids Without Going Insane." The article explains the general costs of a nursing education, the length of time in school, and what to expect from the workload. It also reassures Connie that the class schedules can be flexible so working students can keep their other jobs. The article states that teachers are generally compassionate and understanding and that nursing training programs provide on-campus resources to help every student succeed. Finally, it touches on time-management skills and ends with the reassurance that it's never too late to pursue your dreams. Connie feels inspired for a moment, like the article was speaking just to her.

A week later, Connie can't get the idea of nursing school out of her head. She turns on her laptop computer and decides to search a little bit more—just to see what's out there. She still doesn't entirely know what she's looking for, but she's searching a bit more specifically now. She tries a few queries: "what is nursing school like," "how much does nursing school cost," and "how to become a nurse." In the privacy of her own home, no one needs to know that Connie is considering making this sort of huge life decision. The content she finds is empathetic, encouraging, and informative.

After a few weeks of searching for information online, she notices The Nursing School often appears as a search result, offering helpful articles and videos that answer her questions and make her feel a little less terrified. Just out of curiosity, she clicks on the "Locations" page and is surprised to realize there is a campus less than 30 miles from her. One day, she decides to just go ahead and fill out the form at the bottom of the page to request free information about enrollment.

After she fills out a simple request form for more information about nursing training, she receives a call the next day from The Nursing School asking if she has any questions about their program. Turns out, she has a lot of questions, and The Nursing School has answers. Within six months, Connie works up the courage to enroll as a nursing student—something that had been a dream of hers for years. Now in a nursing training program, she appreciates the regular emails and content she reads about life as a nursing student. It helps her feel connected to a community of people on a similar life path. She even feels so good about her choice in life that she starts posting about her accomplishments on social media.

Though Connie is not a real person, she could be. Her fictional story is based on actual audience research from a real nursing school. "Career-Change Connie" is a *persona* within the audience group of 30- to 45-year-old working mothers who make up one of the school's primary audience groups (Career-Seeking Moms). Personas help us understand the emotional needs, desires, and motivations of different audience groups on a deep, personal level.

Adele Revella, author of *Buyer Personas*, asks the question: "What if understanding and addressing your buyer's expectations—working together to tell a story that builds trust between your company and your customer—became the new common ground to align sales and marketing?"[1] We believe it must be, and we've seen it work time and time again.

WHAT ARE PERSONAS?

Personas are advanced consumer psychology tools created from real interviews with real people. Essentially, they're fictional characters designed from actual customer interactions and insights, archetypes of a kind of person who is among your audience group.

Personas were developed in the 1980s and 1990s by Alan Cooper and are an often-underutilized research tool in marketing efforts. They offer a way to gain a deeper, more specific, more visual, and richer understanding of the people you are trying to reach with your content and your products. Because it's impossible to have a real, live customer in the room with you all the time when you're mapping out your content strategy and business objectives, a persona is a stand-in for that real customer you are trying to reach, attract, and then keep.

Personas can help you recreate real scenarios to better answer your customers' actual questions. And the better you can answer their questions with content, the better you can achieve your content marketing goals—to **communicate** intentionally and **connect** meaningfully in the **context** where you want to have a **conversation**.

In order to tell a story your audience wants to hear—or, rather, to cocreate that story with them—you'll need insight. Insight into why they chose your purple design over the blue. Insight into what they loved about your YouTube contest. Complaints they've had about your product packages. This type of specific insight can give you a better understanding of not only *what* types of content your audiences want but also *how* they want to consume it—like whether they prefer long-form articles or short videos, for example. This type of information can even tell you which social media platforms they prefer.

Personas are not based on what you *think* your customers want but on what you have *actually discovered* they want through tried-and-true research. Just like audience groups, personas are always based on actual data. While it may seem easier to simply pull together a persona from some observations about your customers, this can actually mislead you in the long run. The entire point is to craft a model that reflects the real needs and desires of your customers. That way, you can use a nuanced, detailed understanding of a certain type of person to help you communicate with that particular audience group online. So, don't skip the research!

> "What people think their constituents are like can be quite far from what actual constituents think and how they behave. Therein lies much madness."
>
> —Kate Rutter

PERSONAS FOR DIFFERENT PURPOSES

Personas are multi-purpose tools and can be applied to many different steps in the content production process to help you:

1. **Understand audience groups better.** Personas are a great way to conceptualize and humanize your audience.
2. **Inform search research.** As we'll see in Part 3 of the book, having a persona can enhance the process of performing keyword and topic research.
3. **Evaluate content.** Once you have topics ready to go, you can use your persona to evaluate how the content might actually resonate with your target audience.
4. **Differentiate content.** Having a persona on hand can help infuse your content with more authenticity and help you dig deeper to put your content above the competition.
5. **Inspire nuanced content ideas.** Personas force content creators to

think about what real people want and need, which can open the door for highly specific content creation.
6. **Expand content topics.** Once you've been producing content for a while, personas can help you mine your current content for more ideas when it seems like the well is running dry.
7. **Support other marketing initiatives.** Once you have a persona created, it can also be used for other marketing purposes, like retargeting or branding, and in other online marketing campaigns, such as persona-specific native ads or banner ads.

Personas Inform the Content Production Process

Personas are a tool that can be used for content production to help writers and content producers visualize who they're speaking to. When a writer has no concept of who they're writing to, the writer will default to writing to themself. It's just human nature. Personas are a way to externalize your audience to connect with them better. At the end of the day, you're not producing your content for your company, you're producing it for your audience.

For example, as your content team is researching content topics, outlining projects, writing copy and headlines, or otherwise developing marketing messages, they can ask, "What would Connie be interested in? Can I see this content being helpful for Connie? What would Connie think?" We can allow personas to become living, breathing additions to the team who help direct us in creating content that lands with who we're trying to reach.

Having a persona can inform:

- Types of content to create
- Platforms to use
- Depth and type of subject matter to present
- Vocabulary and diction
- Length and formatting

- Writing style, voice, and tone
- Business goals of the content

Personas Keep Your Focus on Business Objectives

When using personas, you can explore a wide range of topics. Just keep in mind that the content should be customized for the perspectives, interests, and desires of your specific audience while achieving your specific business goals. You're not just producing content to produce content—you're producing content to connect with an audience and drive engagement.

Let's consider a scenario (one we have, unfortunately, seen way too often) in which audience grouping and personas are left out of the equation. To continue with The Nursing School example, imagine a room of content producers brainstorming topics to write about. They start to think about what's trending, what's popular, and what's going viral because they think that getting a huge boost in traffic would be great. It's the holiday season, and they want to write a timely article that will be very popular, so they decide on the topic of "Gluten-Free Christmas Cookies" because gluten-free anything is all the rage. They figure that it's loosely related to the health field, so it wouldn't be strange to post on a nursing school website. They spend dozens of hours working to get it right: They reach out to experts for the best recipes, test a few recipe options, finally settle on one, and then produce a blog post, YouTube video, and an infographic to share on social media.

While we can understand the logic of this thinking, it is unfortunately very misguided. Maybe the article would be very popular and fun to create, but we wouldn't expect it to drive business results. Just think: How much of that traffic would consist of people actually interested in what the business has to offer, which is nursing training (not cookies)? Most likely, not much. The audience is too general, and the topic of gluten-free cookies does not support The Nursing School's realm of expertise—nursing training. We would more likely expect to see this type of content from a cooking, baking, or recipe website. Even though it's not a bad topic in itself, it's not related to The Nursing School's business objectives, which is to enroll students in nursing training. Content should support this objective.

To illustrate the value of personas, consider what would happen if you ran this topic idea by Connie. Would "Gluten-Free Christmas Cookies" help Connie make the decision to enroll in nursing school, inform her about nursing training, or empathize with her concerns? The answer becomes obvious. Connie may or may not care about this particular topic. But even if she does, it's not relevant to her concerns about whether to apply for nursing training nor would it support her as a current student.

Personas help give us focus and direction so we don't waste hours and hours producing content that has nothing to do with our business goals. Something like "Meal Prep Tips for Busy Working Students During the Holidays" would be more relevant to someone like Connie, The Nursing School's audience. She might actually benefit from an article like that because it considers her needs as a working student and offers her solutions. Connie is who The Nursing School should care about, not gluten-free consumers. Even if an article that's popular attracts a small amount of viral success, that traffic is not necessarily going to convert. (Remember, we want *relevant* traffic from our target audiences.) Personas help us better understand our target audience groups for higher-quality engagement.

> As a caveat, Jon, one of the book's co-authors, wants to point out that there could be some good reasons to do a post like this from a brand-marketing perspective. If you're already killing it in search, it could be useful to branch out, do something socially friendly, and produce a trendy piece just to get more eyes on your brand. However, it's not a first priority when trying to grow your business through search. No one thinks to themselves, "This gluten-free cookie recipe makes me want to become a nurse."

HOW TO BUILD A PERSONA

Crafting a solid persona relies on the quality of three things: your audience research, customer insights, and audience feedback. Since creating personas is the specialty of some marketing agencies, you can find in-depth guidance from resources like Adele Revella and her book *Buyer Personas: How to Gain Insight into Your Customer's Expectations, Align Your Marketing Strategies, and Win More Business*. This is a fantastic resource that walks you through the entire process of gathering audience data to create personas. For companies with a budget dedicated to audience research, doing in-depth persona research can be a fantastic investment for the long haul, and we think Revella is an excellent resource. To go all-in, here's a general overview of what the process might look like:

1. Decide what types of questions you want to ask and what insights you hope to gain, then design a series of questions for your customer interviews.
2. Find contact information for potential customer interviews from places such as sales databases or focus groups.
3. Decide how many interviews to conduct, then use a professional recruiter to schedule interview appointments for market research.
4. Hire a professional to conduct customer interviews. Record and transcribe every interview.
5. After you have a certain number of interviews, review them all together, looking for similarities or common pain points across different customer profiles. Pay special attention to the reasoning behind a buying decision, problems or challenges that prevent a buying decision, and positive and negative feedback about the buying experience.

However, we understand that level of research might not be the top priority for every business. To provide an alternative way of crafting personas, use what you have available to you. Look at any kind of qualitative data you have: customer surveys, personal feedback, sales conversations, reviews. If you can, conduct some interviews and simplify the above process to suit your needs. Because the data-gathering part of the persona-building process is so essential to creating a workable persona, and because your needs may be specific to your customer base, we recommend you find the process that works best for you. What's important is simply sifting through whatever kind of customer feedback is available to you to create your persona, rather than making uninformed guesses that could lead you in the wrong direction.

Using the insights from whatever customer data you have, you'll want to pay special attention to the following categories to differentiate and create personas:

- **Goals:** What are my customers reaching for? What do they want to achieve?
- **Motivations:** Why do they want to reach these goals? What is spurring them into action?
- **Frustrations:** What is keeping them from reaching their goals? What are their worries and concerns?
- **Demographic:** What is the relevant demographic information for my customers? This may include age, gender, marital/family status, ethnicity, socioeconomic status, occupation, location.
- **Background/bio:** How did they get to be where they are?
- **Personality/lifestyle:** What is their lifestyle like? What kinds of choices do they make? What types of activities do they prefer?

You can take this information and break it out into a simple Word doc easily and use those categories as your guide, or you can get more creative. We like to use an online persona template to make a visually appealing document that includes a stock photo, with each category clearly broken out so it's easy to see. We love using Xtensio templates for our personas. Xtensio is a project of the Los Angeles design agency Fake Crow, and they provide simple, beautiful document templates to take your work to the next level. The following three personas for The Nursing School—shown in Figures 10.1–10.3—were created using Xtensio.

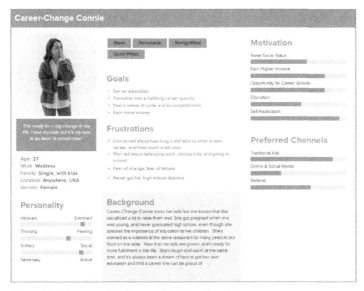

Figure 10.1: Persona for Career-Change Connie

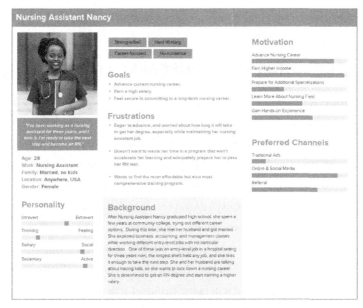

Figure 10.2: Persona for Nursing Assistant Nancy

Figure 10.3: Persona for High School Heather

These personas are based on actual market research for a nursing school. When in doubt, do more research, post a poll online, or go back into your archives to get customer feedback. Ask; don't make it up!

ARE PERSONAS REALLY NECESSARY?

Imagining your ideal customer encountering your content—their mindset, their emotions, their reactions—is an essential mental strategy for content marketing. Personas offer a structured way to transform a vague concept of your audience into a real, living, breathing person who is trying to connect with you. While it's obviously your call where to spend your resources, if you are committed to a long-term content marketing campaign and long-term growth, personas are worth the investment. However, if you're just starting out, you can get by with just audience grouping and go deeper with personas later. Even if you're not ready to do the research for personas right now, having a persona mindset will surely help you as you create your content—remembering that real people are encountering your content, not an abstract group of people.

Switching away from a demographic-centric approach to a persona-centric approach will help put you among the ranks of online content creators who are making waves—getting relevant clicks because they used intentional language targeted to their particular audience's needs. This is partially because, as Revella articulates, "defining markets based on demographics—data such as a person's age, income, marital status, and education—is the legacy of 60 years of selling to the mass market."[2]

Demographics are helpful, don't get us wrong. But solely relying on external characteristics simply won't cut it for effective content marketing. To be successful, you'll want to use audience research that is motivation- and purpose-driven. This allows you to create content that comes alive in your reader's mind, connecting in a real and personal way, and adding value to your customer's story.

Take our Nursing School example; certain other nursing schools out there may not have addressed the anxieties that someone like Connie would have. The Nursing School's content showed Connie that the school empathized with her and offered solutions, and this made her feel welcomed, understood, and trusting. At the core of it, content has the power to make your customers feel good and want to continue a relationship. People want to know how saying yes to business with you will positively impact their lives. Your job is to show them through your content. It's not just important to know your audience before creating content for them, it's absolutely necessary.

POINTS OF DISCOVERY

In this chapter, we explained how a persona is an in-depth extension of one audience group and how using personas could help you take your audience research deeper. Consider creating personas based on actual audience data for your audience groups:

1. Create a persona for each valuable audience group you identified in Chapter 9. Fill in as much as you can based on actual audience data.
2. Choose a persona and take a few minutes to brainstorm questions this persona might be asking about your product or service.
3. Repeat Step 2 for each persona.

Chapter 11

YOUR AUDIENCE ASKS QUESTIONS

Content builds relationships. Relationships are built on trust. Trust drives revenue.

—**Andrew Davis**

Once you have an idea of who your audience groups are and what motivates them, it's time to put that knowledge to use! With a clear idea of who our ideal customers are, we can begin imagining what they are searching for online. Our audience groups and personas are such great tools because we can use them like stand-ins for real customers to anticipate what questions they might be asking online and what their reactions to certain content might be. This is the backbone of our search strategy: Knowing what questions our audience is asking will help us create content to guide them.

Remember the Search Cycle? (We talked about it in Chapter 3.) Each of your audience groups is searching for information at different stages, looking for content that will answer their questions, inspire them, make them feel good, and, ultimately, move them closer to the point of purchase. In this chapter, we'll show you how to start creating the bridge between your audience research and your content topics. Now that you know who your different audience groups are and their unique qualities (and maybe you even have some personas, which was covered in Chapter 10), you're ready to begin moving into the real heart of your content strategy: identifying search-focused topics.

APPLYING THE SEARCH CYCLE

To refresh your memory, the five stages of the Search Cycle are shown in Figure 11.1 and include:

1. Awareness
2. Information Gathering
3. Evaluation
4. Commitment
5. Support

Understanding Search | Search Cycle and Behavior

1. Awareness	2. Information Gathering	3. Evaluation	4. Commitment	5. Support
Need	Solutions	Specifications	Decision	Use
Want	Explanation	Comparisons	Purchase	Evaluation
Problem	Options	Alternatives	Inquiry	Post-purchase
Issue	Service	X vs Y / Pro vs Con	Sign-up	Tell Others
Opportunity	Provider	Quality	Schedule	Recommend
Improve	Supplier	Reputation		Review

Figure 11.1: The Five Stages of the Search Cycle

The goal of audience research in any form of marketing is to help you understand why a customer makes a buying decision, including understanding their thoughts and hesitations. We can learn a lot by understanding what *searches* occur at each stage of the Search Cycle, and this becomes even more precise when using audience groups and personas. Some topics may be relevant to all your audience groups, while other topics may be better suited to specific types of potential customers. Armed with this data, you can make informed decisions about who to target with specific content at specific stages in their search journey. Keep in mind, the "cycle" is not always a linear process and people may enter at any stage.

Let's walk through two of our personas—*Career-Change Connie* and *Nursing Assistant Nancy*—through each stage of the Search Cycle to understand how their questions may differ slightly. If you don't have fully formed personas, that's okay. You can easily imagine that using the audience groups of "Career-Seeking Moms" and "Nursing Assistants" would work just as well as the persona names.

Stage 1: Awareness

The awareness stage involves simply becoming aware that there is a problem, desire, or need for change. People in this stage may not even entirely know what they want, so their thought process might be especially general and vague. This can happen in an infinite number of ways, and it might not always occur online. What's important to know is that, in the awareness stage, your audience is just beginning to discover what they want, so their questions and searches may be unclear—even to them.

In the awareness stage, Connie is starting to become aware of the possibility of a career change, including attending nursing school. Remember, Connie had always had nursing in the back of her mind, and, during this stage, she's now considering it more seriously. The awareness stage involves having private thoughts to herself as well as asking some questions and conducting searches online, such as:

- What's a good career?
- How hard is it to go back to school?
- Is nursing a good career?
- Career change for adult women
- How to balance work and school

In the awareness stage, Connie is entering into a new frame of thought, investigating a burgeoning idea. It might not be fully formed yet, so she's just starting to pull back the curtain to see what she can find. She might be thinking to herself, "I've always wondered what it would be like to be a nurse. Why don't I find out what a nurse does and see if I'd like it?" She's not convinced of anything yet, and so your content isn't trying to make a sale. Your content, at this point, should be solely focused on answering her questions and relaying information that's relevant to her *current* needs, which are, primarily, to find out more about a subject she's not fully committed to yet.

Now, what about Nancy? As a nursing assistant, she's already well aware of the possible career paths for nurses. Since she works in a hospital, she might have already asked some of her colleagues what their nursing training was like and why they decided to become a nurse. Her awareness stage most likely happens offline in her work environment. Since she's already aware that it might be a good idea to advance her career from nursing assistant to nurse, if she does conduct any sort of online awareness searches, they might look something more like:

- Nursing career options
- Nursing training for nursing assistants
- What kind of nursing training is best?
- Should I become a registered nurse?

Nancy might also skip these sorts of searches altogether and jump straight into Stage 3 (evaluation), where she might perform a comparison to determine which path to take (for example, LPN vs. RN). Understanding the differences between the starting points of these two personas ensures your content is intended for a real audience of live humans, not just search engines, and that your content topics address their needs. Understandably, Connie will likely have more awareness-stage questions than Nancy.

Stage 2: Information Gathering

After becoming aware of a problem or desire, a potential customer will start gathering more information to help them understand their options.

As they are trying to solve one problem, they might realize they have other problems, questions, needs, or desires they weren't even aware of before, propelling them into different stages of the Search Cycle. A user will typically spend the most time in the Information Gathering stage as they are thinking through a purchase or exploring their options, and it can be fruitful to focus on this in your content marketing strategy. Creating quality brand interactions and answering key questions for potential customers during this stage can help them choose your brand when they're ready.

Moving our focus back to Connie, at this point, she has become aware of her desire for a possible career change, specifically considering nursing among other options. She decides to gather more information about this possible new career direction. She may also be gathering information about other options, as well, like medical assisting or dental assisting. We're focused on her investigation of nursing, so her searches on this topic might look something like this:

- What is being a nurse like?
- How to become a nurse
- How long does nursing training take?
- How much does nursing training cost?
- How to pay for nursing school
- How much does a nurse make?

Once Connie has done some initial research, she finds her interest piqued. She'd like to know more about the actual possibility of entering a nursing program. It would be a huge decision, so she does as much research as she can possibly handle. At this stage, your content should be focused on giving specific types of information that a searcher might be looking for. Connie learns there are different types of nursing careers, like RN and LPN. As she investigates the broad wealth of information available to her, her searches expose her to many different options, including other related careers, like medical assistant or nursing assistant.

Nancy would likely be doing her own information gathering, and many of her questions may be very similar. She would also probably want to learn about the cost of nursing training and the length of the programs. However, she might be looking for specific information that's been informed by her current experience. Understanding her background, we can imagine some of her possible queries. These might include:

- Career paths for nursing assistants
- How to become an RN from nursing assistant
- Is a nursing degree worth it?
- What certifications does a nurse need?
- Nursing requirements in [X location]

Again, some of the same searches will occur for all personas at each stage, but Nancy would have some specific questions that Connie wouldn't. These differences can inform which topics you choose, as a content creator, for which purposes.

Stage 3: Evaluation

In this stage, your audience has enough information to start comparing specific options, and they're getting close to making a decision. Searches often contain specific phrases about different buying options or different brands they could choose. Evaluation searches could also involve looking for reasons for or against a potential decision. Content at this stage is important for persuading the user to choose the option you want them to choose by highlighting the benefits of that particular choice.

For Connie, she has done enough research at this stage to have a general understanding of what a nursing career is and what nursing training involves. Now, she is trying to decide which choice would be best for her, and she's looking for supporting evidence for that decision. She starts getting more specific with her searches to compare and contrast her options. At this stage, her queries might include:

- Pros and cons of nursing training
- Vocational school vs. community college
- Vocational School X vs. Vocational School Y
- Cost of Vocational School X vs. Vocational School Y
- Nursing training vs. medical assistant training

After Connie has learned what she needs to know about nursing training—such as length of training, cost of training, etc.—it's up to her to decide whether this is something she really wants to commit to. This would naturally be a deeply personal decision. Your content can empathize with her fears, desires, and motivations and speak to her on a real human level that understands her hesitations while encouraging her to take the next step.

Nancy, similarly, would be comparing her options. Again, she might be already highly attuned to nursing career paths, so she might start her searches here. If she already knows she wants to advance her career, she might start her research with searches like:

- LPN vs. RN training
- Nursing assistant vs. certified nurse
- Best nursing programs in [city]
- RN salary vs. LPN salary

Pro Tip: The evaluation stage is a great stage to run a paid advertising campaign because the user is close to making a purchase and is actively comparing alternatives.

Searches like "best nursing programs" qualify as evaluation searches because the query indicates the searcher's desire to find a specific buying solution. Nursing Assistant Nancy would be looking for information to help her decide which degree to get, which program is right for her, and which school would best suit her needs. This is a key stage to create supporting content for your business. Understanding the needs of your personas can help you make these appeals.

Stage 4: Commitment

Alright, so the problem has been identified, the information has been gathered, the options have been evaluated, and your customer is about to commit to the next step in the buying journey. At this stage, the content can be very supportive, encouraging, and reassuring. Make it as easy as possible for your users to make that commitment—because they're ready.

In the commitment stage, Connie is ready to pull the trigger and commit to at least some level of decision-making. This might be making a call, filling out a contact form, making an appointment, or filling out an application. The school can make it really easy for her to engage in this stage by laying out some key steps, such as filling out an application or filing forms for financial aid. When this happens, Connie transforms from a user to a lead or a conversion. The same holds true for Nancy. She's ready and excited to take the next step in her career, so she requests more information, signs up, or enrolls.

If there are any searches at this stage, they may be navigational in nature, such as the name of the business, like "nursing school" or "enroll at [nursing school]." We might also see something like "[nursing school] financial aid application" or "apply for [nursing school] scholarships." For some businesses, these types of searches might contain the phrase "buy" or "purchase" as in "buy [product]." This indicates the user is ready to make that purchase and just needs to find the right web page to take the next step. However, the goal of all the other stages is to get a user to this point, so this is actually the least search-heavy stage. The primary focus of this stage is having supportive elements in place to capture the conversion, such as user-friendly pages that explain the process, easy-to-use application forms, and clearly highlighted calls to action.

Stage 5: Support

We can't overstate this or say it enough: Don't overlook the value of support content that targets the post-purchase experience. As we've mentioned before, the Search Cycle stages are not necessarily linear, and they are all working together. Connie could move back and forth between many stages along the journey, requesting information from a school, then going back to do more information gathering and evaluation, asking new questions to help her understand any new information she's received. The bottom line: Create content to support every moment of the experience with your brand.

In the post-purchase support stage, Connie is enrolled in nursing training or has graduated from the program. The content cycle doesn't end just because the buying decision has been made. Connie is now a potential advocate of The Nursing School, and content can be tailored to reinforce her buying decision. Every email Connie receives to help her through nursing school and every interaction she has online with the school *after* she's already enrolled supports her decision and strengthens that relationship. It also creates more opportunities for the school to maintain their reputation, help their customers, and provide value at every level. Perhaps Connie is so inspired by her life-changing experience with The Nursing School that she leaves a review online, a review that another potential student comes across in their own evaluation stage.

Here are some things that both Connie and Nancy might be searching for once they've already signed up:

- Nursing school career services
- Nursing school resume tips
- Nursing training job applications
- Nursing school textbooks
- Nursing school study tips

Depending on what the query is, these could still be valuable topics to target. Remember, we're thinking about these terms now under "post-purchase" support, but these topics could be relevant to someone else along their own informational journey. This stage opens the door to think about what your audience might be interested in beyond the precise point of purchase so you can maintain that relationship far beyond the point of sale.

PRIMARY VS. SECONDARY TOPICS

Walking each persona along the Search Cycle helps us uncover their thought processes and the types of searches they're conducting. This, in turn, informs the kind of content we'll create for them. Keep in mind, some of the questions your potential customers will ask are top-level, general sorts of questions that can apply to all of your audience groups. For example, perhaps all three personas—Career-Change Connie, Nursing Assistant Nancy, and High School Heather—would ask, "How much does nursing school cost?" We call this a "primary" topic because it's not specific to any one audience group or persona in particular, and it's a primary question anyone might ask related to the business. Another example is, "What is nursing school?" This is also such a broad, general question that content could apply to any of the audience groups you've identified.

Primary questions are the obvious ones—the ones that you'd absolutely expect your business to address. So you definitely should. These content topics can be general, answering the question for anyone who is asking.

To take your content strategy to the next level, virtually every primary topic can be expanded into secondary topics to address specific concerns for each audience group or persona. Secondary topics are where the value of your audience groups and personas really become apparent. For example, the primary topic "How much does nursing school cost?" can be reworked into three separate content pieces for each of your three personas. You'll want to focus on a specific angle for each of them, such as:

- How to pay for nursing school as a working mother
- What high school graduates need to know about the cost of nursing school
- What is the cost of nursing school for nursing assistants?

While the core information may be fairly similar (how much does nursing school cost), the angle of each topic is slightly different to address each different persona's unique needs and desires. The "working mother" piece may highlight a flexible schedule, supportive resources, and scholarships as ways to help ease the burden of nursing school. The "high school graduate" article might focus more on the difference in cost of tuition between a vocational training program and a four-year degree. The "nursing assistant" piece could compare the differences between the salary of a nursing assistant and the salary of a Registered Nurse, highlighting the return on investment. Each one of these topics can be highly specific to each persona's needs.

If you want to try out this exercise, you can use the format shown in Figure 11.2.

(One caveat: Make sure to keep reading into Part 3 where we talk about search, as it's important to verify all of your content topics with *search evidence*. This template and these examples are designed to give you a conceptual idea of how to use personas to differentiate your primary content topics. Everything should still be substantiated with search research. You may want to bookmark this page and come back to it after going through Part 3.)

Primary topic: _____
Secondary topic for Persona 1: _____
Secondary topic for Persona 2: _____
Secondary topic for Persona 3: _____

Figure 11.2: Spinning a Primary Content Topic into Secondary Topics for Different Audience Groups

Essentially, every time you come across a valuable topic idea, you can use personas to cover it from different angles to speak to a specific audience group. This not only expands the value of one topic (you only need to perform one round of research to produce multiple content pieces), but it also serves the specific types of customers you want to attract by focusing on their interests. Remember, your content is not meant for everyone; it's meant for specific people—*your potential customers*. Not every topic will be perfectly suited for each persona, but it gives you an easy and actionable way to create search-informed content titles based on your persona research.

Audience groups/personas and the Search Cycle are two powerful tools to help you identify content topics to target. You can, theoretically, run every content topic through these two screening filters by asking a couple of important questions:

- What would my audience group/persona think about this?
- What stage of the Search Cycle am I targeting?

In Part 3, we'll build on these ideas and show you how to verify your content topic ideas with search research so you can choose the topics that are most likely to drive the organic traffic you want.

POINTS OF DISCOVERY

In this chapter, we took personas even deeper and explored ways to apply personas to content ideas. Consider the following questions about your audience groups:

1. Brainstorm: Make a list of "primary" content topics or questions you can imagine any of your customers asking. Remember, these can be broad, general questions that your business would be expected to answer, such as "What benefits does X have?" or "How much does Y cost?"

2. Take one of your personas and brainstorm some questions they might ask at each stage of the Search Cycle. Remember to consider their interests, background, needs, and desires.
3. Research: How does each of your personas prefer to receive information online—social media, email, videos, podcasts, etc.? Start thinking about the types of content that would appeal to each of your personas and where they would go to access it. Can you support any of your hunches with data?

PART THREE
SEARCH

Chapter 12

UNDERSTANDING SEARCH ENGINES

Without SEO, a website can be invisible to search engines.

—Moz

As a result of the overwhelming amount of information available online, consumers today live in a perpetual state of tension between *searching* and *filtering* (or *scanning*). On the one hand, they're searching for the information they need at a particular moment to accomplish their goals. On the other hand, they do not want their attention scattered with distracting, irrelevant, useless information. They're actively filtering that out, pushing it away, and rejecting it. The average user spends less than 15 seconds on a website before deciding whether to move on.[1] People *expect* the answers they're looking for, and tech-savvy business owners have the opportunity to provide those answers by understanding how search engines work.

SEARCH RESEARCH OPTIMIZES CONTENT PRODUCTION

Businesses that adopt a **search mindset** are better equipped to grow relevant organic traffic, engage appropriate audiences, and streamline their content production processes. **A search mindset leverages data from search engine research to optimize content for greater exposure online.**

Once you integrate a search mindset into your content production process, the quality of your traffic is much more likely to be relevant and productive, driving more conversions and inspiring better engagements. This is because you can validate your content ideas with *evidence*—that is, you can determine whether people are searching for a particular subject (or not), and this enables you to go forward more efficiently and with greater intention. We've worked with dozens of companies that simply didn't know what they didn't know. They had the right ideas and the right energy, but they were missing strategic knowledge on how to use search to drive results.

As two professionals with an SEO background who have been doing content marketing for 30 years combined, it's our mission to help businesses understand how to get their content to perform well and become visible to the people looking for it. **The bridge between your audience and your content is *validating your ideas through search*.**

Our stance is simple: You shouldn't be producing any content until you've at least done some preliminary search research. We recommend doing keyword research so you can discover the questions your audience is asking—and then answer them. Understanding search is the key to getting your content seen and your website visited more frequently. It is essential to driving organic traffic growth and attracting targeted engagements.

> While optimizing content is definitely crucial to improving your rankings, the focus of content marketing is producing high-quality content that your users want to engage with. The more users engage with your content, the more your website will be perceived by Google as having *relevance* and *authority*—two important elements that determine ranking factor.

Traffic for the sake of traffic is meaningless (unless you're a media company, perhaps). But if you're a business website, you want increased traffic from *people who will help you fulfill your business goals*. It's better to attract 100 visitors who are truly interested in who you are and what you do and whose expectations are reasonably fulfilled when they arrive at your website than it is to draw 1,000 visitors to your site who immediately bounce because what they came across was different from what they expected based on their search results. (This is why clickbait is rarely effective, and it's why you shouldn't waste time trying to chase down "popular" topics.)

It is in your best interest to produce content that fulfills these three requirements:

1. Content that's relevant to your business
2. Content that's relevant to your audience's interests
3. Content that people are searching for

You may be surprised once you do your research. What you *think* would make a good subject for a piece of content based on your product may *not* actually be what your audience is searching for. For example, let's say you're a business that offers green cleaning products using the latest green technology, one of which is called micellar technology. This seems like something people could be interested in, right? Why not write an informative article highlighting how this technology works? Sounds like a fine idea, but if you do your research, you may find there's no actual evidence of people searching for subjects like "what is micellar technology?" It turns out this subject is too nuanced and scientific to be of interest to your audience, so it's unlikely an article like this would drive any significant results.

Instead, once you conduct some research, you might find topics that people *are* interested in, such as "how to remove tar from skin." As a green cleaning company, this appears to be a specific topic that's both relevant to your product and a subject people are searching for. People who are interested in ways to remove tar from their skin are likely an audience that would be interested in a green cleaner that does exactly that.

So, what does this search research reveal? It's quite simple: Unless your audience consists of chemists, it's not helpful to your content marketing efforts to write an article on the intricacies of micellar technology, even though it may be part of your product development. Micellar technology could be a selling point, but it's not a commonly known topic—at least not enough that someone would be seeking it out. It's a great idea to include this discussion in your product pages, but there just might not be any demand for independent content around this topic—yet. Save the micellar technology content to support the product pages and landing pages to educate your customers of the product's benefits. If your products become very popular, you might see demand for new content emerge. That would be a good time to focus on this topic specifically. Until then, use search-focused research to identify topics your audience is interested in already.

Just a little bit of research can save you a lot of headache, and we cover this topic in depth over the next few chapters. Despite how well a piece of content is written or produced, it still needs to appeal to your audience using their language and targeting the terms they use. If you're not validating your content topics with search research, how can you be sure anyone is searching for them, or that anyone is even interested?

> You are anywhere from 10 to 100 times more likely to attract a higher volume of relevant traffic to your website when you consistently incorporate a search mindset into your content strategy.

How Search Engines Work

While it's not necessary for the purposes of this book to understand the technical logic behind how search engines work, it's helpful to know what search engines are looking for and how they choose which results to show on a Search Engine Results Page (SERP).

"SERP" is a fancy SEO term for any page that appears after you type a search query into a search engine. This is the page with the ad links at the top and maybe a map or some images. The SERP will look different depending on the query, which determines what type of information Google will serve up. If you search "restaurants near me," the SERP will probably offer a map with some nearby options. If you search "why are frogs green," you're more likely to see some images and perhaps an encyclopedia entry. When it comes to shopping, whenever the word "buy" appears, the SERP may show a scrolling list of items for purchase. And so on. Just remember, the SERP is the page that appears after you search for something—the search engine results page.

A search engine's job is to effectively build a fast-moving, accurate information highway, connecting users with the information they "think" they want. Through complex algorithms, a search engine sends "robots," or "spiders," all over the web to "crawl" pages and create a massive index of information. By categorizing the information these spiders find on web pages, the search engine algorithm returns the most relevant results to the user based on a variety of factors.

SEO uses tactical strategies to increase a website's placement in search engine results. It's a complex process that utilizes HTML structure, website architecture, page content, anchor text and keyword usage, and internal and inbound links, among other things, to increase visibility through search. While a discussion on the proper ways to formulate and optimize your website is beyond the scope of this book, a well-functioning website with clear organization and intentionally optimized pages should be in place already for effective content marketing.

SEO AND CONTENT MARKETING GO HAND IN HAND

Even before "content marketing" was a major industry buzzword, online marketing had always been about quality content. If you put effort into content, it typically performed better. Quality was always the tipping point. Even well-optimized content can fail if it's not structurally robust.

In the past few years, Google has developed smarter algorithms to detect the difference between "good content" and "bad content." Algorithmic evolution demands higher quality content. Content that performs well on the web has always possessed similar traits. For example, quality content:

- Answers users' questions
- Engages users
- Proposes new ideas
- Shares insights and expertise
- Is well-researched
- Is well-optimized
- Is easy to read
- Is unique

Just as content is integral to any SEO campaign, SEO is a crucial part of content marketing. Content marketing and search optimization are not separate industries; we propose they are one and the same. A search mindset should be in every content marketer's toolkit. In the next few chapters, we'll show you specifically how to use keyword research to answer your potential customers' questions online.

The foundation of our content strategy is this: **Drive organic search traffic by answering questions relevant to your audience and your business.**

> "Just as wheels without an engine leaves you pedaling, content without an SEO strategy can't keep up in a digital marketplace. And just like an engine with no wheels, SEO without content is a shiny machine that goes nowhere."
>
> —Nate Dame, SearchEngineLand.com

GOOD CONTENT: AS DEFINED BY GOOGLE GUIDELINES

Sure, there are some other search engines that can drive traffic to your site, but none have as much influence as Google. As of June 2020, Google has maintained more than 90% of the global search engine market share.[2] When we're talking about search engines, we're talking about search engines in general, but we would be mistaken not to focus on Google. Using a variety of tools to analyze traffic sources, it's clear that Google directs the most traffic to sites across the web.

Therefore, it's important to know what Google is looking for when they "reward" websites with high rankings. Google's long-standing mission statement is to "organize the world's information and make it universally accessible and useful."[3] That's a pretty simple statement for a fairly lofty goal. How exactly does Google accomplish this? Even though Google's algorithms are "black box" secrets, the search engine is relatively transparent about what quality guidelines they use to "organize the world's information." In short, Google's mission is to ensure that content is useful, valuable, engaging, and relevant *for the user*.

Google's Basic Principles page includes this statement: "Make pages primarily for users, not for search engines."[4] This is very important! Content that isn't focused on the user and their search behavior is not going to drive the growth that we know you're looking for. At the time of this writing, Google has laid out five main criteria for achieving "high-quality content" (paraphrased):[5]

- Make sure your content is useful and informative.
- Include your own unique and valuable perspective that is different or better than your competitors.
- Use credible sources and cite your work appropriately.
- Give your users a positive experience through specific and unique content.

- Engage your audience through professional execution and interactive components.

If we can agree that the technical aspects of web design, user experience, and SEO are all necessary, then we can also remember that, with those elements in place, *people are your priority*. Search engines are the tools that connect people to products, and we wouldn't be writing this book if search engines didn't exist. But keep in mind, they are a means to an end. (Don't worry, search engines can't have their feelings hurt.) Search engines aren't going to shop online or sign up for your monthly subscriptions; your target audience consists of *people*, and search engines are just one very important avenue to reaching them.

The goal of search engines is to satisfy user queries, and the goal of your business is to satisfy your customers. By identifying your customers' needs and focusing on providing solutions to their questions online *consistently*, you show search engines that your content meets users' needs, and momentum to your site grows.

What's good for the user is typically good for search.

Google is an ever-evolving company that adapts to changing user needs and technological innovations, which means algorithms and guidelines may change suddenly over time. But the most important rule to remember is this: *Put the user first.* If you were around for the infamous Panda updates, you probably learned that it's not worth it to try and "game the system" because Google eventually identifies and filters out low-quality content. Once you're on Google's "naughty list," it's extremely hard to get back into the search engine's good graces, so it's better to keep aiming for consistently superior content in the first place.

> For best results, don't chase algorithms.

When you focus your energies on improving the lives of your audience by answering their questions in your content, this is what will actually improve your rankings. It's very important to note that this search section is not about relaying SEO tactics to *increase your rankings* necessarily; it's to understand search behavior and inform your content strategy with search research in order to *better meet your audience's needs*. If you're producing content that's intelligently informed by how search works and what your audience wants, you're well on your way to simultaneously satisfying Google's requirements, building your audience, and generating more relevant traffic.

> Gimmicks and shticks don't work, but quality lasts.

Quality, targeted content has the power to outlast any algorithmic storms that might threaten less content-driven sites. If you take a look at the gigantic success of Wikipedia, you'll see what we mean. Wikipedia is the largest encyclopedia on the Internet, and Google consistently returns Wiki results for thousands of subjects. So, what is the key to their success? Well, even though Wikipedia is a user-generated encyclopedia that anyone can edit, they maintain consistent quality because of the website's high internal standards. According to their own guidelines, content must be "factual, notable, verifiable with cited external sources, and neutrally presented."[6] Wikipedia's content is a feast for integrity-driven search algorithms.

Google's guidelines and Wikipedia's quality criteria are largely compatible: Both companies make it their mission to ensure that accurate, verifiable, and high-quality content are presented to the people who come across the information on the web. Think about it: Without quality guidelines, the Internet would be overrun by self-promotional clutter (and, in the past, it was, which is why Google keeps cleaning it up). While the Internet is largely open to anyone to do what they please, the systems that Google and websites like Wikipedia put in place help keep the Internet valuable to the people searching for information (which, let's face it, is all of us). Stick to the principles laid out by Google and Wikipedia, and you should have a pretty good yardstick for determining whether your content is serving the people it's meant for.

Search research gives you the tools to validate interest in any particular subject or question so you can write about what your audience wants to know, not what you *think* they want.

A search strategy considers these four components:

1. It gives your audience something of value (informs, educates, inspires, engages, etc.).
2. It fulfills your business's goals (leads, conversions, downloads, calls, etc.).
3. It uses language and terms that your audience uses (keyword research).
4. It offers higher value and quality than your competitors (evaluation, competitor analysis).

Audience Needs + Business Goals
+ Relevant Terms + Value
= Search Strategy

POINTS OF DISCOVERY

In this chapter, we discussed the role of search engines in content marketing. Consider the following questions as we begin navigating search research:

1. What do you hope to discover about what your audience is searching for?
2. What are some of the key phrases that would describe your business offerings?
3. Brainstorm some questions you expect your audience to be asking.

Chapter 13

SPEAKING THE LANGUAGE OF SEARCH

> With a good product, marketing can all be boiled down to education. Effectively educating people about any good product will create the desire needed to produce action.
>
> —**Jeffrey Harmon, Chief Marketing Officer, Orabrush**

Isn't it amazing how Internet access has opened the door to millions of people to buy pretty much anything they want online? There's a product or service for nearly everything nowadays (and if there isn't, there could be soon). Somewhere on the web, your business exists, and, every day, people search for topics related to what you do, whatever that may be. The role of search research is to discover the language your customers are using to find you online.

WHY THE RIGHT KEYWORDS MATTER

Imagine you're a niche producer of special artisan products featuring Norse mythology. We're talking elven lamps, luxurious rugs with ancient battles depicted on them, Thor figurines—the whole deal. Now, imagine you've been labeling everything in your product catalog and on your web pages with labels like "Norse Rug" and "Norse Art" because, obviously, that's what they are.

Now, imagine an SEO guy walks into the room, sits down with you for a few minutes, and blows your mind when he tells you that, all this time, you could have been optimizing your products for another descriptor, "Viking," because—as it turns out—way more people search for "Viking" than "Norse" when they want to find out about Scandinavian seafaring pirate culture. And you could have been driving double or triple the amount of traffic to your website just by adjusting the way you label your products, switching from "Norse Rug" to "Viking Rug."

In this example, it's not *wrong* to label everything Norse, but it's more *effective* to call things by what people are searching for. It turns out that the search term "Viking" is roughly four times more popular than "Norse." It makes sense, though, why the owner of the store would miss this tiny yet impactful detail. He's so deeply involved in the particulars of Norse mythology that he could give you a lecture on why calling something "Viking" isn't totally accurate. However, search research is not about being technically correct. It's about driving more people to your website. Sometimes too much expertise can actually alienate us from our audience if we don't know how to relate to them.

> **A NOTE ON SEMANTIC SEARCH**
>
> Search engines are now smart enough to understand more than just the words you type into a search bar. They can use the context, the intent, and the relationship between words to make an educated guess about what you're looking for. In other words, search engines are better able to understand conversational queries to deliver more accurate results. This is, in part, influenced by the rise of voice search and how we speak to virtual assistants, like Siri and Alexa.
>
> Search engines might also factor in your search history, your location, and spelling variations to try and figure out what you want. So, having robust content means your web page might get delivered even if it's slightly different from a user's query—if Google thinks that's what they want. Still, keywords matter. They are still the most direct route to understanding the needs of your audience and crafting topics to reach them.[1]

Purists, be warned: This section is about finding the language people use to search for the things they want. Your average Joe searching for a cool hat on the Internet might not know the exact difference between the term Viking and Norse. He just knows he wants something awesome. So, the lesson is this: If you want to be found online, it's worth it to find out what language people are using to find you. And it might come as a surprise sometimes, which is why keyword research is so essential.

There's a slight disclaimer here, which is that Google is probably smart enough to help users find your content if it's really solid quality—even if it's not a perfect keyword match. But, in general, your content needs to be able to speak your customer's language. There's another reason why the Norse shop owner might overlook the Viking vs. Norse detail: He simply didn't know to question it. He wasn't employing a search mindset. Knowing the actual words your customers are using to look for things—and, ultimately, to find what you're offering—is crucial.

KNOW WHICH KEYWORDS TO USE

If search engines are information highways connecting users to content, keywords are the signposts that connect users to the information they're searching for. In ordinary language, the term *keyword* refers to a word that embodies the essence of meaning in a larger text. In digital marketing, it means much the same; a keyword is a word or phrase that describes the content of a document.

In the language of the Internet, **a keyword is a word or phrase used to perform a search.**[2] Colloquially, a keyword is typically one word, but the keywords we are talking about—search terms—can actually be comprised of one word or many. A keyword can be a phrase, like "how to play piano," or a string of words that might not normally occur in natural speech, such as "best happy hour Minneapolis." By knowing what keywords to target, you can increase your chances that a search engine will deliver your content to the people searching for it.

Any term that is used to find information through a search engine is considered a keyword, and **keywords are one of our most valuable links to our target audience because they show us what people want to know more about.**

> Keywords are "the voice of your potential customers."
>
> —SEMrush

DIRECT TRAFFIC TO CORE PAGES

Proper search research ensures that your content is relevant to both your audience and your business goals. Let's back up a moment here and connect the dots. We want to target relevant keywords to drive traffic to our website, and we want that traffic to be meaningful. Ultimately, we want our amazing audience-focused, search-researched content topics to direct users to the most important section of any business website: our products or services pages.

We call these revenue-producing pages *core pages*, and we call the main keywords that direct people there *core keywords*. Everything we do for content marketing to educate and inform online searchers is ultimately about getting the right people to land on these core pages—the place where they may convert into a customer. Here's how the concept breaks down:

- **Core pages** are your main product or service pages—those key web pages that explain your services, highlight products, or invite a lead or conversion.
- **Core keywords** are keywords determined to be the most relevant and valuable to your business and are closely related to your core pages.
- **Modifiers** are words added onto a core keyword that increases the specificity of the search.

Now, let's take a deeper look to understand how they work.

Core Pages

Core pages (most often, landing pages) are typically designed to sell. These are the main pages where we expect to see conversions. Let's return to the example of The Nursing School since we've already started thinking deeply about that business model. The Nursing School has four main core pages:

- *Nursing School:* Home Page
- *Nursing Training Programs:* Top-Level Category Page
  - *LPN Training:* Program-Specific Page
  - *RN Training:* Program-Specific Page

> Remember our earlier discussion about Norse vs. Viking, and knowing which terms to target? Here's another really good example: LPN training is also sometimes called LVN training. At the time of writing, more people are searching for "LPN" training than for "LVN training," even though they are essentially the same thing. LVN is the term used in California and Texas—the only difference is geographic. So, since the Nursing School did their research, they named their program appropriately, capturing the greater search volume for their national brand.

Obviously, the home page is a core page—it's the front door to any website. The next core page is a top-level category page simply called "Nursing Training Programs." This page links to the two program pages that The Nursing School Offers: LPN Training and RN Training. Each of these program-specific core pages includes in-depth descriptions about the type of nursing training offered and are designed to capture the conversion. A user may enter the website anywhere, but we want them to eventually wind up on the page(s) where conversions happen. These core pages should be optimized to capture the sale.

Core Keywords

Core keywords most closely reflect the business goals of those core pages. Oftentimes, they're actually the same exact phrase, such as "nursing school," "nursing training programs," "LPN training," and "RN training." In other words, core keywords are closely related to your services, ideally as transactional in nature as possible and as close to conversion as possible. You may have a few different variations for each core keyword, such as "nursing training" and "nursing classes." These core keywords are your primary keyword targets. Consider these the top of the pyramid (as pictured in Figure 13.1) that all other keywords support.

"Wait a minute," you might be asking. "Where did these core keywords and core pages come from?" And that'd be a very good question. The short answer: There's a whole research process involved in identifying the best core keywords for your business and industry—like finding out the differences between Viking and Norse from our example above—and how slight nuances in phrasing can produce dramatically different results. There's also a strategy for setting up your core pages and determining an effective page hierarchy.

As SEO guys, we know this initial foundation can be a whole chapter in itself, but we don't want to stray too far off topic. Remember, we're here to discover topics for content marketing. If you want to do some research on your own or hire an SEO company to set up your core pages and determine core keywords, that's great (maybe you already have!). Otherwise, you can still get started with us now. Or, visit ContentShift.com/Resources for some introductory tutorials on setting up core pages and core keywords.

For the purposes of this book, you just need to have a few main products or services identified. These can easily be your working core keywords. They should just be one to three words long. Your core pages will be your home page and any other pages specifically describing your products or services. As you can see in Figure 13.1, we've identified core keywords for each core page on The Nursing School website.

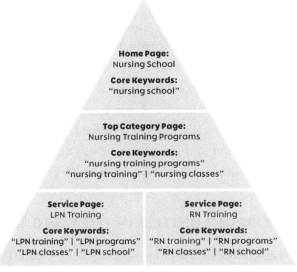

Figure 13.1: Core Keywords and Their Relation to Core Pages

If you haven't already done it, clearly identifying your business goals will help you determine the direction of your core pages and which core keywords and modifiers to target. Do you want people to sign up online? Do you want to make sales through an ecommerce platform? Do you want to drive phone calls? Do you want to increase your email list? These goals may naturally change over time, and your goals should direct your content strategy. But whenever you sit down to drive traffic, you'll want to have a clear goal in mind to focus your content marketing efforts around.

Depending on what you do, your site may have lots of core pages and lots of core keywords, or just a few. For example, a law firm may begin a campaign to focus on driving phone calls for leads, and they might offer to answer legal questions for free to find potential clients. An optometrist may decide to focus on increasing their email list to maintain customer loyalty through newsletters about eye health, glasses care, and promotions. Your business goals will direct your core pages, core keywords, and content strategy.

Modifiers

Modifiers are often adjectives, adverbs, verbs, slang, locations, shopping terms, or parts of a question added onto a core keyword. In the search term "nursing classes Detroit," the city name (Detroit) modifies the core keyword (nursing classes). In another search term, "where to find the best reading glasses," the core keyword is "reading glasses," and the rest of the question (where to find the best) is the modifier. Keywords that contain multi-word phrases and modifiers all exist in what is called "the long tail."

FINDING OPPORTUNITIES IN THE LONG TAIL

Google processes trillions of keyword searches each year, and 15% of them are brand new.[3] Most of these new keywords are likely long tail keywords. In his groundbreaking book, *The Long Tail*, author Chris Anderson proposes that the Internet has actually changed the nature of commerce.

For most of the 20th century, markets favored a small number of items that sold widely to mass markets (the era of big brands). Now, Anderson proposes that markets have shifted their bulk to long tail: the large number of items that sell in small quantities to niche markets. In other words, small producers are able to compete and even flourish right next to the big brands because the Internet has opened up doors of communication and accessibility that didn't exist before. You can find artisan soap or Dove products equally online, depending on what you search for.

Any long-term content strategy starts with the long tail. For businesses of any size, targeting specific long-tail keywords in your content can open the door to finding customers in your specific niche and start building traffic to your website. For larger businesses that compete in popular locations with popular keywords, it's important not to overlook the value in the long tail. No matter the size of your operation, or the extent of your customer base, long-tail keywords open doors to varied, nuanced subjects.

The long tail is as much an economic theory as it is a search tool, but we'll be referring to it in terms of how information is distributed on the Internet. Refer to the following long-tail graph, illustrated in Figure 13.2.

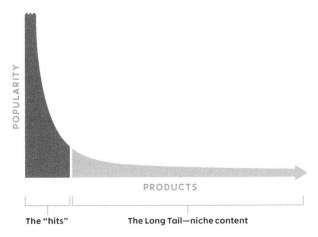

Figure 13.2: The Long Tail

As you can see, the "hits" are high on the popularity scale. These are extremely popular and heavily searched terms online. They're usually very short, general terms—often only a word or two. We call these types of searches *head terms*. "Birds," "window panes," and "shoes" are all head terms. A **head term** is a popular keyword with high **search volume**—meaning, lots and lots of people are typing that term into Google.[4] Search volume measures the number of searches for a given phrase during a given time frame, usually measured on a monthly basis. (Core keywords are often head terms.)

Lower in popularity but extending outward is the "long tail." The **long tail** consists of search phrases that are less heavily searched and more specific, resulting in lower search volume. "North American bird watching guidebook," "where to find the cheapest window panes," or "women's size 5 black Nike running shoes" are all examples of keywords that would fall into the long tail category—longer, more detailed, more specific, less popular terms that are usually more indicative of the real question the user is asking. (Long-tail keywords often contain a head term and a modifier.)

Think of the head of the graph (the hits) as containing the term "Nike." As you move down the graph towards the tail, the search terms become progressively longer and more specific until you end up with something like "women's size 5 black Nike running shoes." Here's another example: If one head term is "cheeseburger," the tail can expand from that starting point indefinitely until someone might be searching for something like "organic grass-fed Wagyu beef Gouda cheeseburger Long Beach." Anything is possible, right? The long tail, theoretically, goes on forever, containing every possible iteration of a search term.

A long-tail keyword can consist of any number of modifiers around a core keyword, such as "where can I find the best nursing classes near me" (where "nursing classes" is the core keyword for The Nursing School). Figuratively speaking, the long tail is a mile wide and an inch deep.

Consider the following long-tail graph, shown in Figure 13.3, in even more detail.

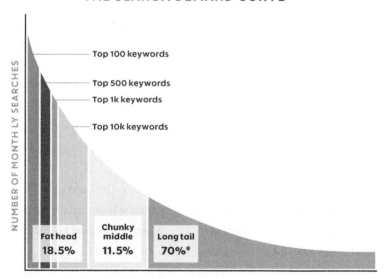

Figure 13.3: The Search Demand Curve. Digital Image. Available from: Moz, https://moz.com/beginners-guide-to-seo/keyword-research (accessed 2016).

On the left-hand side of the graph, you'll see that the most popular keywords on the Web—head terms (or fat-head terms)—generate millions of searches but only account for 18.5% of all searches. On the right-hand side of the graph, as popularity trails off, you'll see the "long tail" of the curve makes up around 70% of all Internet searches. And in between is "the chunky middle," or search terms that are in between head terms and long-tail terms, accounting for the remaining 11.5% of all searches. In general, the more popular a keyword is, the more competitive it is. Likewise, the less popular a keyword is, the less competitive it is.

It is here in the long tail that specific audiences search for specific topics related to your specific business. The opportunities to connect with an audience online are virtually endless—if you know how to position yourself strategically for maximum exposure *and* create irresistible content. Long-tail keywords will form the basis of our content strategy.

"A long tail is just culture unfiltered by economic scarcity."

—Chris Anderson

> Savvy Tip: Businesses often focus on transactional searches to the exclusion of other types, but it would be foolish to neglect informational searches, which often fall into the long tail. "Why" queries, for example, dominated Google search in 2020.[5] Rather than dismissing non-shopping related searches, savvy content marketers recognize the potential of informational searches as indirect marketing channels. Useful and appealing informational articles support brand loyalty, trust, and sales now as well as down the line.

Here's a breakdown of the three different types of search terms:

- **Head terms:** Short, heavily searched, competitive phrases (also called body, fat-head, or short-tail terms).

- **Mid-tail terms:** Also called "chunky middle," these are phrases that generally fall somewhere in between long-tail and head terms regarding length and intent.[6]
- **Long-tail terms:** Long phrases with multiple words that are highly specific but less competitive, for example, "women's black Nike running shoes" versus "running shoes."

LONG-TAIL KEYWORDS ARE SPECIFIC QUESTIONS YOU CAN ANSWER

Think of every search query like an implied question. The user wants to know something, whether that's general information about a topic or a specific answer to a specific question. **User intent** describes what a user hopes to achieve when typing a query into Google. Though we aren't mind readers, search marketers can often determine what the user's intent is based on different keywords. At the very least, we can usually determine if it's transactional, informational, or navigational.

With a head term, the question is usually vague. If someone types in the head term "birds," your guess is as good as ours when it comes to deciphering intent. Does that person want to know about different types of birds? Are they looking for images of birds? Do they want to know about the mating habits of birds? There's really no way to tell.

It's any search engine's guess, too. As you can see in Figure 13.4, out of the 742 million possible results for "birds" at the time of this writing, Google serves up a sampling platter, showing us a definition from Wikipedia, a few news articles, an article from National Geographic, a knowledge graph, a bird database, and a few local businesses related to birds. The user's intent is unclear, so the results are fairly all over the place to try and give the user what they want.

Long-tail terms generally show clearer user intent, which is helpful for us as content marketers in a lot of ways. "North American bird watching guidebook" exists under the long tail, and we can reasonably infer that the searcher is either looking to purchase a bird-watching guidebook for this region (wanting to generally learn more about bird-watching guidebooks) or even wishing to compare different types of bird-watching guidebooks.

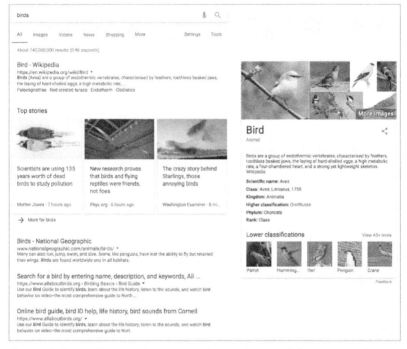

Figure 13.4: Google's Search Results for the Head Term "Birds"

There could be an intent to purchase or an intent to learn more about the product, but we know that there is at least a specific item in mind. That's definitely something we can work with as content producers—if that keyword is relevant to our business. Sure enough, Google delivers a fairly streamlined yet diverse array of results for this query, as shown in Figure 13.5. The top result is a list of items you can buy, and below that is an article from the Audubon Society (a brand authority) entitled "What Bird Guide Is Best For You?"—a resource post on buying the right guidebook.

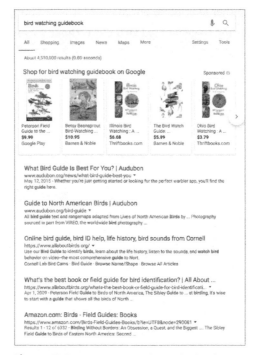

Figure 13.5: Google's Search Results for the Mid-Tail Term "Bird Watching Guidebook"

It's easier to answer a question if we know what the question is, right? Long-tail keywords essentially have the question built into them and are more indicative of user intent. And, for the purposes of this book, we are going to treat every content topic as a question. You'll see in Chapter 14 how simple this can be: Find the questions your audience is asking, and then answer them. For most businesses just starting out with content marketing, as well as for those who want to become more intentional, *targeting long-tail keywords* is going to compose the large majority of your strategy. Utilizing the long tail will help you build traffic, target specific audiences, and build brand authority on specific subjects.

> The long tail is the land of opportunity where specific audiences seek specific solutions to their problems.

TARGET LONG-TAIL KEYWORDS FIRST

When you first start producing content, we recommend that you avoid trying to rank for those one-word head terms like "shoes" that millions of people search for every month. "Why?" you ask.

- Those terms are too vague.
- They don't indicate user intent.
- They're too competitive.
- They might not be serving your business goals.

Sure enough, you might be thinking: "Well, what about those core keywords?" These are often head or mid-tail terms, such as "nursing training." So, here's where it gets interesting: We want to target those specific core keywords *for the long haul*, working those into every piece of content we produce in order to build authority for those keywords over time while, *at the same time*, targeting long-tail terms for specific topics and questions.

Long-tail keywords support your core keywords. Modifiers can turn a core keyword into a long-tail phrase and can open up windows of opportunity to capture leads you might have otherwise missed if you were *only* targeting head terms, which are wildly competitive. So, in other words, you want to target your core keywords while expanding into the long tail, knowing that it takes longer to rank for head terms, catching all the wins you can in that long tail of opportunity as you go.

Producing solid, quality content consistently over time for your core keywords can eventually place you among that competition. Once you're a trusted authority in your field, your website might naturally show up for head terms like "shoes," but that should be an eventual benchmark, not a starting point. Ranking for head terms is a great aspiration and a sign of a website's well-earned authority. It's something to build towards over time.

Start by engaging your audience with specifically tailored posts around nuanced subjects. This will increase your organic search traffic steadily. Most long-tail keywords offer a lower barrier to entry, allowing you to rank for that term because the search volume is lower, there is less competition, and user intent is generally clear.

If you identify the *right* long-tail keywords that are relevant to both your business and your audience, you can think about that like a clear, unfettered connection between what you have to offer and what people are looking for. This is the goal! Long-tail terms are often a direct question, which is what we'll focus on in the next chapter.

If you're a brand new site, or if you're new to content marketing, it's important to start where you are and grow from there. If you can bring in 100 new visitors to your website every month, consider that a win. In 6 months, if you can bring in 1,000 new visitors, that's progress. Eventually, maybe your content is shining so brightly that you're attracting tens of thousands of visitors every month. To get there, you have to start somewhere. And that starting point is in the strategic long tail. In the chapter ahead, we'll move into the discovery phase and begin conducting actual keyword research for content marketing in the long tail.

POINTS OF DISCOVERY

Now that you're familiar with the language of online searches, consider the following questions for your business:

1. What types of words can be used to describe your business? Brainstorm a list of all possible terms you or your customers may use to describe what your business does. Think about synonyms or related phrases that can be used to describe the same thing, like "Viking" and "Norse."
2. Brainstorm a list of what you might expect to find as popular head terms related to your business, such as "shoes" or "cheeseburger." Start thinking about how to use modifiers to turn these competi-

tive head terms into long-tail questions. Brainstorm some long-tail keywords that can be formulated from your head terms.
3. Does your website already have clearly defined core pages and core keywords? If so, great. Have these close at hand as we go through the next chapter. If not, visit ContentShift.com/Resources for tips on how to get your foundation in order.

Chapter 14

KEYWORD RESEARCH TO DISCOVER CONTENT TOPICS

"[T]he behavioral-driven marketer is mapping out multistep interactions over time designed to support the buyer's intent."

—Dave Walters, *Behavioral Marketing*

In the mid 1700s, a man named Thomas Bayes challenged the emerging scientific method at the time with a bold theory. He proposed we start with a guess. Nothing can be absolutely determined, he posited; yet, some things may be closely estimated. Bayes believed that rather than aiming for perfection or for complete knowledge, we can aim to be *less wrong over time*.

We think this is a brilliant principle to apply to content marketing because our aim is to use informed data to create productive content and to keep improving over time. That's the nature of evolution and growth. It's our job as content producers and businesses to roll with the tide and keep a pulse on the trends, like what people are searching for at different moments in time. One keyword may show no search volume today, but that can change completely in six months. Queries can also evolve as Google better understands intent. Keyword research educates and informs us about our audience's changing needs, interests, and questions.

Keyword research is not an exact science; instead, it is a tool we use to gather aggregated data, which provides us with the evidence we need to make informed choices. There's no way to concretely determine exactly what your audience wants at any given time, but you can certainly use educated trials to be "less wrong over time."[1] In order to regularly meet our audience's needs and provide them with valuable content, we begin by relying on what we already know, expect, or believe to be true about how they might be searching for information online (including the audience research we discussed in Part 2), and then we validate those ideas with search research.

> "[Y]ou need to get comfortable taking in data points and building educated hypotheses based on them. Do not get hung up on needing bullet-proof evidence before acting."
>
> —Dave Walters, *Behavioral Marketing*

Doing keyword research is not a one-time-only experience but rather an ongoing method to help you refine your content strategy as you go. There will always be new data to encounter. Like a sailboat adjusting its sails with the wind, you can adapt to the changing needs of your audience by consistently checking in to see what interests them and what resonates with them, and this will allow you to identify even more opportunities to connect. Similarly, checking in with your audience might alert you when it's time to go in a different direction. If your audience is the wind, keyword research and metrics are the sails—the well-designed methods that keep you steering in a logical, audience-focused direction.

> "Marketers need to come to terms with the fact that, in a digital world, control has become an illusion. Rather than acting like traffic cops, directing data flows to predetermined silos of demographic and behavioral characteristics, we should see ourselves as offering a concierge service, assisting and enriching personalized experiences."
>
> —Greg Satell

THE GOALS OF KEYWORD RESEARCH FOR CONTENT MARKETING

To be clear, the process of doing keyword research can be applied to a few different goals. As SEO professionals, we want to clarify that this chapter is about doing keyword research specifically for content marketing, not for on-page web optimization. (Hopefully, you've already done that! And if you haven't, don't worry, you can still apply everything you learn from this chapter to your content marketing.)

What we're going to teach you is how to find content topics based primarily on evidence that people are, in fact, actually searching for that topic, and then we'll show you how to prioritize those topics based on their relevance to your business. We'll be using our core keywords to kick this process off, but even if you haven't done any initial SEO research, that's fine. As long as you know what products and services your business offers, you will have a starting point. Whether you're a company with a huge marketing department or a startup, you can apply this process to your content marketing strategy.

The goals of keyword research in content marketing are to:[2]

- Support core keywords and increase traffic to core pages
- Identify questions users have about your product or service
- Discover valuable questions to answer in your content
- Validate topics of interest with search volume
- Drive traffic to a particular area of the website

CONTENT STRATEGY: ANSWER CUSTOMER QUESTIONS

Our goal as content marketers is to use keyword research to identify the questions our audience is searching for so we can show up in the search results when they ask those questions. If someone were to walk into your brick-and-mortar store and ask a salesperson questions like, "Hey, can you tell me more about this product? How much is it? How long will it last?," it's a no-brainer that you'd want to answer those questions to help them move toward a purchasing decision. When a searcher types a question into a search bar, it's a similar dynamic; it's just happening online.

If a searcher is asking a question that's relevant to your business, then they're probably a potential customer—someone who's interested in learning more about what you do. This means you definitely want to appear in their search results with a clear, informative answer. This is the basis of our content marketing strategy: *Use your content to answer questions your audience is already asking about your business.*

We will use keyword research to identify the main questions your audience is asking, then prioritize your content creation around those vital questions using relevant criteria, like search volume, relevance to your core pages, and the Search Cycle. We'll talk about evaluating those keyword questions in the next chapter, but, for now, let's start with gathering the research.

Sounds simple, right? We hope so. Maybe a little boring? That's okay. When you think about what's going to drive business to your website, it's not necessarily going to be super-exciting, trendy topics, unless you're a news or lifestyle publication. For example, we can imagine The Nursing School's potential students asking questions like: "Where should I go to nursing school?," "Why should I become a nurse?," "Are there jobs for nurses?" These may not be the most titillating topics for the average person, but content marketing is not about going viral and becoming Internet-famous; it's about finding and connecting with potential customers to grow your business. **When answering customer questions, focus on creating content that is useful, timeless, relevant, and valuable—both to your audience *and* your business.**

USING KEYWORD TOOLS

How do we know what questions our audiences are asking? We use keyword tools to do this research. There are a ton of online tools out there, some free and some paid, which provide all the information you could possibly want to know about keywords.

Essentially, these tools aggregate data from across the web and search engines to provide a snapshot of a particular keyword's popularity. Each one offers its own particular wealth of data and style of information. You don't need to get hung up on all that. What we're most concerned with right now is using these tools for two purposes: 1) finding the exact language of the questions people are asking and 2) identifying the search volume for each keyword.

These are our three favorite tools that we recommend for keyword research:

1. **SEMrush:** This is by far our favorite tool and the one we consider essential to our business. SEMrush is a global competitive research service for online marketing, and their mission is to "make online competition fair and transparent, with equal opportunities for everyone."[3] SEMrush offers a free trial, but, ultimately, this is a paid tool for professional marketers. We love it because, as search and content marketing professionals, we are constantly taking advantage of their huge variety of SEO tools, especially in-depth ways to conduct keyword research. There are so many ways of filtering information and seeing trends in keyword data. SEMrush allows you to group keywords by question type, which is exactly what we need for this process. For anyone who wants to invest in a wealth of functionality, this tool takes the cake.

2. **Moz Keyword Explorer:** Our second favorite tool is Keyword Explorer by Moz. The dashboard for this tool is fairly simple, offering a few different data points for in-depth SEO research, like keyword suggestions and SERP (search engine results page) analysis. We like Moz because this tool gives you the option to type in a core keyword and then filter by questions, which is our priority for this process. You can also "group" questions by lexical similarity; meaning, you reduce the number of redundant questions that ap-

pear. The caveat? Like SEMrush, you get some free search queries per month, and then you'll need to sign up for a pro account to access unlimited searches.

3. **Ubersuggest:** We recommend this free keyword research tool for anyone who wants to skip the advanced functionalities of paid tools and just get straight to the business of search volume. We love it because, for a free tool, you get access to search volume and suggestions for related keywords—two of the most valuable pieces of data for content marketing—and you don't even need to create an account. Designed by online marketing guru Neil Patel, Ubersuggest offers some other great options for added value, but, for our purposes, we mostly care about the fact that you can find search volume for any keyword out there—*for free*. Though Ubersuggest doesn't specifically report on questions, you can easily supplement with some simple Google research.

Here's an extended list of other tools out there at the time of this writing:

- Google Ads Keyword Planner
- SEOToolSet
- Answer the Public
- Google Trends
- Keywordtool.io
- Searchmetrics
- Ahrefs
- SpyFu

As we all know, software and online tools change often. Free tools sometimes become a paid service only, dashboards change, and functionalities are updated. Basically, each service is constantly improving their product and updating their platform. So, when you're ready to get started, be sure to check out these different options for yourself, or visit ContentShift.com/Resources for an updated list.

At the end of the day, it doesn't matter to us what tool you use; the process we'll teach you can be applied to any keyword research platform. Whether it's SEMrush, Ubersuggest, Moz Keyword Explorer, or a combination of multiple tools, the goal is to discover relevant questions your audience is asking (keywords) and roughly how many people are asking that question every month (search volume).

Because it's our preferred research software, we'll be walking you through the keyword research process using SEMrush. Even if you decide not to sign up for SEMrush, these examples are meant to give you an understanding of how to sift through keyword research.

Most keyword tools have a staggering array of options and a wealth of data. To keep it simple and relevant to our goal of using keyword research for content marketing, we don't need to go over everything; otherwise, this would be a course in SEO. Instead, we're going to focus on discovering those relevant audience questions and identifying the search volume for each one. So, seriously, don't worry about all the other information you might come across. Keep your focus on your questions surrounding your core keyword.

HOW TO DO KEYWORD RESEARCH, STEP BY STEP

Keyword research is a massively valuable tool for all of your future content marketing efforts. This is what both of us (Mark and Jon) geek out on all the time. We're SEO guys, so this is our deep end of the pool. We know that keyword research is a vast field that has many nuances, so the process we're about to walk you through isn't the be-all and end-all of keyword research. Here, we'll walk you through the process of keyword research to help you find content marketing topics. We hope we've made it simple, clear, and easy for you to follow.

Step 1: Define a Business Goal

Depending on how frequently you update your business goals and redefine your content strategy, you may find your content process changing fairly often or not very often at all. Some businesses like to check in on their content production process quarterly, some biannually, and some annually. When you're focused on driving traffic for a specific outcome, it's important to give the process some space and expect that results will come over time. That being said, the focus of your efforts is extremely important to consider. Before we move into the actual keyword research process, we want to make sure you have a clear goal in mind every time you embark upon keyword research.

If you're just starting out, your goal could be as simple as "start driving organic traffic overall." In that case, you would focus on driving traffic to your core pages. At other times, your business goal may involve driving traffic to a specific area of your site for a specific conversion. Whatever your focus is, it should be clear and should direct the rest of your content strategy.

With that in mind, let's go through a hypothetical example for the Nursing School to show you what we mean. The Nursing School has been around for a while, but they're finding that their classes—which operate out of a few different places across the country, including Awesometown, USA—have only been seeing enrollment rates at around 75% capacity for the last few years. They have a fully optimized website already, and they've decided to tackle this business problem with multiple marketing strategies, one of which is content marketing. Their business goal is to improve enrollment rates in nursing classes over one year so that they reach 90% of their enrollment capacity on average across both of their offered programs, RN training and LPN training.

With this business goal in mind, we would focus on content marketing efforts that would increase this likelihood. If we want to increase enrollment, our general content strategy would look like this:

1. Produce content to attract the relevant audiences (as discussed in Part 2).
2. Drive organic search traffic to the pages where interested students can request more information.

In other words, we produce content that will lead people toward those conversion opportunities. In order to create that content, we'll focus our search research around keywords and questions that will both attract and inspire those potential students to enroll.

Step 2: Choose a Core Keyword to Start

With your business objective for your current content marketing campaign in mind, choose a core keyword related to that end. For example, any of The Nursing School's core keywords would probably be a good starting point to work towards increasing enrollment. We think it's best to start out at the top level, especially if you're just starting, so we're going to choose the core keyword "nursing school" to continue this example.

What happens if you haven't outlined your core keywords? If this is the case and you're just getting started, take stock of what your business does to find a core keyword. What is your business? What is it that you offer your customers? For example, do you sell mattresses? Your core keyword might be "mattress sale," "best mattresses," or "cheap mattress." Are you a life coach? Your starting keyword might just be "life coach." Don't overthink your starting point. Keep it simple and focus on what your business offers. Just start somewhere. (Later, you would want to validate your core keywords with research, but it's fine to just choose a starting point.) Write down a one- or two-word phrase that describes a product or service you offer. If you offer multiple items, start with one of the broadest, most popular, and in-demand aspects of your business. This is now your first core keyword.

If you're further along in this process and have done this a few times—

or perhaps you're shifting focus to drive traffic to a specific area of your site—still choose a top-level, broad core keyword to begin. We'll start getting more specific in the next step, but it's important to choose a keyword that's a head term and directly related to your business as your starting point. This is so you can focus your efforts around a relevant, competitive keyword and build towards competing for that term. It also helps to keep your content production focused around your business goals and conversion opportunities.

Step 3: Make a List of Questions Related to That Keyword

Using your core keyword as a starting point, you'll research the questions your audience is asking related to that topic. Ever heard of the Five Ws? This is the *who/which, what, when, where,* and *why* that journalists, researchers, and police investigators use to make sure they're getting a *complete* report on a subject. We can use this same concept for content marketing. (*Note*: We've added "which" to the modifier "who" because these are sometimes very closely related. "Who" is a question asking specifically about a person or people, while "which" can ask similar questions about things or inanimate objects.) Like an investigator, you can use these Five Ws to help you discover the questions your customers are asking. For the purposes of content marketing, we're going to add a few more categories to our list of primary questions. These additional categories are based on some of the most common search modifiers and include: "How," "Does/Do," "Vs/Or," and "Miscellaneous (Is/Can/Are/Best/Top)."

You want to be an authority in your field, so you want to *completely answer* the pressing questions your audience is asking. If you're a business, people are going to have questions, such as:

- *What* you do
- *Who* your services are for (or *which* applications they can be used for)

- *When* is a good time to consider your business
- *Where* to find you
- *Why* you do what you do and why they should care
- *How* to use what you offer
- And more

They might also be asking questions about what your business *does*, how your business compares with others (*vs/or*), information about what things *are*, and what the best options are. Focusing on the Five Ws plus these key modifiers will help you create content that answers the core questions any potential customer might be asking. And as you learned in the previous chapter, these highly specific questions are generally in the long tail, which gives you a better chance of appearing in search results. To keep track of your research, we've provided a template you can use, as shown in Figure 14.1. Please visit ContentShift.com/Resources to download this template.

Figure 14.1: Keyword Research—Subject Discovery Template

CORE KEYWORD:

CORE QUESTIONS:

Who/Which

Research			Evaluation		
Keyword Question	Search Volume	Relevance	Search Cycle	Notes	Priority

Notes:

What

Research			Evaluation			
Keyword Question	Search Volume	Relevance	Search Cycle	Notes		Priority

Notes:

When

Research			Evaluation			
Keyword Question	Search Volume	Relevance	Search Cycle	Notes		Priority

Notes:

Where

Research			Evaluation			
Keyword Question	Search Volume	Relevance	Search Cycle	Notes		Priority

Notes:

Why

Research		Evaluation			
Keyword Question	Search Volume	Relevance	Search Cycle	Notes	Priority

Notes:

How

Research		Evaluation			
Keyword Question	Search Volume	Relevance	Search Cycle	Notes	Priority

Notes:

Does/Do

Research		Evaluation			
Keyword Question	Search Volume	Relevance	Search Cycle	Notes	Priority

Notes:

Vs/Or

Research			Evaluation		
Keyword Question	Search Volume	Relevance	Search Cycle	Notes	Priority

Notes:

MISC: Is/Can/Are/Best/Top

Research			Evaluation		
Keyword Question	Search Volume	Relevance	Search Cycle	Notes	Priority

Notes:

Whatever your core keyword is, type it into your preferred keyword research platform. We'll use SEMrush. The following screenshot, shown in Figure 14.2, is from SEMrush's Keyword Magic Tool. Observe: What are the most popular questions surrounding a particular phrase? For our example, we're using the core keyword "nursing school" to discover relevant customer questions.

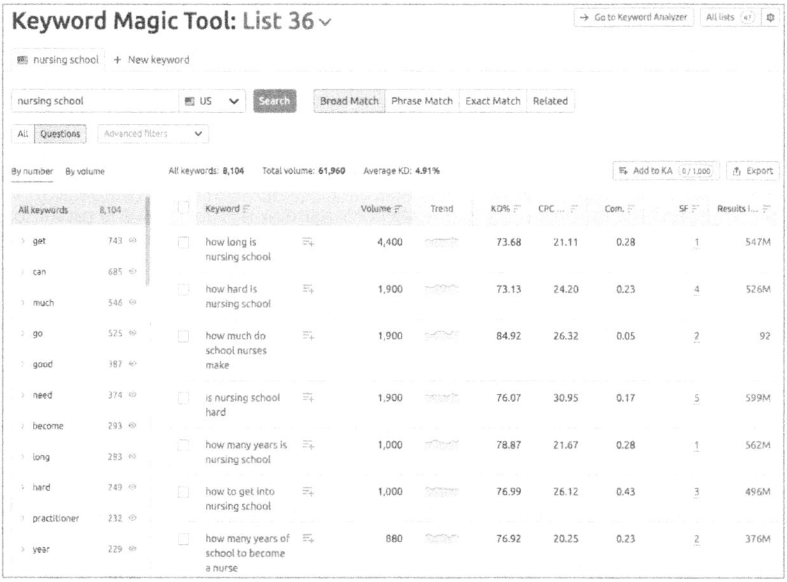

Figure 14.2: SEMrush's Keyword Magic Tool

Whichever tool you're using, you're probably going to see something similar: A LOT of results. How do you choose which questions to add to your list? While at first this may feel like less than a complete answer, *use your best judgment.* You know your business and your audience best. You can sift through your results, looking for questions that make sense to answer for your business needs and target audience(s). Play with your options and search results, and take advantage of your filtering options.

The results in Figure 14.2 are the "broad match keywords" shown in the form of "questions" for the keyword "nursing school." This means SEMrush is delivering ALL the keyword questions that are broadly related to your original query, with some differentiation in phrases, such as nurse AND nursing, school AND schools. You can also toggle "phrase match" or "exact match" to limit results to the exact phrase in different orders or in the exact order the phrase appears, respectively.

From your initial results page (in whichever search tool you're using), sift through the queries to compile a list of what you think might be the most relevant, timeless, compelling, and important questions you should be answering for your potential customers. Put them on your list. Here are our tips for choosing keywords to add to your initial list:

- **Not all Ws will be equal.** You can aim for a certain number of questions for each of the modifiers. However, you might not get results in equal measure for each question. Maybe you find that you're seeing mostly "what" questions and not many "who/which" questions. Maybe you have 10 questions for "what" and only one for "how." That's fine. Work with what you find.
- **Notice what stands out.** You don't necessarily need to go in any particular order. We like to skim over the results, looking for questions that seem to be the most relevant to the business and the audience, filling them into our "Subject Discovery" template as we find them. Use your best judgment to determine which questions are relevant to your audience and business, letting these extra modifiers guide you.
- **Use search filters.** You can sometimes "filter results" for a particular question. In SEMrush, you can click "advanced filters" and search within these results *just* for a word, such as "when." This can help you more easily see the different question categories. You can also filter by search volume if you want to see the highest search volume at the top.
- **Stay focused on your core keyword.** You're certainly going to come across really great questions you'll want to answer that aren't super related to your core keyword at hand. For example, you might come across something like "what schooling is required to become a nurse practitioner." This is a very nuanced topic, specific to one particular type of nursing career path. We recommend you stay on track with your core keyword at hand and not add these auxiliary terms to your list now. Instead, save those related phrases you come across in another spreadsheet. It's a great idea to make a running list of other good questions you come across, and keep adding to it! Consider creating a separate "master" list for any "etc." keywords you come across to return to later. Sticking to one core keyword at a time can keep you from getting overwhelmed and help you stay organized and focused.

- **Use Google.** If you're not finding exactly what you want, simply type your keyword into the Google search bar. Look for the box that says "people also ask" and see what kinds of questions are being delivered. If you click on one, it expands a few more beneath it, so the list is essentially endless. This is a great way to supplement your keyword tool. You can also scroll down to the very bottom of the SERP to see "searches related to." Here you'll find similar searches delivered by Google for even more ideas. Obviously, you won't have search volume for these keywords from Google, but if a question shows up in Google, it's safe to imagine it's popular enough that people are searching for it. This is also a great way of supplementing your keyword research if you're using a free tool with less functionality. You can *always* check against Google for more insight, and we recommend it.
- **You don't need to target every single exact phrase with an individual piece of content.** Some of your questions may end up being subheadings within a larger post, so don't be overwhelmed thinking you have to create a post for every single topic. At this point, use your best judgment to choose questions that feel vibrant, relevant, and robust.
- **Choose the higher search volume between two similar phrases.** When you come across questions that are similar in meaning but slightly different in how they're phrased, such as "how long is nursing school" and "how long does nursing school take," choose the phrase with higher search volume. The exact phrase isn't absolutely essential since Google is usually smart enough to figure out that someone searching for something like "what is a nursing class" would also likely be interested in results for "what are nursing classes." You don't need to clutter your research with too many similar or identical terms. Speaking of which, let's talk about another important metric: search volume!

Step 4: Identify Search Volume

Search volume describes the number of searches expected for a keyword in a certain time frame. This data is used to measure search engine traffic for that keyword.[4] The number usually refers to a monthly number of searches. For example, SEMrush provides a monthly average compiled from the last 12 months of data. So, if you see that search volume for "nursing school" is 49,500, that means that around 49,500 searches for that phrase are currently performed every month, on average, in the United States. Numbers may vary across different platforms, though not widely. For example, Moz Keyword Explorer gives a range of searches rather than an average.

Search volume tells you approximately how popular a keyword is. This is important information to know when deciding whether to create a piece of content. The more search volume there is, the more people are searching for that particular phrase, and the more likely you are to drive increased traffic to your website. This metric is really helpful in getting an idea of how much traffic you might stand to gain and how many people are asking similar questions.

Take note of which terms are more heavily searched than others. You'll use this information to help you decide which topics to target. You might find that some terms are very popular, while others are not. How do you know what's "good" or "bad" search volume? Generally speaking, higher is better for long-tail terms. But, if you find that a seemingly awesome keyword has little or even zero search volume, that's okay. For now, just focus on gathering the data and adding it to your "Subject Discovery" document to evaluate later.

Keyword research is a constantly changing field, so identifying search volume should be helpful and not an absolute metric. If you come across a query that seems like a relevant question to your business, you can ask yourself these questions:

- If people aren't searching for this question now, do I think they would in the future?
- Is it relevant to my core business?
- Could answering this question help a potential customer learn more about what my business does?

If your answer to any of these questions is yes, keep it on your list.

A NOTE ABOUT NO DATA OR ZERO SEARCH VOLUME

If you discover keywords that have either no data or zero search volume, the general rule of thumb is that there isn't a lot of interest in that topic currently. While higher search volume is generally better, our caveat will always be that if the question is out there regarding your business, then it's worth answering, regardless of how many people are searching for it today. Search volume is changeable and can grow over time, so even low search volume shouldn't necessarily deter you from answering an important question.

You may be wondering, "Why isn't there any search volume?" It could be due to a few different reasons:

- The data might not be available yet. Keep in mind, 15% of searches on Google are brand new searches—never before seen.[1] Especially if you're a B2B business or in an emerging field, the awareness may not be fully there yet.
- The keyword might be a new "trend." You can check Google Trends to see how popular a keyword is over time. It's possible the keyword may gain traction. You can also check the question in your Google search bar to see if Google populates answers for it. If so, that could be evidence that people are searching for it.
- If you're getting mostly zeros, consider if you're using the best core keyword? Remember our earlier conversation about semantics and the "Norse" vs. "Viking" discussion? It's possible you want to go back to the drawing board and investigate your semantics to make sure you're using the terms that people are actually searching for.
- There could always be a technical error.
- It's just not something anyone is currently searching for.

Another tip: While you're looking for a strong keyword question to focus a piece of content around, keep in mind that once this content is published, it will be full of other keywords, both naturally and strategically, which will help it be seen. Think holistically about what a good topic is—using high search volume as a data point that interest is there—with the understanding that "no data/zero search volume" should be carefully considered before discarding a topic altogether.

So, that's essentially it for your keyword research: Find questions and note the search volume for each one. In Figure 14.3, we show an example of the research we've done for our example keyword, "nursing school."

Figure 14.3: Identifying Search Volume for Our Example Keyword, "Nursing School"

CORE KEYWORD: nursing school

CORE QUESTIONS

Who/Which

	Research		Evaluation		
Keyword Question	Search Volume	Relevance	Search Cycle	Notes	Priority
Who started the first nursing school	70				
Who gives nursing school loans	0				
Who should write letters of recommendation for nursing school	0				
Which nursing school should I go to	90				
Which nursing school is easy to get into	40				

What

Research		Evaluation			
Keyword Question	Search Volume	Relevance	Search Cycle	Notes	Priority
What is nursing school like	390				
What do you learn in nursing school	210				
What to expect in nursing school	210				
What is nursing school	170				
What are the prerequisites for nursing school	140				
What classes do you take in nursing school	90		/		
What to bring to nursing school interview	90				
What to do after graduating from nursing school	90				

When

Research		Evaluation			
Keyword Question	Search Volume	Relevance	Search Cycle	Notes	Priority
When do you start nursing school	70				
When do you start wearing scrubs in nursing school	50				
When do you apply for nursing school	40				
When did Florence nightingale open her school of nursing	10				
When do they drug test you for nursing school	10				
When do you start clinicals in nursing school	10				

Where

Keyword Question	Research		Evaluation		
	Search Volume	Relevance	Search Cycle	Notes	Priority
Where to get immunizations for nursing school	50				
Where to get a physical exam for nursing school	40				
Where can I go to nursing school for free	30				
Where to go to nursing school	20				

Why

Keyword Question	Research		Evaluation		
	Search Volume	Relevance	Search Cycle	Notes	Priority
Why is nursing school so hard	320				
Why is nursing school competitive	70				
Why do you want to go to nursing school essay	50				
Why go to nursing school	10				
Why am I having trouble getting into nursing school	0				

How

Keyword Question	Research		Evaluation		
	Search Volume	Relevance	Search Cycle	Notes	Priority
How long is nursing school	4,400				
How hard is nursing school	1,900				
How many years is nursing school	1,000				
How much is nursing school	880				

How to prepare for nursing school	480
How to pay for nursing school	260
How to apply for nursing school	210
How to be organized in nursing school	90
How to find out if a nursing school is accredited	70
How to get scholarships for nursing school	70
How to go to nursing school as a single mom	70
How to prepare for first semester of nursing school	70
How to stay healthy in nursing school	70
How to write a personal statement for nursing school	70
How to get into nursing school after high school	140
How to pass nursing school exams	140
How does nursing school work	110

Does/Do

Research		Evaluation			
Keyword Question	Search Volume	Relevance	Search Cycle	Notes	Priority
Does CNA experience help for nursing school	70				
Do employers care where you went to nursing school	20				
Does it matter where you go to nursing school	10				

Vs/Or

Research			Evaluation		
Keyword Question	Search Volume	Relevance	Search Cycle	Notes	Priority
Nursing school vs other degrees	0				
Dental hygiene school vs nursing school	0				
Radiology tech school vs nursing school	0				

MISC: Is/Can/Are/Does/Do/Best/Top

Research			Evaluation		
Keyword Question	Search Volume	Relevance	Search Cycle	Notes	Priority
Is nursing school worth it	210				
Should I go to nursing school	170				
Can you do nursing school online	90				
Is it possible to work and go to nursing school	90				
Which nursing school should I go to	90				
Am I too old to go to nursing school	70				
Can you have piercings in nursing school	70				

What do you notice after you do some initial research? It should be very interesting to see what types of questions people are asking. In our example, you can see that there's a pretty wide variety of questions, from wondering about how long nursing school will take, to how much it costs, to whether it's hard or easy, to what types of classes to take and whether it's worth it. These are all pretty logical questions for someone investigating nursing school as a potential career investment. These questions can give us really good insight into the broad, top-level questions that we can expect most people in this audience group to be asking.

And then there are the more highly specific questions, like, "Can you have piercings in nursing school" and "When do you start wearing scrubs in nursing school." These types of questions might surprise you, and they provide heightened insight into the nuances within this audience group. Maybe it's never occurred to you that potential students may wonder about piercings or when you start wearing scrubs. If there's evidence that these questions are being asked (which there is), you may consider answering them. This will show how in tune you are with your audience's needs as a company, and it'll help build trust, as your customers are looking for answers they can trust. These specific questions may be a little lower priority than your top-level questions, but they are important to discover nonetheless.

You can glean extremely valuable insight from the questions your audience is asking. Rather than shooting in the dark, you can let these questions guide your content, helping you create a valuable connection between your business and your potential customers online.

Step 5: Repeat This Process for Any Core Keyword You Have Related to a Current Objective

Though it sounds simple, you can actually uncover A LOT of questions in this process and plenty of content topics to work with. In our current example, we may have plenty to work with, so we may not need to repeat the process for another keyword. But we always could. Just know that after you've exhausted the questions surrounding one core keyword, you can repeat this same process for any other core keywords (or products/services) related to your business. These simple steps can be repeated over and over again with different terms to, theoretically, keep you discovering topics *ad infinitum*.

We absolutely love this process because it is highly accessible to any business, big or small—whether you're just getting started in content marketing or have been doing it for years and want to learn new methods. For those businesses that have already been producing content for a while, this is such a valuable exercise to continue validating your content topics and making sure you answer all the important questions your audience has. New questions may arise over time, so it's a good idea to keep this process front of mind.

Perhaps for The Nursing School, we would go down the list and choose "nursing training" next. These keywords are fairly closely related, but the differences between them will reveal new and different questions.

YOUR BUSINESS GOALS DIRECT YOUR FOCUS— EVERY TIME

From a top-level business perspective, the core keywords you choose to focus on may change depending on what kind of traffic you want to drive to which areas of your site. These business goals might change quarterly, or monthly, or however often your content team determines. Just don't forget to let the business goals drive the process, and not the other way around.

For example, if The Nursing School decides driving more leads to a specific program—say, an RN program—is a primary business objective for the current quarter, they might decide to focus their content efforts on targeting keywords around that keyword phrase. We could repeat this process for the core keyword "RN classes." The next quarter, perhaps the focus becomes a different program. You can group keywords by business objective at any time.

You can focus on other elements that you think would open up new doors as you see fit. You could choose a stage of the search cycle to focus on or a specific persona to reach. You can go off the beaten path and do this for related keywords that arise or other topics relevant to your business. The possibilities are endless! The important thing is that you now have a process for finding questions that would be worthwhile for your business to answer.

After doing a phase of research like this, the next step is to weed through all this information to evaluate topics and choose which ones to execute on, which we'll go over in the next chapter.

POINTS OF DISCOVERY

Voila! Now you know the basics of keyword research for content marketing. Why not get started?

1. Go through Steps 1–5 of the keyword research process for one of your core keywords, writing down any information you come across using the template (you can download the templates at ContentShift.com/Resources). What are your initial impressions? What do you discover?
2. If you encountered any keywords with no data, why do you think this might be? Put these "no data" keywords aside.
3. Take any one of your keywords from your list and use that phrase to do a Google search. What do you notice about the types of websites and content that appears on the first page of search results?

Chapter 15

EVALUATING KEYWORD QUESTIONS

> Although it's vital to optimize your content for maximum discoverability, your primary focus whenever attempting to rank for a keyword—regardless of its search volume or competitiveness—should be on creating the most exceptional content you possibly can. Every time, all the time, now and forever.
>
> —Dan Shewan, WordStream

Once you start digging into keyword research, you may find that you're coming across so many content ideas and relevant keywords that it seems like you'll have a never-ending supply of topics to write about. This is great because it easily resolves one of the common issues that businesses run into: *What do I write about?* Through keyword research and evidence-backed data, you can uncover a plethora of subjects just waiting for you to publish and share with your company's unique and compelling perspective.

In this chapter, we'll answer three key questions:

- Which subjects should you prioritize and write about first?
- Which subjects are most closely related to your business?
- Which topics are most relevant to your audience?

Answering these questions will help you prioritize the topics you've found. We'll take the keyword research process from the previous chapter and dig through the data to chart a path forward—using both data *and* instinct. Calling back to Bayes, remember that our aim is to be *less wrong* over time and to make educated, informed guesses. Use your best judgment, always.

Not every keyword is created equal—some will be more relevant to your business, some will have higher search volume, and some will resonate more with your particular audience. So, how do you specifically create content that cuts through the clutter and provides value to your audience, thereby establishing your brand as an authority in the field and inspiring trust and loyalty in your customer base? The short answer: *specificity*. Another short answer: *organization*.

Remember, traffic for the sake of traffic is meaningless. Content for the sake of content is ineffective. You want to drive *relevant* customer traffic to your website and produce *relevant* content to attract the right audiences. Identifying specific, evidence-based, keyword-researched topics to focus your content around is a step towards attracting more of the right customers and driving more conversion-oriented traffic to your website. And remember, always bring it back to your goals.

HOW TO DECIDE WHICH CONTENT QUESTIONS TO ANSWER FIRST

When it comes to deciding which questions to answer with your content, there are a lot of factors to consider depending on your particular business objectives and content strategy. We encourage you to evaluate your search topics based on your unique goals. However, since we can't materialize in front of you with specific recommendations for your individual business (not yet, anyway!), we've identified the three most important factors that *anyone* can use as evaluation criteria, especially if you're just starting out. So, when you're deciding which topics to prioritize, consider these three things first:

1. The relevance of the topic to your core business pages and keywords
2. The topic's search volume
3. What stage in the Search Cycle the topic falls into

Certainly, you can find other metrics that can be useful—and you will—but our goal is to make the search research process straightforward, simple, and useful for you and your marketing department. **We contend that if the question is relevant to your business (and, therefore, to your audience) and if it has enough search volume to make it worthwhile, you'll want to consider producing content for that topic.** Additionally, understanding where in the Search Cycle a searcher would be coming across this content is key to determining any kind of projected results.

And here's where the "educated guesses" come in: Only *you* can determine, using your best judgment, which topics are the most relevant to your business and your goals for this campaign—the topics robust enough to attract the type of customers you want. And only you can decide what range of search volume is "worthwhile" to you. Similarly, you can use the Search Cycle to determine which stage of the buying cycle to target. In the next chapter, we'll provide some additional food for thought, but even if you're just working from these three criteria, you should be in pretty good shape to get a working list of content topics.

Evaluation Criteria #1: Relevance to Your Business

When evaluating a keyword, ask yourself, "Does this keyword support my core pages and core keywords?" Because you're starting with a strong core keyword, most of the phrases you'll find are probably related in some part to your business's core pages and keywords. However, we can start becoming even more selective and discerning at this point. *How* relevant is a term to your business? More specifically, would answering this question help move you toward your campaign goals?

If you recall our earlier example, The Nursing School's campaign goals are to increase enrollment over the period of a year. While some questions in your research may be wonderful for achieving a different goal, we're specifically targeting questions that would help someone make a decision to request more information about enrolling. For this reason, we would target content topics that answer potential students' enrollment-related questions rather than other questions that may be relevant to the business and audience but work towards another goal (such as purchase reinforcement or thought leadership). A content question such as "what is nursing school like?" would be a better topic to bolster enrollment than "how to pass nursing school exams." The first one speaks to a potential student's reservations and interests before enrolling, while the second one speaks more to *current* students about their anxieties around passing tests. Both may be relevant to the business, but the first topic is more urgently related to the current goals.

Use your campaign goals as a compass for evaluation. Make an educated guess based on what you know about your audience and your business, and keep a running list of topics. You don't need to discard the topics you won't be targeting now; keep them in mind for the future. They might be highly relevant to a campaign down the road.

You may wish to use "low, medium, and high" to assign relevance to each keyword in whichever keyword-tracking document you're using (the Subject Discovery template we mentioned in Chapter 14—available at ContentShift.com/Resources—or another). In some cases, there might be "no relevance" to your particular objectives, and that is an easy way to eliminate a content topic. For example, you might have come across a topic about "pediatric nursing" in your research phase, and it may have high search volume, but if The Nursing School doesn't offer this program, it has no relevance to your business, so there is no solid business reason to write about it.

The "high" relevance topics should be easy to identify. "How hard is nursing school?" would likely be a high relevance topic since we can imagine a lot of people are asking this question. It's general and relevant to someone making a decision about whether or not to attend nursing school.

The "medium" and "low" relevance topics aren't necessarily off topic, but they could just be slightly peripheral to your audience and business needs, not specific to your current goals, or more nuanced versions of a high-relevance topic. For example, in our Nursing School case study, we came across a few different iterations of questions wondering how hard the math and science in nursing school would be. We can understand that the audience might have some anxiety about being able to pass their nursing classes if the math is too hard, and this would be a good topic to cover to assuage those fears and provide some emotional reassurance. It's relevant.

However, because this is a more nuanced topic with a potentially smaller audience base, you might decide to score it as "medium" relevance. Something like "does nursing school require physics?" is even more specific, so it might be deemed "low relevance." These topics, even if they're marked as medium or low relevance, can still be great topics to target. But, for the sake of prioritizing, you might decide to target the bigger, broader topics first and come back to these more specific questions later—or place these lower-relevancy topics as subheadings within a broader framework.

Think about finding connections between related topics and potentially collapsing multiple topics into one post, using an "umbrella" method. For example, "what kind of math is required for nursing school?" could be the content title (the top of the umbrella), and you could have subheadings addressing specifics like physics, calculus, and other math-related subjects (spokes under the umbrella). If topics are closely related, you can also plug them into Google and see what results you get for "related searches." This is a tactic we often like to use to find links between questions.

The bottom line is this: Check and double-check the relevancy of a content topic against your business goals and your audience's interests. Always use your best judgment and consider what you are trying to accomplish with content marketing. Also consider what you know about your audience and the types of topics that could help inform them about what you're offering. It doesn't need to be perfect, just informed by reason and "less wrong over time."

Evaluation Criteria #2: Search Volume

When evaluating a keyword, ask yourself, "Is this keyword worth targeting based on ideal search volume?" There's no hard-and-fast rule for the perfect search volume, but you can make informed decisions based on the numbers you've compiled during the research stage. Obviously, the higher the number, the better (usually) because it means more people are searching for that term every month, which translates to more opportunity for traffic to your website. The general rule: Target questions with higher search volume first. High search volume is an indicator that people want to know about this topic.

The caveat: Let the topic guide you. You might come across a great topic that shows zero search volume, but you can see there are some results on Google. Or maybe you know people are asking about it from talking to your customers, or perhaps you see search evidence for the topic on different platforms, like Google's "People Also Ask" or other software that doesn't show an exact number. Like we mentioned in Chapter 14, "zero/no data" doesn't mean you necessarily need to throw the topic away. Search volume shows you where the interest is, now, but this could always change. Even keywords with low search volume can become part of a content outline as subheadings or keywords in the body text.

The bottom line: Search volume is a key part of deciding what topics to write about because it is a data-driven metric showing you where your audience's interests lie. Consider search volume like the gutters in bowling. Your goal is to shoot the ball down the alley to hit all the pins. Search volume can help guide you toward your target (and avoid the gutter) by providing helpful limits and guidance.

"Eh, fuck it, Dude. Let's go bowling."

—Walter Sobchak

Evaluation Criteria #3: Search Cycle

Let's not forget about the Search Cycle and the importance of understanding where we are meeting our audience (potential customers) in their search journey. As you are evaluating content questions to target first, identifying which stage of the Search Cycle the question falls under can help you determine a content strategy.

While every keyword can be tagged as belonging to one or more of the Search Cycle stages, we are intentionally asking you to think about the Search Cycle *after* determining search volume and relevance. This is because, if you are pressed for time, you don't need to waste resources thinking through every single content question for the Search Cycle. We want you to identify your top priorities based on search volume and relevance first, and then go deeper. You may choose to do the following process only for medium- or high-relevancy topics with high search volume, or you may choose to do it for all of them.

At this point, look at your high-priority/high-relevance keywords and ask yourself, "Which stage of the Search Cycle does this question target? Where does it fit in the user's journey? How close to conversion is this question? What are my business goals for this round of content production?" In our experience, most businesses benefit from choosing an area to focus on for each content marketing period—typically a quarter, a half-year, or a year—which can help you choose topics based on where they fall in the Search Cycle. Your goals can shape which questions you choose to target.

For example, if your current goal is to generally drive leads, you may choose to focus on the questions that most closely align with the comparison stage, which is closest to conversion. If your content marketing strategy is focused instead on building thought leadership, you may decide to focus on topics that allow your unique perspective to shine, which may be the awareness or information stage. On the other hand, you may have identified a need to support existing customers, so your content strategy would benefit from producing content around the fifth stage of support. We want you to always keep in mind that anyone visiting your web page is arriving at a specific moment in their search journey, and remembering this will help you become more intentional with your strategy.

ALL SEARCH TERMS ARE IMPLIED QUESTIONS

This seems like a good time to remind you of a small but crucial detail that will help you continue thinking about this research and evaluation process. We've been harping all along about finding the right questions—the ones your people are asking. But what about search terms that aren't in the form of questions? For example, "best nursing schools for continuing education." We had the modifier "best" on our questions template (which we covered in Chapter 14), but, clearly, this phrase is not a direct question. It's actually an implied question. The implied question is, "What are the best nursing schools for continuing education?" As we know, online searchers don't always use "proper" English syntax and grammar. Searchers will often condense their questions into shorter phrases, as noted in this example, which makes sense considering the platform.

There's always a question behind a query, and it's typically easier to discern the full question behind keywords in the long tail than it is to determine the questions behind head terms. For example, what is the question behind "nursing classes" (a head term and core keyword)? It's kind of hard to tell. The searcher wants to know something about nursing classes, but we're not sure what exactly (they might not know either). As you go forward, remember that sometimes the question will be implied rather than direct.

CONTENT STRATEGIES FOR THE SEARCH CYCLE

Now, let's apply some practical strategy to what you already know about the Search Cycle. The Search Cycle helps us understand which stage(s) in the buying journey someone might encounter your content. This tool can help us meet our customers where they're at to facilitate a continued interaction with our brand, hopefully leading in some cases to a conversion or sale. Here, we'll help you apply the keyword research you just did with the different stages of the Search Cycle so you can make informed decisions about which keyword questions to target, depending on what your goals are.

Stage 1: Awareness

Searchers in the awareness stage are generally just becoming aware of a problem or need. They don't really know what questions they're asking. They don't have a particular brand or solution in mind; they're just looking for information.

Breakdown of Stage 1 Awareness Search Terms

- Awareness terms generally have higher volumes of searches every month.
- They are less specific and relevant to a specific business goal.
- They are often head terms, and very competitive.
- They are often implied questions.
- They may cover a broad range of topics as the searcher tries to figure out what they want to know more about.

In our Nursing School example, some general awareness terms may include the following: *best careers, jobs in demand, what careers are good*. You can see these are top-level questions and pretty far from the specific "answer" of nursing school, but they are the initial questions someone might ask when looking for another career.

While awareness terms are the farthest from the point of conversion, this stage casts the widest net for those "just browsing" people. Have you heard of the Marketing Rule of 7? This is the idea that your brand needs to get in front of people seven times before they remember you enough to make a purchase.[1] Considering the oversaturated digital age, this number may even be double now. Creating content for the awareness stage is primarily about getting your name in front of more people, more often, and for more broad-level searches. As Google continues to evolve, they are also recommending more content to people based on their previous searches (as in Google Discovery), which is helpful to us as content creators.

The bottom line: Awareness searches span the farthest reaches of the web, where you may get in front of new audiences.

Content Strategy for Stage 1

- The advantage of targeting this stage is that, if you reach people here, they may remember you when they're ready to take action.
- If you want to cast a wide net, targeting the awareness stage generally reaches more people.
- If your goal is to become a thought leader and authority in your field, targeting this stage can be useful for expanding your reach and attracting audiences in related professional fields.

Stage 2: Information Gathering

Most searches occur in the information gathering stage. A user is actively researching a topic or train of thought, trying to find the information they need to make a decision. Alternatively, they could just be browsing a topic of interest to them. They may or may not be "shopping around," but they are definitely searching for information to help them learn something, find something, or do something.

Breakdown of Stage 2 Information Gathering Search Terms

- Informational searches account for about 70% of all Internet searches.
- Informational searches may not necessarily lead right away to a transaction or conversion, but this is the stage where you can provide valuable insight and resources to your audience.
- Informational searches often fall in the long tail and can provide specific clues as to what your audience is interested in.

Helping a user understand something, teaching them how to do something, or shining light on a question can establish your brand as an expert source of knowledge. The information gathering stage of the Search Cycle is a great place to direct a lot of your content energy. Since most searches occur in this stage, you can imagine that it would only make sense to spend most of your content marketing energy specifically attempting to answer users' questions. Most of our discussion will center around the information gathering stage, and we recommend spending most of your content marketing time or budget producing content that targets search terms in this stage.

Content Strategy for Stage 2

- Generally speaking, most questions will probably fall into the information gathering stage. Here, you have the opportunity to answer the questions people are asking about your business before they commit.
- Focus on providing accurate, relevant, and helpful information to your audience rather than selling. The conversion point comes after someone has learned what they need to know to say yes. Build trust in your audience by providing them with honest, insightful answers to their questions.
- Consider this stage your wide net of leads, specifically focused on your audience's questions about various elements of your business.

Stage 3: Evaluation

The third Search Cycle stage is so important that it has its own category in our keyword research template: "Vs/Or." The evaluation stage is all about whittling down two or more options toward a final decision. Searchers have some options in mind, and now they are fine-tuning their research to be swayed in one direction or another.

Breakdown of Stage 3 Evaluation Search Terms

- Evaluation searches tend to be transactional and fairly close to the point of purchase.
- Informational searches make up the bulk of online queries, but of the 30% of searches that fall in other categories, the evaluation stage is the closest to conversion.
- Evaluation searches are often implied questions, like wondering what the "best" or "top" option is or comparing X "vs." Y. Searchers might also use modifiers like "or" to compare two things or "review" to find other people's recommendations.
- Searchers have typically already done enough research (or have enough of an idea about what they want) to be ready to make a decision between two or more options.

For most businesses starting out with a content marketing plan, creating content for the evaluation stage might actually be your first priority even though it's the third stage. Yes, the information gathering stage consists of around two-thirds of all searches and should fill most of your time and energy in the long run, but the evaluation stage has the largest influence on conversion, so it's not a bad idea to focus at least some time and energy targeting this stage.

This is why we've created a category all on its own for "Vs./Or" searches in the Subject Discovery template. They are so common and important that we want you to have the evaluation stage high on your radar. As you're researching, be on the lookout for those comparison searches that indicate someone is close to making a purchasing decision, and consider how to approach that topic without being overtly salesy while still focused on providing value for the searcher. Sometimes these are branded searches like "X business/product" vs. "Y business/product." They may also be wondering about different types of options, for example, "online vs. in-person nursing school." Search queries like this provide a great opportunity for you to create content that goes over the benefits and drawbacks of each option to help potential customers make an informed decision (hopefully toward your brand). Once you understand the comparison, create content that helps your audience weigh their options.

Content Strategy for Stage 3

- If you have to choose between producing content for the evaluation or awareness stages of the Search Cycle and you want to begin increasing conversions, focus your energies on the evaluation stage because these searches tend to land closer to the point of purchase.
- Look for specific terms that indicate intent to buy and comparison topics that you would have an easy time answering.
- Content you can create for the evaluation stage may include reviews and stories of satisfied customers, links to information that confirms the value of your product as compared to others, and specific incentives to purchase.

Stage 4: Commitment

The commitment stage is ultimately where you hope your audience becomes a customer. You've done everything else right so that, when they're ready to pull the trigger, they already have you in mind.

Breakdown of Stage 4 Commitment Search Terms

- Commitment stage searches are often navigational. They occur after a user has already done the research needed to make a decision. The search may be exact and directive, such as "order from X business online."
- There's not much you really need to do in your content marketing efforts to direct people to this stage. Everything you produced in the other stages will support your audience's decision to commit to engaging with you online.

The strategy is now less focused on drawing the right people in and more focused on keeping them with you through the purchase. Make sure you have all the other supporting elements in place. For example, check that your website is functional and easy to use, the copy on your product and ecommerce pages is clear and accessible, and the checkout or conversion process is seamless.

Content Strategy for Stage 4

- A content strategy at this stage includes keeping your pages up to date, producing valuable informational content, optimizing your website, and providing a user-friendly experience.
- Make sure to have your core product pages optimized for your core keywords so people can find you at this stage. Keep your website, shopping cart, and any other conversion tools up to date, clear, and easy to use.

Stage 5: Support

Your online campaign doesn't end when the customer converts. After the customer says yes, the support stage begins. This is the time to confirm the rightness of the decision they've made and help them become evangelical, loyal, word-of-mouth marketers for your brand. When it comes to search, support may also sometimes look like information gathering, so keep this in mind: Your job as a content creator is to answer questions and help your customers know what they need to know—both before *and* after the purchase.

Breakdown of Stage 5 Support Search Terms

- Support questions may revolve around how to use your product or what to do at a later stage in their relationship with your business.
- Support terms are about the post-purchase customer experience.

The goal here is to maintain customer interaction and continue to create positive messages around the brand while continuing to provide value to the customer. Make sure that you have content in place to answer your customers' post-purchase questions—which are also sometimes *pre-purchase* questions. Whether a user is *considering* buying your product or *already* has, they may search online to see what kind of support is available.

For example, before Google, if you had a question about, say, adjusting the radio settings on your new Honda Accord, you probably would've reached straight for the glove box to pull out the user's manual. While those physical user's manuals are still included with most vehicles, today you might actually find it easier to pull out your phone and do a quick search for "2017 Honda Accord radio settings." Someone just taking a test drive might *also* perform this exact same search.

In the support stage, consider how your company is helping people and highlight those accomplishments and resources. Consider what your customers want or need once they're already with you. Support content can take the form of direct contact with the customer immediately post-purchase, like a follow-up email, asking for feedback or a review, or sending coupons. Support content might also highlight features of the product just purchased, or a personalized recommendation of complementary products.²

An attitude of positive customer engagement—not only *before* and *during* the sale but especially *after*—is an important ingredient to long-lasting content success. Remember, you are creating and maintaining relationships and experiences beyond the POS (point of sale). You are engaging with your audience as human beings and showing them you care about their lives. This means you produce content for a well-rounded, holistic brand experience.

Content Strategy for Stage 5

- You can create how-to guides, user manuals, FAQs, and other support materials to anticipate these post-purchase questions. Especially if you are offering complex products or services, you'll want to help people with some sort of supportive quick-start content.
- You might also consider featuring user reviews and testimonials. For example, The Nursing School might feature a Student Spotlight on the blog every month or produce articles specifically designed to help students succeed in their nursing program. This type of content shows both post-purchase users *and* pre-purchase users that the company cares about its customers beyond the sale.
- Content for this stage may highlight satisfied customer reviews; offer contests, competitions, or coupons; or otherwise engage your audience in an interactive way beyond the sale.

The Search Cycle allows us to conceptualize the needs of our customers at various points in time. It can certainly help inform our decisions about the type of content to create, for whom, and for what end goal. On your Subject Discovery document (the one you created in Chapter 14), fill in which stage you think the question in mind is targeting, and let that inform your production strategy. Identifying each Search Cycle stage for your developing list of questions can help you decide what content to produce this round, which questions to save for later, and which to possibly even eliminate.

NEXT STEP: ASSIGNING PRIORITIES

Armed with these evaluation criteria, you should be able to see, at a glance, which questions satisfy both a reasonably high search volume and a high relevance to your business, and where they fit in the Search Cycle. Now, you can prioritize the "high" search volume and "high" relevance topics as your top priority. You can use either a numerical system, like 1–5, or continue with a "high, medium, low" demarcation to fill in your "Priority" column on your spreadsheet.

Depending on your capacity and goals for content production, you now have a working plan for which content topics to prioritize first. How many pieces of content you decide to produce is entirely up to you, so your numbers will reflect your particular plan. We'll take you through some other considerations in the next chapter, but these criteria can be your baseline.

In Figure 15.1, you can see an example of our template filled in for The Nursing School. Remember, you can find this information using your preferred keyword research tools; our favorite is SEMrush. This research has been compiled by finding questions around the initial keyword "nursing school." As you can see from the template, we've organized the questions based on the system of questions we developed in Chapter 14.

Out of our initial research, we've narrowed our priority topics down to 17 high-priority content titles and 4 medium-priority titles (shown in bold).

Figure 15.1: Keyword Research—Subject Discovery Template

CORE KEYWORD: nursing school

CORE QUESTIONS

Who/Which

Research			Evaluation			
Keyword Question	Search Volume	Relevance	Search Cycle	Notes		Priority
Who started the first nursing school	70	Low	N/A	Not relevant to audience, could be a general question		Low
Who gives nursing school loans	0	Med	Info Seeking	Low search volume but relevant to someone ready to enroll, closer to conversion		Med
Who should write letters of recommendation for nursing school	0	Med	Info Seeking	Low search volume but relevant to someone ready to enroll, closer to conversion		Med
Which nursing school should I go to	90	High	Awareness	Broad question		Med
Which nursing school is easy to get into	40	Med	Awareness	Broad question with application focus		Med

Notes:

What

Research			Evaluation			
Keyword Question	Search Volume	Relevance	Search Cycle	Notes		Priority
What is nursing school like	390	High	Awareness	Decent search volume and relevant to a broad audience		High
What do you learn in nursing school	210	High	Awareness	Decent search volume and relevant to a broad audience		High

Keyword Question	Search Volume	Relevance	Search Cycle	Notes	Priority
What to expect in nursing school	210	High	Info Seeking	Decent search volume and relevant to a broad audience (this is slightly similar to the previous query and may be combined)	High
What is nursing school	170	High	Awareness	Early in conversion journey but important top-level question	Med
What are the prerequisites for nursing school	140	High	Info Seeking	Important question, closer to conversion	High
What classes do you take in nursing school	90	Med	Info Seeking	Good to answer	Med
What to bring to nursing school interview	90	Med	Info Seeking	Could offer high value to those ready to enroll	Med
What to do after graduating from nursing school	90	Med	Support/Info Seeking	Support graduates and also pre-enrollment important question for decision-making	Med

Notes:

When

	Research			Evaluation	
Keyword Question	Search Volume	Relevance	Search Cycle	Notes	Priority
When do you start nursing school	70	Med	Info Seeking	Practical for application process	Med
When do you start wearing scrubs in nursing school	50	Low	Info Seeking	Interesting but not essential to conversion	Low
When do you apply for nursing school	40	High	Info Seeking	Important to decision-making, conversion	High
When did Florence Nightingale open her school of nursing	10	Low	Info Seeking	Not specific to business goals but interesting	Low

When do they drug test you for nursing school	10	Med	Info Seeking	Low search volume	Low
When do you start clinicals in nursing school	10	Med	Info Seeking	Low search volume	Low

Notes:

Where

Research			Evaluation		
Keyword Question	Search Volume	Relevance	Search Cycle	Notes	Priority
Where to get immunizations for nursing school	50	Med	Support	Seems post-purchase	Low
Where to get a physical exam for nursing school	40	Med	Support	Seems post-purchase	Low
Where can I go to nursing school for free	30	Med	Awareness	Intent does not align with business goals	Low
Where to go to nursing school	20	High	Awareness	Could be combined with other topics	Med

Notes:

Why

Research			Evaluation		
Keyword Question	Search Volume	Relevance	Search Cycle	Notes	Priority
Why is nursing school so hard	320	Low	Support	Student-focused, could be valuable to offer encouragement	Low
Why is nursing school competitive	70	Low	Awareness	Application-focused, could be valuable to help ease application stress	Low
Why do you want to go to nursing school essay	50	Med	Commitment/ Support	Ready to apply or post-application help topic	Med

| Why go to nursing school | 10 | High | Awareness | Opportunity for benefits but low search volume | Med |
| Why am I having trouble getting into nursing school | 0 | Low | Support | Post-application help topic | Low |

Notes:

How

	Research			Evaluation	
Keyword Question	Search Volume	Relevance	Search Cycle	Notes	Priority
How long is nursing school	4,400	High	Info Seeking	Lots of people asking this question. Definitely answer	High
How hard is nursing school	1,900	Med	Info Seeking	Opportunity to assuage fears	High
How many years is nursing school	1,000	High	Info Seeking	Can be combined with "how long"	High
How much is nursing school	880	High	Info Seeking	Top-level, important question to answer	High
How to prepare for nursing school	480	High	Support/Info	Could be post-application or information seeking	Med
How to pay for nursing school	260	High	Info Seeking	Could be combined with "how much," key to decision-making	High
How to apply for nursing school	210	High	Commitment	Close to conversion	High
How to be organized in nursing school	90	High	Support	Could be post-application support for students	Med
How to find out if a nursing school is accredited	70	High	Info Seeking	Practical	Low
How to get scholarships for nursing school	70	High	Info Seeking/Support	Could be combined with other funding questions	Med
How to go to nursing school as a single mom	70	Med	Info Seeking	Specific to Connie persona	Med

Keyword Question	Search Volume	Relevance	Search Cycle	Notes	Priority
How to prepare for first semester of nursing school	70	Med	Support	Post-enrollment support	Med
How to stay healthy in nursing school	70	Med	Support	Post-enrollment or info seeking	Low
How to write a personal statement for nursing school	70	High	Commitment	Ready to apply, needs help with decision-making	Med
How to get into nursing school after high school	140	High	Info Seeking	Close to conversion, specific to Heather persona	Med
How to pass nursing school exams	140	Med	Support	Post-enrollment support	Med
How does nursing school work	110	Med	Info Seeking	Broad, general question, may be combined	Med

Notes:

Does/Do

Research				Evaluation		
Keyword Question	Search Volume	Relevance	Search Cycle	Notes	Priority
---	---	---	---	---	---
Does CNA experience help for nursing school	70	Med	Info Seeking/ Commitment	Specific to Nancy persona	Med
Do employers care where you went to nursing school	20	Med	Awareness/ Support	Could be post-graduation or early in the search	Low
Does it matter where you go to nursing school	10	Med	Awareness/ Support	Same as above, could be combined	Low

Notes:

Vs/Or

	Research		Evaluation		
Keyword Question	Search Volume	Relevance	Search Cycle	Notes	Priority
How hard is nursing school compared to other degrees (read: Nursing school vs other degrees)	140	Med	Evaluation	General, broad question	Med
Nursing school vs medical school	260	Med	Evaluation	Close to each other in health field but very different	High
Paramedic school vs nursing school	70	Med	Evaluation	Close to nursing field	High
Nursing school vs business school	50	Med	Evaluation	Very different options	Low
Nursing vs PA school	50	High	Evaluation	PA = pharmacy assistant, closer to nursing field	High
Dental hygienist school vs nursing school	30	High	Evaluation	Close to nursing field	High
Private nursing school vs community college	20	Med	Evaluation	Depending on business goals, can be relevant	Med
Law school vs nursing school	10	Low	Evaluation	Very different options	Low
Nursing school online vs campus	10	Med	Evaluation	Might be relevant depending on business model and goals	Med
Nursing school vs college	10	Med	Evaluation	Top-level question but low search volume	Med
Nursing school vs medical school difficulty	10	Med	Evaluation	Important to decision-making but low search volume	Med
Nursing school vs nursing program	10	Med	Evaluation	Needs more thought	Low
Nursing school vs pharmacy school	10	High	Evaluation	Close to nursing field but low search volume	Med

Notes:

MISC: Is/Can/Are/Does/Do/Best/Top

Research				Evaluation		
Keyword Question	Search Volume	Relevance	Search Cycle	Notes	Priority	
Is nursing school worth it	210	High	Awareness	Opportunity to discuss benefits	High	
Should I go to nursing school	170	High	Awareness	Can be combined with above	High	
Can you do nursing school online	90	Med	Info Seeking	Depending on business goals, answer	Med	
Is it possible to work and go to nursing school	90	High	Info Seeking	Can use Connie persona	Med	
Am I too old to go to nursing school	70	Med	Info Seeking	Can use Connie persona	Med	
Can you have piercings in nursing school	70	Low	Info Seeking	Can use Heather persona	Med	

Notes:

Out of this list of 67 questions we found through keyword research, we've green-lighted 21 of them. Seventeen of these titles we've marked as high-priority because we think they are especially relevant to prospective students who are already interested in learning more about enrolling in nursing school or close to the point of conversion.

Then, we actually went back to our original list after we discovered we had not chosen any of the Support stage titles to approve. It's very easy to overlook the Support stage, as we've mentioned before, because when we're focused on driving leads, we can forget to address our *current* customers. So we went back and green-lighted four content titles for the Support stage. Even though they were medium-priority, we believe it's important to allocate a portion of your content resources to nurturing the customers you already have.

Of course, you will use your own judgment and current business objectives to determine which of your initial content titles get the green light to move forward into production!

POINTS OF DISCOVERY

Now that you have some guidelines and recommendations for evaluating your content questions, go ahead and complete that step.

1. Fill out the rest of your Subject Discovery template, focusing now on the evaluation table. What is the relevance to your business? What stage of the Search Cycle does the keyword target? Mark any other notes, and assign a priority for that content topic based on current business goals.
2. Indicate somehow, either by bolding or highlighting with a color, which topics are on the table for this round of content creation.
3. Are you noticing any patterns with this data? Are you getting any ideas about what future content marketing campaigns might look like?

Chapter 16

TAKING SEARCH RESEARCH EVEN DEEPER

Watch your competitors, but don't follow them.

—**Arnoldo Hax**, *Inbound Marketing*

By now, we hope we've given you a clear, identifiable process for researching and evaluating content topics based on audience interests and business goals. Using keyword questions, you can target content topics that drive results. Of course, any SEO professional reading this will ask, "Well, what about *this?* And what about *that?*"

We know there are plenty of other factors to take into consideration, which is why we encourage you to take advantage of the Subject Discovery template we shared in Chapter 14. (You can also find it at ContentShift.com/Resources.) As you'll recall, we provided you with a worksheet so you could keep track of content titles you found while researching keywords. This worksheet is organized around the questions model of content marketing. There was a "notes" section at the bottom of each worksheet as well as a "priority" column on the far right. Our intention is to make the process of research and evaluation simple and straightforward, without *oversimplifying*.

We included the "notes" column so you could capture any *other* important factors you'll also want to consider when evaluating topics, such as:

- Determining whether a topic is evergreen
- Filling in the gaps by performing competitor analysis

- Drawing from personas and audience research
- Grouping related topics together
- Jotting down anything else you may find useful to remember

If you have the capacity to think through these items as part of your prioritization process, that's ideal, but as we've said before, the only metrics you *really* need to get started are search volume and relevance. We understand you might be working with dozens or even hundreds of content ideas. Do what makes the most sense.

You can consider this an "advanced" chapter, although we highly recommend *not skipping* this chapter because it contains lots of useful information that we hope you'll integrate into your overall content strategy. Our goal is to give you what you'll need to get started quickly and strategically while providing enough information for you to take your process deeper every time.

NOTE #1: EVERGREEN CONTENT IS ALWAYS GOOD

There's one very important type of content topic we've alluded to but haven't yet defined. What do you call content that's entirely relevant to your business goals, answers your audience's questions, has consistently significant search volume, likely won't ever become completely outdated, and will continue bringing in traffic and converting customers long after you've published it? This, my friends, is the holy grail of content marketing: *evergreen content.*

Evergreen content stays relevant and fresh to search engines and users long after it's been published because the subject is both *popular* (among your audience) and (relatively) *timeless*. Evergreen topics are not based on trends or timely news. Like the name implies, these content topics are "always in season." For example, consider the difference between the two following topics:

- Nursing job outlook for 2020
- What does an RN do?

The first post title is timely, journalistic, and newsy—relevant to the audience of The Nursing School and compelling for someone considering becoming a nurse. It's a great topic, but it will eventually become outdated. It still may be a worthwhile topic to cover, but it's good to note that it does have a limited shelf life.

The second post title is an evergreen topic because it will continue to stay relevant even as time passes. You can reasonably expect that this audience would continue to ask questions about the job duties of an RN. The topic won't go out of style for people pursuing nursing as a career. People will be searching for this topic long after it's published, and if the post offers good value to its readers, it will (hopefully) keep appearing in the search engine results pages (SERPs) for new people to discover as time goes on.

Evergreen content is one of the best types of content you can create because, theoretically, even after initial publication, it will continue to attract relevant traffic. Your investment into one piece of strategic content can potentially show you returns for years to come. Evergreen content keeps working for you long after you've hit "publish."[1]

Consider these questions to identify evergreen posts that are relevant to your business:

- Is this a question or topic that someone would've asked five years ago or will continue to ask five years from now?
- If someone is new to your product or service, would they ask this question?
- Could there be potentially other related topics that could support this subject?

Evergreen topics tend to feel very natural, especially helpful, and organically robust. You can imagine very easily that a lot of people are asking this question because it makes sense given your specific product or service.

Remember The Nursing School topics we identified in our spreadsheet in Chapter 15? Most of those topics would be considered evergreen, even if the content might change over time. For example, "how long is nursing school?" is a question we can imagine people asking in ten years, even if in ten years certain requirements for nursing have changed. The topic is evergreen, and that is what we are looking for. If you want to tag a topic as evergreen, go ahead and put that in the notes section of your spreadsheet.

(**Note:** Sometimes, rules or requirements do change over time, which is why it's a good practice to regularly conduct content audits and update your previously published pieces with new information—which we'll talk about in Part 4.)

NOTE #2: FILL IN THE GAPS WITH COMPETITOR ANALYSIS

Performing *competitor analysis* can help us determine whether we're able to produce content that's different, better, more robust, or more unique than the content being produced by our search competitors. There's so much content already out there; you don't want to produce the same old thing that someone else already did five years ago that's still ranking #1 on Google. That would be extremely hard to outrank, and probably not worth your time. But what you *can do* is figure out where there are opportunities to fill in the content gaps and determine if you have a competitive angle. This consideration deserves some thought, so it's a good thing to spend some time on, especially once you have a content topic identified.

You can learn a lot from what content is already out there and how it's performing. First and foremost, competitor analysis can actually save us time and energy if we determine a content topic is *too competitive* to target right now. In this way, we learn to direct our energies away from dead-ends. But, more importantly, competitor research can help us refine our topic strategy by informing the quality and direction of our content. We want to know what's already out there in search results so we can do it differently or better.

Conducting competitor analysis during the evaluation stage can help you decide two things:

- Whether a content topic is worth targeting
- What elements your content would need to have to compete on the SERP

Here's a list of a few ways to use competitor analysis to inform your strategy and determine your competitive angle:

1. **Check what content appears in the top spots for your keyword.** First, simply type your keyword into Google and see what pops up. Take note of the brands or companies in the top 5 or so spots on the SERP. Are they huge brands that you probably won't outrank, or smaller to medium-sized operations? Click on the titles and consider, how good is this content? How well does it answer the question? Could we do better?

Also, you can input your keyword in SEMrush and check the "Organic Search Results" section to see the top-ranked spots for any given term, with links to those web pages.

2. **Consider what your competitive angle would be.** You can use this information to decide whether you want to produce content that's similar but better, or whether you think you can do something different to stand out. For example, let's say the results for a search were all websites that had "Top 5" or "Top 10" in their titles. There must be a reason why that topic ranks well for lists. Would you be

able to make a better list than those already out there, or might you try some different angle to be unique? Can you be competitive by making an infographic, or a video, or adding visuals, or involving an expert opinion, or citing better sources, or making it more fun to read? There are tons of ways you can ensure your content will be competitive, and they'll be unique to each situation. What opportunities do you notice?

3. **Analyze their content structure.** You can observe your competitors' content to inform your own. What headings and subheadings are they using? What is the quality of the writing? How long are the posts? How interesting or insightful are they? What's missing? What can you *add* to the conversation?

4. **Analyze the URL:** You can take the URLs of these competitor websites and conduct a "URL discovery search" in SEMrush. This will show you any *related keywords* that the post is ranking for. Are these posts ranking for any keywords you don't already have on your list? If so, maybe take note of those ideas. You may decide to add them to your running list for further research later.

The bottom line: Check out what content is already out there as you move through your evaluation process. Use your best judgment to determine whether you can add to the conversation with your unique perspective, or produce something better—whether that means creating content that is longer and more in-depth, or more well-researched, or covering more ground. You've got to do something *different* and more *unique* if you want to compete online. The best way to do that is to understand what's already been done so you can keep pushing the envelope. Make a note in your spreadsheet of any ideas you come across, as they may be helpful later on.

NOTE #3: DRAW FROM PERSONAS AND AUDIENCE RESEARCH TO GET EVEN MORE SPECIFIC

So far, we've been talking about search research for your *general audience*. Your top-level questions are typically broad and relevant to most of your persona types and audience groups. For example, "how much does nursing school cost?" would likely be a question that Career-Change Connie, Nursing Assistant Nancy, and High School Heather would ask. In other words, a lot of the initial questions you find from your core keywords won't have a specific persona focus.

Personas become super helpful down the road once you've answered all the essential, top-level questions you can possibly find. From there, you can start researching specific topics for specific audience groups, using your personas to lead the way.

However, even if you're at the beginning stages of your content strategy, it's helpful to always keep your personas in the back of your mind. Ask yourself, "Is there a specific persona or audience group that would really appreciate this content? Is this question geared towards one persona or audience group over another?"

You can use your knowledge of your audience to make notes wherever it might be helpful. For example, let's say that, as a content strategist, you already know from the sales department that students are constantly asking about whether going to nursing school guarantees a job in nursing. If you come across this question in your search, it should be high on your radar. You might make a note such as "students often ask this question."

Alternatively, returning to our example from a previous chapter about student anxiety over math, this is where knowing your audience can really help you make decisions about which content to target and why. Even if the search volume is low, you might make the note that "students are often anxious about math;" therefore, you have extra reason to believe it's a worthwhile topic to target.

Finally, once you start following all the different topic threads, you can use our exercise from Chapter 11 (noted in Figure 11.2) to spin one content topic into multiple posts for different audience groups. "Study Tips for Nursing Students" can also become "Nursing School Study Tips for Working Mothers," "How to Prepare for Nursing School as a High School Student," and "How to Excel in Nursing School for Working Nurses." Each persona (Connie, Heather, and Nancy) inform each of these content topics based on what we know about who they are, where they are in life, and what their needs/motivations are.

Personas are a great way to get more mileage out of a single content topic and show your audience you are speaking to *them*. These persona strategies might not apply to all topics, but when you see an opportunity, take note.

NOTE #4: GROUP RELATED QUESTIONS INTO OUTLINES WITH SUBHEADINGS

As we mentioned before, you're probably going to come across similar questions asked in slightly different ways. Typically speaking, just choose one. You don't need to note every single iteration of any question. You want there to be *slight to significant differences* amongst the questions to give breadth and depth to your content.

If you do come across a few different questions that seem closely related, you can make a note in your template about grouping topics together in one piece of content. Often, some of the closely related questions we come across can become subheadings within an article. This is great because subheadings are like the signposts for search engines.

Closely related subheadings show Google that there are multiple topics that could be of interest to a user searching for that topic. And this is a great start to constructing a content outline, as we'll talk about in Part 4. So, take note of where there are opportunities to combine or collapse relevant topics. You may even start some rough content outlines as you do this, which will help you in later steps.

NOTE #5: USE WHATEVER TOOLS YOU NEED— EVERYTHING AND THE KITCHEN SINK

As we've mentioned already, we're only giving you a small glimpse into what's possible using SEO keyword research tools. Remember, that's intentional. There's a lot of stuff you don't necessarily need to know about SEO in order to produce high-quality content that resonates with your audience, and we believe that paring it down to the essentials will help you in the long run.

As SEOs, however, we would be remiss not to mention at least a few other tools and things to consider when doing your research and making your decisions. If you have time, you can throw in anything—including the kitchen sink—as part of your evaluation process.

Here are a couple of other things we tend to consider:

- **CRO:** Conversion Rate Optimization (CRO) is the next step after SEO and content marketing. Once you choose your topics and keywords, hit publish, and share, you can test out certain things—like calls to action, button colors, different verbiage, and more—to determine how to increase your conversion rate. Once you start bringing in traffic, you want to be constantly testing and improving. While CRO is outside the scope of this book, it's also very important. CRO is an entire field in and of itself, and it's worth investing in *after* you're driving significant traffic to your site if you want to make that traffic work even better.
- **Difficulty Score:** A lot of SEOs like to look at the difficulty score as another way to determine how viable a content topic is, or how easy or hard it will be to compete with existing content. The difficulty score takes a lot of different factors into account, such as the page authority (PA) and domain authority (DA) scores of the top 10 links in Google's SERP. If this sounds like more industry speak, don't worry too much. Our opinion is that the difficulty score can be helpful sometimes, but it should be considered a periphery factor along with other elements of

competitor research. Take it with a grain of salt, and use your best judgment.

WHAT ABOUT PAID ADS?

Google offers plenty of ways to advertise and market through their channels, including paid advertising. A company pays to have an ad placed at the top of a SERP for certain keywords. Ads are a quick and easy way to draw traffic to your site, and the benefits may be immediate, but they're also usually temporary. Paid search ads typically return more conversions than organic search results during an ad campaign. It's convenient for people searching for a specific goal to click the sponsored links. However, once an ad campaign is over, that traffic is often gone as well.

> According to data compiled by SparkToro, 65.6% of desktop searches resulted in a click on an organic search result, and only 3.7% resulted in a click on a paid ad.[2]

Meanwhile, the content you create for organic search keeps working for you long after you have paid for and published it. Here's what we mean: When you're in the middle of a paid campaign, you might end up stuck in a cycle where you feel like you have to keep paying for ads to keep attracting website traffic. The associated costs per click typically become more expensive over time.

On the other hand, content marketing for organic traffic typically incurs a cost up front to produce the content, but once a piece of organic content ranks, its visibility can last for a very long time, especially with periodic updating. That content will always be there on your website, aging and gaining visibility with minimal further effort on your part. As long as you're strategic and intentional about the content topics you choose, producing one piece of valuable content can be a long-term investment that keeps driving returns on that investment for years to come.

> Over time, paid advertising becomes more expensive, while organic content becomes more valuable.

This isn't to say that paid search marketing is for the birds. In fact, paid and organic marketing strategies can certainly complement each other. Paid advertising online can do wonders for your business in the near-term because it presents an opportunity to expand your brand's exposure. For example, it could be a good strategy to run a paid ad campaign for certain keywords targeted to the comparison stage of the Search Cycle when people are closer to a point of purchase. Paid ads can also complement the user's decision journey and provide brand awareness during the early stages of information gathering. Especially if you don't currently rank for those broader queries, paid ads can help you get traffic quickly and dominate in more of the SERP.

Paid advertising online and content marketing are equally valuable approaches, but they require different mindsets, processes, and skill sets. Paid advertising is focused on selling, while content marketing is focused on providing information and building trust. A paid ad's landing page is typically written to capture a sale rather than provide education.

If the rest of the content across your site is interesting, valuable, and relevant, diversification across multiple marketing approaches is fantastic (paid ads, social media marketing, affiliate marketing, etc.). You could, theoretically, occupy multiple spots on the SERP: a paid ad, a search feature, an organic position, or more. Still, while paid ads, SEO, and social media should be seen as the arms and legs of digital marketing, content is the primary focus—the main circulatory system. Content marketing is the umbrella term that could arguably describe all marketing efforts that use content—which, again, is everything.

RECAPPING THE CONTENT STRATEGIES WE'VE COVERED SO FAR

Alright, so we've covered a lot of ground. To conclude this section on search strategies for content marketing, let's recap some of the main things to remember when doing keyword research:

- Higher search volume is usually better, but even content questions with little to no search volume can be valuable if the question is strong.
- Content questions that have the highest relevance to your business should be targeted first.
- Understand which stage of the Search Cycle you're targeting.
- Stage 3 of the Search Cycle (evaluation) is the best stage to target for conversion.
- Stage 2 of the Search Cycle (information gathering) is where the bulk of searches will occur and will likely compose a large percentage of your content efforts.
- Don't forget to pepper in some content targeted to Stage 5 of the Search Cycle (support) to show your audience you value staying connected.
- Evergreen topics are a great investment.
- Long-tail terms are more specific and less competitive than head terms.
- You can do some competitor analysis to determine the viability of a topic.
- Personas can give you even more opportunities for content expansion.
- Learn from your competitors about how to make your content stand out.

ALLOCATING TIME AND RESOURCES TO THE SEARCH RESEARCH PHASE

How much time should you spend gathering all this data? Dave Walters, author of *Behavioral Marketing: Delivering Personal Experiences at Scale*, recommends spending 125% more time than you think you need to collecting data. We would agree. There's no hard and fast rule, but the more research you do, the better your content is going to be—always. This could mean sitting down with your content team once a month to document your plan for the next four weeks, or you could plan ahead every quarter. We recommend scheduling time within your workflow to regularly update your keyword research. This will keep your content strategy fresh and forward-moving at all times.

In Part 4, we'll get into the meat and bones of content creation: understanding different types of content, outlining articles, hiring writers, ensuring quality, constructing a timeline for publishing, honing a strategy for sharing, and defining metrics to keep you improving every step of the way.

POINTS OF DISCOVERY

Every business will have different targets and priorities for content marketing. As you make some decisions about which content titles to produce, consider some of the following questions:

1. Which stage of the Search Cycle do you think your business should target first with content marketing? Why?
2. How many of your possible content topics are evergreen?
3. After doing some competitor research, which topics seem to have the best chance of competing, and why?
4. Which of your content questions are closely related enough to potentially be grouped together into one piece, using subheadings to organize the information?
5. Which topics may be well-suited for one or more of your personas?

PART FOUR
PRODUCTION

Chapter 17

DOCUMENTING YOUR CONTENT STRATEGY

Marketers who document their strategy are much more likely to accomplish their content goals and be successful. It really is that simple.

—Joe Pulizzi, Content Marketing Institute

Okay, so you've probably heard over and over again that it's important to have a "documented content strategy." That's entirely true. But what does that look like? How do you create one? And what will it do for your company? The good news is, you've already been doing a lot of the legwork throughout this book to gather the materials, ideas, and research you need to draft your documented content strategy. And if you're familiar with putting together any sort of marketing or business plan, just consider your content strategy as part of your marketing plan—the part that's specifically dedicated to content marketing.

A content strategy outlines how your content will achieve your business goals. It's the blueprint for your entire content production process. In short, it's the written plan of action that outlines *how* you will achieve your goals and *what* those goals are based on your objectives and capacity. While there's no one-size-fits-all template for a content strategy—and yours may range anywhere from one to 20 pages, depending on the level of detail you wish to include—you *will* need some sort of written plan that outlines what you hope to achieve with your content marketing.

Now that you have a solid grasp of what content marketing is—what it does, who your audience is, how to understand them better, and how to research and evaluate content questions to target—it's time to put it all together. In this chapter, we'll walk you through the basic elements of a content strategy. We'll also provide you with a template you can use and adapt to fit your needs. Throughout Part 4 of this book, we'll focus on putting all the pieces together so you can implement your plan, including setting goals, optimizing content, streamlining your content production process, and measuring your progress.

ALIGN CONTENT STRATEGY WITH BUSINESS GOALS

One of the most important elements of a documented content strategy is the explicit acknowledgment of your business objectives. Amazingly, we've seen well-respected companies jump straight into producing content for the sake of producing content without ever stopping to consider how it relates to the bottom line. Your business goals inform every aspect of your content production process, like which types of content to produce and through which channels. We've been touching on these topics throughout the book, and now it's time to get specific.

A **business objective** is a general, measurable target for the company overall, such as "increase leads" or "sign on new clients." Your company's top-priority business objectives will direct your content marketing goals and your production process.

A **content marketing goal** is what you intend your overall content marketing to accomplish, such as "educate potential customers on product specifications." This is a general vision for your content marketing efforts, informed by your business objective. In turn, this goal will inform your production goals and methods.

A **content production goal** sets out to determine your output schedule, such as "publish one blog post per month." Your production goal will be determined by your overall content marketing goal and will be the most actionable part of your strategy—essentially directing your day-to-day activities and methods.

It's absolutely essential that we start at the top level—your business objectives—and not the other way around. There's no point in choosing an arbitrary starting point like "publish daily blog posts" if you're not sure whether it's likely to meet your business goals. We always want to start with what you want to accomplish and then lay out a content strategy informed by your objectives.

As your business objectives change, so too might your content marketing goals or your production methods. Let's take a moment to identify which of your business objectives is currently driving your content. These can be general and top-level because they describe, overall, the direction of growth you wish to focus on now.

Examples of business objectives may include:

- Create awareness of your brand
- Educate people about your products
- Generate leads
- Drive sales
- Increase revenue
- Decrease customer service costs
- Become a thought leader in your industry
- Reach new markets
- Generate referrals
- Increase sign-ups/subscriptions

Business objectives often naturally change over time. For example, your business may want to increase relevant leads now, but, in two years, you may be happy with your regular inflow of leads, and you may wish to focus your efforts towards building thought leadership in your field. It's important to regularly take stock of your company's progress, growth, and shifts and make any necessary adjustments as you go. When you decide to invest in content marketing, you'll want to focus on the most pressing business needs driving your company at any given point in time.

Make a list of your primary objectives for content marketing. Some organizations may be primarily focused on establishing or expanding brand recognition within their industry, while others may want to focus on reaching new markets and generating new sales or leads. Multiple goals are also normal.

Now, prioritize. What are the top 1–3 most important, pressing business goals for your company at this time that you want content marketing to achieve? Here's a prompt: "The top three factors driving my organization to invest in a content marketing strategy are . . ." Write these down.

Are there ways to quantify these objectives? For example, The Nursing School knows they want to increase enrollment to fill 90% of class capacity (up from the 75% capacity of the previous years). Having some sort of quantifiable goal will be helpful when it comes time to check in on your progress. So, even if it's as simple as "increase website traffic overall by 5%," it's good to have at least some sort of objective that can be measured at your next content audit.

THE IMPORTANCE OF A DOCUMENTED CONTENT STRATEGY

"Remember, content is a team sport."

—**Kristina Halvorson and Melissa Rach,**
Content Strategy for the Web

A documented content strategy can mean the difference between reaching your target and drifting away. You know how when you write something down, you're more likely to actually do it? This principle applies to content marketing. As we've been advocating this whole time, if you're serious about making headway with content marketing, spend the time upfront to get clear, focused, and ready to succeed.

In short, a documented content strategy helps you stay on track:

1. **It keeps your content production focused on business goals.** It's important to know where you want to go and what you want your content to achieve. Documenting your strategy helps keep you focused on the results you want.
2. **It keeps your content production process organized and effective.** If you're producing a lot of content, organization is key to maintaining a steady and smooth output across multiple team members.
3. **It maintains a historical record for reference.** A content tracker and documented strategy can help orient any new content managers in the case of a personnel shift. It's also useful to have a reference point to look back on at any point in the strategizing process.

Content marketing, when done well, is inherently connected to other aspects of your marketing endeavors—and not separate. These content marketing documents you create—your content strategy, content tracker, and content calendar—can be strategically shared with other departments in your organization. For example, sales and customer service departments can communicate to the content team what audience needs and concerns they experience, which can inform your search research for relevant topics.

Strategic content marketing pushes you to refine and focus your messaging. Maybe a sales team member notices that customers seem to be highly interested in some specific aspect of your products. If this message can be effectively transmitted to the content developers, they can align their content around this customer interest. Aligning resources in this way puts content at the forefront, not on the sidelines, as a vital piece of your company's momentum.

A content strategy is not unlike a business plan. It can inform everyone of the purpose of content creation, keep high-level executive communication on the same page, inform budgets, and keep everyone on track. Content marketing doesn't work as well if it operates in a silo or in a separate division from the rest of marketing. Everybody needs to be on board, understanding the value of producing high-quality, relevant content that's on message.

Someone—whether that's a content strategist, the head of the web department, or the marketing director—needs to have ownership of the content strategy. Whether that's you or someone else, there needs to be at least one voice in the company driving the strategy forward and streamlining the efforts of different departments. This person, ideally, has a deep understanding of content strategy and can make informed, high-level decisions when necessary; communicates with other departments regularly; and keeps the content team aligned with the business's goals. As Lee Odden says in *Optimize*, "content isn't king, it's the *kingdom*."[1] Any successful kingdom needs some sort of centralization. Consider your documented content strategy the central focus for your content marketing as it evolves.

PUT YOUR CONTENT STRATEGY INTO WRITING

As promised, we've designed a content strategy template you can use as a blueprint for your organization, as shown in Figure 17.1. (You can also download it from ContentShift.com/Resources.) This is a fairly simple, straightforward, top-level document that can serve as a starting point—you can fill it in with as much detail as your heart desires, or you can keep it simple and just make brief notes for now. It's all up to you.

The main goal of this content strategy template is to motivate you to put your content strategy into writing so you know *why* you're doing what you're doing. This template prompts you to move toward your goals by acknowledging your unique business objectives, your specific target audiences, your precise search research, and your particular content production resources and methods (we'll talk more about this last one in Chapter 19).

You'll notice that most of the template is fairly high-level. Each one of the categories can be expanded upon with its own research and documentation. All we need to see in this template are the most important bullet points, knowing we can access deeper information elsewhere. This template is designed with three spaces for each question, but you may wish to fill out more or less than three. Anywhere between two and five bullet points for each question is a good range. More, and you might start to get overwhelmed and unfocused. Less, and you might unnecessarily limit your options.

Much of the information you may be able to fill in already using the research covered earlier in the book. The last section on the template called "Production" includes questions that will be covered in the next few chapters, so don't worry—we will explain how to fill those in. You can leave them blank for now and come back to them later.

If there are other categories you have identified as essential to document in your overall content strategy, add them as you see fit. Add notes where you need them. Your content strategy should be a living, breathing document specific to your needs.

We recommend checking in on your content strategy once every six months, or however often you feel is necessary to monitor your progress and keep on track. Whatever you do, don't just fill it out once and let it collect virtual dust on your computer. Your content strategy should evolve with your company and your audience, so keep your eyes open for changing trends and goals within and outside of your organization—and update it accordingly.

Figure 17.1: Content Strategy Template

Name of company: _____
Date: _____
Completed by: _____

Company Information

Type of Company: Basic background information.

1. What does your company do or sell?
   _____

2. B2B or B2C?
   _____

3. Legal structure of company?
   _____

General Business Objectives: Overall, the type of growth you'd like to see for your company.

1. Tangible result you'd like to see:
   _____

2. Tangible result you'd like to see:
   _____

3. Tangible result you'd like to see:
   _____

Specific Business Objectives: Take each item from above and add numbers and dates (if applicable).

We'd like to (achieve tangible result) by (amount or degree) in (time frame).

1. We'd like to _____ by _____ in _____ .
2. We'd like to _____ by _____ in _____ .
3. We'd like to _____ by _____ in _____ .

Audience Research

Audience: Identify your primary audience groups.

1. Target group #1:
   _____

2. Target group #2:
   _____

3. Target group #3:
   _____

Personas: Write down your primary personas.

1. Persona #1:

2. Persona #2:

3. Persona #3:

Audience Needs: Identify some of the most pressing needs or questions you have discovered across all audience groups.

1. Audience Need #1:

2. Audience Need #2:

3. Audience Need #3:

Refer to audience research documentation.

Search Research

Priority Focus: What is your marketing team's business direction during this time frame? These goals will direct the search-focused topics you'll write about.

Core Pages to Support: Identify the pages on your website that are most relevant to meeting your business objectives.

1. Core Page #1:

2. Core Page #2:

3. Core Page #3:

Core Keywords: List the keywords most relevant to your core pages and audience needs.

1. Core Keyword #1:

2. Core Keyword #2:

3. Core Keyword #3:

Refer to search research documentation.

Production

Content Marketing Goals: These should both fulfill your audience's needs and meet your business objectives.

Content Goal #1: _____
Content Goal #2: _____
Content Goal #3: _____

Primary Content Types: Determine the best types of content to reach your audience.

Content Type #1: _____
Content Type #2: _____
Content Type #3: _____

Content Production Goals: Identify reasonable goals to hit your business objectives.

Production Goal #1: _____
Production Goal #2: _____
Production Goal #3: _____

Content Auditing Schedule: Determine how often to check in on your content strategy.

Conduct a content audit with metrics reporting every _____ months.

One-Sentence Vision Statement: Express the big vision of your content marketing plan. Use this as an ideal to strive for, and base it on the reality of your audience's needs and your company's business objectives. Think big and envision what your greatest content marketing success would look like.

_____
_____

This content strategy is scheduled to be assessed and updated by _____.

IDENTIFY YOUR CONTENT MARKETING GOALS

As you fill in the "Production" section of your template, you'll want to identify your primary *content marketing goals* (related to but slightly different from business goals). Your content marketing goals should arise from a logical blend of two things: your audience research and your business objectives. Your content should add value to your audience's lives while working toward your business objectives. For example, if The Nursing School wanted to increase leads (a clear business objective) and also help potential nursing students learn about the nursing career path (a clear audience need), a content marketing goal might read: "Inform and educate potential nursing students about the benefits of a nursing training program."

Your content marketing goal should be a win-win: good for your business and good for your audience. If you're unsure what your audience's needs are, go back and do more audience and search research until you feel confident. Once you have the tools down, you'll find that crafting a content strategy that works for you is less of a one-time procedure and more of a constantly evolving, multi-faceted process.

Take a look at the example content strategy template that we've filled out for The Nursing School (shown in Figure 17.2). You'll notice most of the fields have been covered in earlier chapters, and we're pulling the information straight from the work we've already done. The rest of the fields in the "Production" section (such as content types, content production, and the content auditing schedule) will be covered in the next few chapters.

Figure 17.2: Example Content Strategy Template for The Nursing School

Name of company: The Nursing School
Date: October 1, 2020
Completed by: Mark Hawks and Jon Heinl

Company Information

Type of Company: Basic background information.

1. What does your company do or sell? Nursing training programs
2. B2B or B2C? B2C
3. Legal structure of company? For-profit corporation

General Business Objectives: Overall, the type of growth you'd like to see for your company.

1. Tangible result you'd like to see: Increase leads
2. Tangible result you'd like to see: Increase enrollment
3. Tangible result you'd like to see: Increase organic website traffic

Specific Business Objectives: Take each item from above and add numbers and dates.

We'd like to (achieve tangible result) by (amount or degree) in (time frame).

We'd like to increase enrollment to 90% capacity by next year's enrollment season.

We'd like to increase website traffic by 10% in 6 months.

Audience Research

Audience: Identify your primary audience groups.

1. Target Group #1: High school graduates
2. Target Group #2: Career-seeking mothers
3. Target Group #3: Working nursing assistants

Personas: Write down your primary personas.

1. Persona #1: High School Heather
2. Persona #2: Career-Change Connie
3. Persona #3: Nursing Assistant Nancy

Audience Needs: Identify some of the most pressing needs you have discovered across all audience groups.

1. Audience Need #1: Financial: Career and income security
2. Audience Need #2: Intellectual: Information and resources
3. Audience Need #3: Emotional: Support and encouragement

Refer to audience research documentation.

Search Research

Priority Focus: What is your marketing team's business direction during this time frame? These goals will direct the search-focused topics you'll write about.

Drive leads to nursing training program pages.
Core Pages to Support: Identify the pages on your website that are most relevant to meeting your business objectives.

1. Core Page #1:   Overview of Programs
2. Core Page #2:   Program—LPN Nursing
3. Core Page #3:   Program—RN Training

Core Keywords: List the keywords most relevant to your core pages and audience needs.

1. Core Keyword #1:   Nursing Training
2. Core Keyword #2:   Nursing Programs
3. Core Keyword #3:   Nursing School

Refer to search research documentation.

Production

Content Marketing Goals: These should both fulfill your audience's needs and meet your business objectives.

Content Goal #1: Inform and educate potential nursing students about the benefits of a nursing training program.
Content Goal #2: Inspire and encourage prospective students to inquire about nursing programs.
Content Goal #3: Show the benefits of a nursing career.

Primary Content Types: Determine the best types of content to reach your audience.

Content Type #1:   Blog posts
Content Type #2:   Infographics
Content Type #3:   Videos

Content Production Goals: Identify reasonable goals to hit your business objectives.

Production Goal #1:   Publish three blog posts per week
Production Goal #2:   Publish one infographic per quarter
Production Goal #3:   Publish two student spotlight videos/month

Content Auditing Schedule: Determine how often to check in on your content strategy.

Conduct a content audit with metrics reporting every 6 months.

> **One-Sentence Vision Statement:** Express the big vision of your content marketing plan. Use this as an ideal to strive for, and base it on the reality of your audience's needs and your company's business objectives. Think big and envision what your greatest content marketing success would look like.
>
> *Become the top online resource for prospective and current nursing students by producing exemplary informational content that helps nurses achieve the career of their dreams.*
>
> This content strategy is scheduled to be assessed and updated by [Month/Day/Year].

TRACK AND SCHEDULE EVERY PIECE OF CONTENT

> "Because content marketing is a long-term strategy and often involves multiple content producers, customers, and outside influencers, keeping track of all the stories and formats (online or offline) can be tricky... and problematic."
>
> **—Joe Pulizzi,** *Epic Content Marketing*

Your content strategy is your bird's-eye-view map. It has all the important elements: your business goals, audience information, search focus, production process, and big vision. Once you lock that into place, you don't necessarily need to update it every day; though, like we said before, you'll want to revisit it every once in a while. It might be helpful for your content team to print out a master copy and have it posted in the office (or otherwise easily viewable). This will ensure these focal points don't somehow evaporate and then everyone finds themselves wondering how they got so far off track. For sure, keep them handy.

As for your everyday content documentation, you'll need a *content tracker*. A content tracker can also be called a *content planner*, or a *content map*, and it may or may not double as an *editorial calendar*. You'll find different people talking about these tools in different ways, but, essentially, you need a way to keep track of all the content you're going to produce, who's producing it, when it's scheduled to go live, and any other important details. It's also a good idea to include the goal or strategy behind each piece.

There are lots of different ways to track your content, but the important thing is that you do it. You might have one master planner—perhaps in Excel or Google Sheets—with different tabs for different projects. Or your content planning system might be multiple documents, each with a specific focus. You might even find software online that works for you. (We've developed our own tracker template, which you can find and download from ContentShift.com/Resources.)

There are a lot of moving pieces, a lot of details, and tons of tiny nuances that come with strategically producing online content, so it can seem burdensome at first to track everything you do. But this tool is nonnegotiable! Find a way that works for your team, and make sure everyone involved in the content creation process is properly trained and consistently using the system.

So, why do we need to have a content tracker? Because investing a few additional minutes upfront to track everything can save you countless hours down the road. Once it comes time to conduct your regular content audit, you'll need to have some way of reminding yourself of what's been published in order to assess whether you're hitting your goals. You'll need to be able to easily see what you're doing and how it's working from a distance.

If you get into the habit of putting every single piece of content into a tracker, it can show you opportunities as well as holes in your strategy. And, as we noted, it can also save you a lot of time down the line when you suddenly need to know where something is, who wrote it, or what happened to that piece of content. No one wants the unnecessary headache of losing any content, which is surprisingly easy to do.

If you're also using the tracker as a calendar, it's vitally helpful to know who's doing what, and when. You can look at data in myriad ways, skim titles to see what's missing, and notice opportunities for improvement. There are so many reasons to keep a tracker, but the bottom line is this: It adds order to what is potentially a very messy process. Without a content tracker, expect content chaos.

Figure 17.3 shows an example of a simple internal content tracker.

Title	Author	Status	URL	Date
Awesome Content	John Doe	Published	www.website.com/awesome	15-Oct-22
There's a Beverage Present	The Dude	In Queue	www.seosavvy.com/beverage	Goal Dec 2022
More Good Stuff	Jane Doe	In Editing	www.interwebs.com	Goal Mar 2023
The Dude Abides	Jeffrey Lebowski	Ideation	http://hero.fandom.com	Goal Jan 2024

Figure 17.3: Simple Content Tracker

Using Google Sheets or Excel is a simple, easy way to keep track of all the content you produce.

As you can see in Figure 17.3, there are just five columns:

- **Title:** Title of the content piece.
- **Author:** The author of the piece.
- **Status:** Publication status, such as Ideation, In Writing, In Editing, In Queue, and finally Published.
- **URL:** Once published, insert the URL where the content is located.
- **Date:** You could update this every time the tracker is updated until the piece is published. Or you can list the publication goal date. Then, put the final publication date once it's live.

Depending on the type of information you want to track, your content tracker may be much more detailed, and that's great. There are nearly endless categories you could choose to add to your tracker, but it's important to only track the information that's going to help you achieve your business objectives. If you try to track everything, you run the risk of overwhelming yourself and cluttering your strategy with unnecessary details. Take stock of the elements you need to track for your goals and process, and build the tracking document into your everyday process.

If you want a more nuanced tracking system, you can mix and match categories to your preference. For example, one advanced tracking system might incorporate workflow status, audience direction, search research, and content goals. It may be a little more effort at first, but a detailed content tracker can provide a central location to document the thought process for each content piece. Here are five main elements we might recommend adding to your advanced content tracker:

Workflow Status

This could be a top-level category to track where the content piece is in production. If you have a more involved production process, like with separate writers, editors, and graphic designers, you could break out categories for each one to include the name and date of each step. This could be helpful if you have a content manager who is responsible for knowing where any given piece of content is at any time. A simpler version could just be columns for "Production Status" and "Date." Tracking workflow status can be helpful to see who is managing a content piece at any given time within a team.

Audience Direction

This top-level category would be a place for any audience research notes. Especially if you have multiple audience groups, this category could help direct the content to appeal to certain readers or viewers. You may have categories for audience groups, personas, or just a broad category for audience notes.

Search Research

This category is meant to use any search discoveries you've already made in the research phase to help guide production. You could create a column for targeted keywords to focus the writing, a column for related keywords to inspire further content ideas, or a column for keyword-focused subheadings to assist with organization. If you are researching your search competitors, you could have a column for notes about how to make your content better or different than what's already out there.

Content Goals

This category is a space to clearly define the goals and direction for every single piece of content. It could be a succinct description of what the content will do, such as "educate and inform about X topic" or "inspire readers to reach out to learn more." Content goals help keep a piece of content on track, especially if production is handled by a few different people. You might want a column for content type (which we'll discuss further in Chapter 18). And to go even deeper, you could add a column for the Search Cycle to determine which stage the piece is targeting.

Optimization

This category is to track any optimization notes that could make post-production run more smoothly. (We'll talk more about optimization strategies in Chapter 18.) We find that people often forget to optimize, so having a dedicated space on your content tracker could be useful. Since driving traffic to product and service pages is often a primary goal of content marketing, you could have a column specifying which core pages to target. Don't forget to cross-link to them! You can also take note of other related pages you've published as additional cross-link opportunities. You could track image files to use with the post, tags, categories, meta-descriptions, or anything else that might help you optimize the published content later.

These are some ideas for creating a detailed content tracker, but you really don't want to get so deep in the weeds that you lose sight of the big picture. Think about what makes sense for your team and your scope. Try out a few things, then adjust as needed.

We want every piece of content we produce to perform, though not every piece will perform the same way. Some pieces of content will generate more sales or leads than others, but each individual page, post, video, etc. needs to have a specific goal or purpose in mind. Your content strategy (your overall compass) will guide each piece of content.

If you don't know why your content exists, then it probably shouldn't. What are you helping people achieve? How are you making your customers' lives easier? A piece of content should satisfy both your business objectives and your audience's needs.

Consider these questions for every piece of content you produce:

1. Why are you producing it? What will the content give to the reader? How does it promote your business objectives?
2. Who is the audience? Who is it primarily written for?
3. Where or how is it going to be seen? What is the platform and distribution plan?*

Having a content tracker helps you get a visual overview of your progress over time. A piece of content should never just be published and forgotten but tracked and updated over time as necessary.

Reasons for keeping a content tracker:

1. It keeps your content organized.
2. You can group content by related subject.
3. It tracks your search optimization strategy (cross-links, page targets, anchor text).
4. It shows you what's been done so you don't accidentally duplicate content.
5. It can help you expand your topics by seeing the connections between ideas.
6. It allows you to revisit content goals at a later date.
7. It keeps your internal team on the same page.
8. It prevents confusion down the line.
9. It allows you to update keywords, links, and news as appropriate.

---

* Constructing a comprehensive distribution plan is outside the scope of this book, but it should definitely be a consideration if you plan on using other channels, such as social media or other forms of sharing.

Even if you aren't sure how to use your content tracker yet, just get started. If you have content already created, start thinking about how to fill in your columns, tabs, and rows with information that will help give you a clearer picture of how your content is working for you. For more information on using your tracker as an editorial calendar, check out Joe Pulizzi's recommendations in his book *Epic Content Marketing* (found on page 204).

POINTS OF DISCOVERY

Now that you know how important it is to document your content strategy, you can use the template provided in this chapter and the following questions to keep moving forward:

1. Make a list of all your business objectives related to content marketing. Next, number them in order of current priority. What are the top three? These will drive your content marketing decisions.
2. Fill in the content strategy template with as much information as you are fairly certain about right now. What is missing? How can you go about filling in those blanks? What additional information or further action is needed?
3. Begin using a content tracker. What are the most important details for you to track given your company's objectives and resources?

Chapter 18

CONTENT TYPES AND OPTIMIZATION

An optimized content marketing strategy is a plan for delivering thoughtful content with certain audiences and outcomes in mind.

—Lee Odden, Optimize

ptimization is an important term in search marketing and generally means using strategies to make your content more easily discoverable in search. We've already done a lot of the work to discover the keywords, related subjects, and opportunities that'll help us create search-focused content. Now, it's time to focus on optimizing that content.

Optimization isn't about stuffing your blog post with keywords to improve your rankings; it's more holistic than that. We want to optimize our content for search, yes, but we also want to optimize our content for the user. In essence, we want to optimize our *strategy* for best results. This includes optimizing our content to support other pages on our websites, especially core pages. We want to optimize everything we do so it becomes more efficient, more effective, and more reliable over time.

And yes, of course, optimization involves using keywords and SEO techniques. But first, we must know which *types of content* to produce for our audience and goals. Remember, you're uncovering what your audience is searching for, and your content should fill that need. For example, if you're marketing to casual diners of classic American restaurants, you're certainly not going to choose whitepapers as your primary content strategy. You need to know what type of content your audience likes to consume and tailor it to those platforms. (That being said, we have a favorite type of content that we believe can be adapted for nearly any business, and we'll share that recommendation later in this chapter.)

CONTENT TYPES BY LEVEL OF ACCESSIBILITY

Different types of content come with varying resource requirements. Generally speaking, the more involved the production is, the greater the investment of time and energy (and money as well). We've broken down some of the major content types into categories based on how resource-intensive they are to create. When we say that anybody can create content, it's true. There are types of content for which the barrier to entry is very low. And there are also some types of content that require huge teams, expertise, and budgets.

If you're looking for a thorough breakdown of virtually every type of content you could possibly create, you'll find a wonderfully comprehensive list by Joe Pulizzi in his book *Epic Content Marketing*. Here, in the sections that follow, you'll find an overview of what we think are some of the most common and useful types of content to consider. You can choose what's appropriate for you.

Level One: Low Barrier to Entry

Some types of content have what's known as a "low barrier to entry." This means they're fairly easy to produce and are accessible to nearly everyone. Examples include:

- Blogs
- Written Articles
- Simple Web Pages
- Graphics (Custom Images, Photography, Headers)

Blogs, Written Articles, and Simple Web Pages

One of the easiest ways for anyone to get started with content marketing is to begin creating blog posts. Just a moment ago, we gave you a little teaser about our favorite content types. Well, it's blog posts! We think they are the simplest, easiest, and best way to get started doing content marketing for any business of any size. You can produce a pretty good amount of quality content relatively easily. If you were to *only* use blog posts as your primary content type, we'd be pretty confident that you'd be in good shape.

Most website platforms are already set up to handle blogs, so there's not a whole lot of extra work to do to get started. If you can write, you can write blog posts, and blogs are great for SEO. Having a blog is absolutely the easiest pathway into content marketing, and it'll fit into nearly anyone's strategy because you can publish at any time, you can optimize your text for keywords, and you can share the post with your network on other platforms, like social media, or via email. (Fun fact: This is how Jon got his start in this industry—writing "web logs" for his band back in the '90s.)

For beginners, we recommend starting with blog posts or web pages and expanding from there. Your website is where your products and services are located, so we want to publish content that will drive traffic to your core pages. Using your keyword research (especially related to subjects of interest to your audience), you can start putting together a content schedule for topics you confidently expect to resonate with your target audiences. Whether you hire writers or produce the blog posts yourself, it's not too difficult or resource-intensive to start publishing high-quality writing to attract the type of people you think will be interested in what you have to offer.

> Did you know the word "blog" came about in 1999 as a shortened version of the phrase "web log," which was originally used to describe the process of "logging the web"?[1]

Graphics

If your blog post says 500 words, then a picture says a thousand. Images are another way to put content out there with your unique stamp. We live in a visual society—images are immediately appealing and can convey a feeling or mood differently than written text alone. Whenever possible, a marriage of text and visuals is best. At minimum, all blog posts should be accompanied by at least one image. Ideally, you use images to break up the text, connect more deeply to the topic, visualize data, and help readers scan the document.

The great news is that you don't have to be a graphic designer to start producing some really sharp-looking images. There are some great websites out there that can help even the most technically challenged among us. Canva.com is one of them, and it's free and easy to make eye-catching visual materials to complement your blog posts (or to feature on their own).

Did you know you can optimize your images so they also show up in search results? All images should be optimized for search wherever possible because it's an easy way to get even more search traction out of your posts. It's not hard to optimize images, but it's easy for non-SEOs to overlook. (Keep reading for more on this best practice later in the chapter.)

Level Two: Medium Barrier to Entry

You might find yourself wanting to invest in creating content that takes a little more planning and effort to produce. For the right audiences and on the right platforms, these content types could yield great return:

- Infographics
- Whitepapers
- E-guides

Some content types require a bit more lead time, capital, resources, or planning to execute well. Infographics, whitepapers, and e-guides fall into this category. They take a little more time and strategy, but, for the right audiences and with the right strategy, they can really elevate your content marketing game.

Infographics

The Internet loves infographics. They are the perfect blend of images, numbers, and text, and they're designed to convey a brief yet condensed amount of knowledge in one visually appealing image. Infographics tend to be really social-friendly and engaging because they don't require a whole lot of investment to enjoy. You can glance over an infographic in a few seconds, enjoy the aesthetic, and easily find the information you're interested in.

Infographics require a bit more of an up-front investment of resources than writing a simple blog post. There are more moving parts: You'll need a graphic designer, a writer, a researcher, and a fact-checker. Sometimes these roles may overlap, and if one person has all these skills, you've hit the jackpot.

The most important element of getting an infographic right is having a great graphic designer to pull the disparate pieces of information together. Following that, you'll want to make sure the research is thoroughly fact-checked and organized. An infographic that looks sloppy or disorganized—or that conveys inaccurate or incomplete information—would be a waste of effort, so be sure to go all the way if you're going this route.

Whitepapers

Whitepapers also take more time and resources to do well. They are especially great for B2B businesses whose audience includes industry experts, as they tend to explore a specific subject more deeply and thoroughly than a regular blog post. It's not uncommon for whitepapers to be anywhere from 10 to 100 pages long. For businesses that could benefit from explaining the nuances of a subject, whitepapers may be well worth the time and effort. They can be excellent lead generators and sales tools.

The most important element of a whitepaper is hiring an excellent writer and researcher. The value of a whitepaper is that it positions you as a subject expert in your field, so you've got to make sure the information you're conveying is factual, current, well-organized, well-researched, and appropriately cited. Because your ultimate goal is to win more business, it helps to write the whitepaper from an angle that conveys your unique perspective. The time and energy you spend creating a really thorough whitepaper could help you nurture leads and convince them of your expertise and value.

E-guides

E-guides are similar to whitepapers but are less academic and technical. They're not quite long enough to be books, but they are substantial enough to be considered long-form content. Often formatted as a downloadable PDF, e-guides are a company's take on a subject matter in their wheelhouse, often used as informative guides or sales tools. The name is what it sounds like: consider them bulky enough to be a guidebook, like a multipage booklet giving an overview of a topic.

The value is that they are long enough for you to explore a topic in depth and convey your expertise to a potential customer or client, including the benefits of your product or service. The benefit to your customer is that (when done well) they can learn what they need to learn for free. Consider it extended space to answer questions in a streamlined, cohesive manner. The range is really flexible, but you might see a three-page long e-guide or one that's twenty or fifty pages long, depending on the scope and goals of the content.

An e-guide might be something like "Guide to a Nursing Career" and might include a few of the most important topics from your keyword research. Once you've produced a substantial amount of blog posts, you could combine the best topics into an e-guide, offering a one-stop shop in a fancy format. Consider the research, organization, writing, editing, formatting, uploading, and marketing to make an e-guide compelling as a guidebook and sales tool. Once an e-guide is out there for people to find, it can be a great source of incoming leads when you offer it to prospective and current clients.

Level Three: High Barrier to Entry

Certain types of content require a substantial investment of time, money, and energy to produce but may have excellent return value. These types of content, when produced with expertise, can go a long way in expanding your audience base and creating long-lasting relationships:

- Videos
- Podcasts
- Online Classes/Webinars

The more complex a project is, the more resources and planning it will require. Producing videos, podcasts, and webinars can be amazing ways to build and engage a consistent audience base. While anyone can potentially record a video or podcast simply on their smartphone or computer, to do these well with a high level of quality might require additional resources and a bit more planning. Producing content like this can be an entire project on its own, potentially involving a recording studio or equipment, cameras, and editing software, or lighting and sound considerations. Though generally more complex with more equipment and technical necessities, if you have the resources, creating this type of content can be one of the best ways to connect online.

Videos

Videos are one of the most popular and engaging forms of content, and online video usage is actually on the rise. According to HubSpot, 72% of consumers polled in a survey said they'd rather watch a video tutorial to learn about a product or service than read written text.[2] (Video is also becoming more prominent in SERPs.) Regularly posting to a YouTube channel or other video platform can help you reach the audiences that love to consume content in that format.

Podcasts

Podcasts have become hugely popular in the last few years, providing a fantastic way to offer valuable insight or information on your topic to the audiences using that platform. According to Statista, 44% of Americans listen to podcasts.[3] And why not? Many of us are often driving in our cars, walking or working out, cleaning, or performing other tasks that don't require our full mental attention. Queue podcasts. With over 850,000 podcasts out there as of January 2020, it's easy to find podcasts on nearly any topic you might be interested in.[4] And if there's not a podcast out there in your specific industry, or if you think you would be able to sustain a consistent and ongoing conversation with a unique angle, why not consider creating your own?

We classify podcasts as "high barrier to entry" for a few reasons. Like videos, you will need to build your podcast platform, which means figuring out where and how often to post, what your angle is, what to call it, and how to attract an audience. Within this process, you will need to decide how and where to record, what recording or editing equipment and skills you will need, and all the marketing that goes along with any product—like copy, graphics, optimization, and sharing.

Generally, you'll need to have a host with a great personality and a good "radio voice." You may decide to do interviews or just share information and insight on different topics each week. Most importantly, you'll need to be consistent. We wouldn't recommend starting a podcast if you're not fully committed to the idea. Podcasts generally need to come out regularly, such as once or twice weekly, or release a certain number of episodes for a "season" to be successful in the long run. Also equally important: Don't be boring! How will you make sure that what you're saying is interesting enough for people to spend their precious time listening to? Figure that part out, and the rest is a cakewalk.

Online Classes/Webinars

Finally, offering online classes is a great way to share your knowledge, build your audience base, and even create another revenue stream if that's appropriate for your business. Webinars and online courses present an excellent opportunity for those companies that have skilled teachers and relevant topics to share.

Like videos and podcasts, there needs to be a lot of upfront energy to produce and market an online class. Are you a trusted authority in your field? Are people already aware of your expertise and want to learn from you? Or can you effectively convey why your class will be valuable? If so, you might benefit from offering an online class. Depending on your model, you may actually charge a fee for this type of content, especially if it's exclusive, high-level knowledge, or if it's a series of classes over a period of time. Or you may offer a free one-day webinar here and there to attract new audiences and build your authority in your field.

Whichever way you do it, you will obviously want to take great care to offer a class or webinar that is truly packed full of value. The process of signing people up for a class or webinar doesn't have to be complicated, but you will need a method of tracking sign-ups, delivering content, and engaging with your participants. This is all simply a process that will need to be managed, as if this were a real college course through a university. Yes, take your class as seriously as a field of higher education because then you will be motivated to provide unparalleled instruction to your attendees, which is the most important element of any online class or webinar.

Each of these content types can potentially have a great return on investment, but there is usually a concentrated investment of time, money, and planning required up front, as well as regular and consistent production. Make sure to do enough audience research to determine whether these are mediums that a high percentage of your audience actually consumes before deciding to pull the trigger, and take the time to create a production and marketing plan to ensure success.

Level Four: Very High Barrier to Entry

Some content types are not accessible to everyone but may be appropriate for some businesses who are focused on growth. These content types may require a specialized skill or expertise and may require a very high level of commitment and investment to produce:

- Apps
- Magazines/Catalogs
- Books (Print or ebook)

Similar to videos, podcasts, and webinars, there are some types of content that exist entirely separately from your actual business, yet are related to it, and are solely meant to complement your products and services without directly bringing attention to them. This type of content can take on a life of its own and become renowned for the value it delivers, pure and simple, without any more than a brand connection to your business.

Apps

Some companies may want to take it upon themselves to become industry experts by offering tools and resources that can help people live their lives better or become more informed in a certain area. Creating an app is not for the average Joe, but you might be in an industry where you can create your own software to complement your primary business services. If you have a great programmer or developer in your corner, maybe they can create online apps to help your audience function more efficiently.

Giving people a new tool that makes their lives easier or better through technology is clearly a way of offering a high level of value. Creating an app may come at a very high cost in terms of time and money—including developing, then testing, then publicizing, then maintaining—depending on how complex your idea is. But the benefits can be exponential. You could decide to offer the app for a fee, creating a passive revenue stream. Or you could create a subscription community around your tools. Either way, this type of content morphs from just "content" to "product," as in something that exists alongside but separately from your primary business.

Magazines/Catalogs

If you want to become an actual publisher of magazines or catalogs whose focus is high journalistic integrity—and not just positioning your products and services—you can take it upon yourself to release a regular publication as a separate addition to your company to build brand trust and authority. The ultimate achievement is when your company becomes synonymous with value in your field. When what you deliver becomes less about marketing and more about the quality you're offering, you may have entered the realm of "publication" in addition to just "content." Magazines or other sorts of quality periodicals operate more like a publishing house than a marketing department, and like apps, this type of content can truly become its own entity.

Think back to our earlier John Deere example. The agricultural resources offered by this magazine excelled in such a way that the content has since become an authority of value beyond any direct tie to the products and services they offer. The magazine is not selling John Deere products; it has essentially become such an authority in the field that the magazine's role is now in service to the industry, more like journalism than marketing. Again, this level of content production would be essentially like running another business, separate but related to your primary products or services.

Books (Print or Ebook)

Finally, if you want to collect your knowledge in a book, you can use this format to share what you know with a wider audience and help people gain in-depth knowledge about a subject you know well. Any writer will tell you that writing a book that people actually want to read is no light task. While e-guides can be published fairly easily, the ease of technology is not the hard part about writing a book. In fact, it is now easier than ever before to publish a book—with print-on-demand and self-publishing tools aplenty—but it is no easier than before to write a book.

Writing a book in and of itself may take anywhere from six months to many years. More than that, you must have something unique, substantial, and worthwhile to say—or be able to research your way into quality. Do you have years of experience in your field and a unique viewpoint or angle that you think will help people? Like podcasts and classes, what are you able to say that people will want to commit time to reading and learning about? If you think you have knowledge or insight that simply must be shared with the world, a book could be a great investment.

Reading a book is a time commitment, but if you are offering true value, a book can be a fantastic resource that people will keep on their shelf and return to again and again. As for production, the writing is the hardest part, most likely, but you will also need a book designer, cover designer, publisher or self-publishing outlet, copyeditor/proofreader, blurbs/foreword, book marketing copy, and a way of getting all your hard work out into the world.

The bottom line: Blog posts and graphics are the easiest and most accessible way to start producing high-quality content consistently. With a dedicated plan and consistent production schedule, you may consider expanding into more complex forms of content creation. Ask what types of content would best serve your audience, and create a plan that will work for you. (The plan part is very important!)

DETERMINING THE BEST PLATFORM FOR YOUR CONTENT

It's always a good idea to research the content that's already out there on the subjects you're interested in pursuing, regardless of the type of content you produce. Researching your topical space online is especially important before deciding to create more resource-intensive materials. Are there already a dozen podcasts out there on your subject? How could yours be different or nuanced? Or, if there aren't any substantial resources in your industry, how could you stand out and fill a niche?

Let's consider Career-Change Connie for a moment—a persona of The Nursing School—and ask ourselves, "What content mediums does she use?" For example, does she watch video tutorials? Does she listen to podcasts on her way to work? Does she flip through mailed magazines in the evening? What else is already out there, and how might you best reach your intended audience, offer unique value, and grow your business?"

Once you've thought about the relationship between the various content types and your audience, return to your content strategy template (the one we shared in Chapter 17, Figure 17.1), and fill in the "Primary Content Types" category with any content types you think would be a good fit for your strategy right now. If you're not sure, web pages and blog posts are the most universal content type to begin with.

Throughout the rest of the book, we'll be focusing on blog posts as our primary content type (our favorite type of content that anyone can use). Blogs are the most accessible vehicle for content—both for content creators and online users—and they offer the greatest benefit to most organizations, regardless of your company type, what your capacity is, or who your audience is. The caveat, of course, is that there are plenty of content types to explore using your available resources and best judgment—not just blogs!—but they're definitely the easiest when you're first starting out.

> 93% of B2B marketers reported using blog posts and 75% said they generated leads with content marketing during the last 12 months.[5]

6 ESSENTIAL SEO ON-PAGE OPTIMIZATION ELEMENTS

No matter which platform or medium you're using, there are ways to optimize the visibility of your content in search. Most content platforms that exist—whether that's a blog post, an Amazon listing, or a YouTube video—offer custom options for posting on the page. This is called **on-page optimization**. On-page optimization includes elements like titles, subtitles, headings, tags, categories, custom URLs, image file name, alt text, and meta-descriptions for the page. Using relevant keywords and linking strategically within the post itself are also ways of optimizing content so that search engines will deliver your content consistently and often to the relevant audiences. Optimizing content for search (on every platform you are using) should be incorporated into your content production process. (We'll talk more about content production in Chapter 19.)

In the next sections, we'll cover what we believe are the six most important elements of on-page optimization—i.e., what you should be doing for every piece of written content you publish. Bear with us as we dive into the weeds just a bit. This is technical information that we believe is highly important to your content marketing success, and we've made it as accessible as possible for the non-SEOs out there. Everyone should have a basic knowledge of on-page optimization. We recommend putting each piece of content through the following checklist before publishing.

#1: Title

First impressions mean a lot! Titles are the first thing a user will see, and it's one of the most important SEO elements. If you're using a platform like WordPress, by default, the title of your post also becomes part of the meta-title, the URL, and the H1 tag, which are heavily used by search engines to determine relevancy to a query.

Titles should be keyword optimized, accurate to the body of the post, and competitive to similar topics already out there. The best titles are not too long. According to HubSpot, blog titles with 6–13 words get the most consistent number of views.[6] If possible, add some creativity and uniqueness as well to pique the interest of your readers. Lots of people make an entire living writing titles for media organizations, which should tell you how important they are. Definitely not an element to be overlooked!

#2: Cross-Links

You'll be creating lots of content across multiple topics, and it's a good practice to always be linking internally to your own content and pages wherever it's relevant and natural. *Internal cross-linking* is a key element of on-page optimization because it helps the spiders and robots connect the dots between topic ideas and increase the topic strength of related posts. Links also provide a helpful trail for users to follow if they want to know more about a subject. Just think about how Wikipedia opens up new doors with every link—you'll want your content strategy to do the same.

Since you'll be creating posts intentionally around specific topics relevant to your business, think about cross-linking as a way to create useful channels for users and search engines to follow. The *anchor text* of a link (the text being linked) should be relevant and keyword-optimized to give a reader and a search robot a descriptive sense of what the linked content or page is about. For example, if you add a clickable link to the word *nursing training*, it would make sense to link to a page about that topic and not something completely different. (This should be obvious.) Because content marketing is ultimately driving your business goals, you'll want to link both to your core product pages as well as to your other relevant content or blog posts. That way, your nursing training link could reasonably point to a core page listing The Nursing School's training programs.

Internal cross-linking is an often-overlooked practice that consistently increases your visibility online because it shows search engines that you have built a wealth of knowledge around related subjects. It also sends a signal to the search engines that you still value this content; if you don't link to your own content, why should search engines? As an advanced tactic, once you have already created a robust amount of content, you can always go back to old posts and find opportunities to add relevant cross-links. No piece of content is an island—always link to yourself when relevant!

#3: Length

People often ask about the ideal length of a blog post or other piece of content. There's no easy answer. Quality is the most important element, so our advice is this: Make it as long as it needs to be. If it only takes 400 words to answer a simple question, don't ramble on just to fill up space. (Jon hates fluff! Fluff is the enemy!) As Dr. Suess says, "So the writer who breeds more words than he needs is making a chore for the reader who reads."[7]

However, here's a good rule of thumb: The more in-depth you can go with a topic, the better. Just make sure you don't lose focus. Outlining and formatting your content based on the questions people are asking about the topic can help you stay on track. Consider how much depth a reader would want from a specific topic. What will it take to answer the question and related questions completely? Use this as your compass.

You can also check out what your competitors are doing and notice opportunities to fill in the gaps. If you hope to outrank them as a subject authority, you probably need to cover a topic from a different angle, offer a unique perspective, or expand coverage of a topic. This generally amounts to a longer post. In general, trends show a typical blogger's post increases in length over time. The length of a typical blog post in 2019, according to Orbit Media, was 1,050 words, compared to an average of 808 words in 2014.[8] Blogging statistics and trends from Orbit Media show that posts are getting longer.[9]

#4: Formatting

Since we're living, writing, and publishing in the digital age, it's essential to consider how your piece of content appears visually on the page. It should be easy to read, appealing to view, and easy to skim through (43% of readers skim blog posts, according to HubSpot).[10]

Especially if you have a long post, breaking up the information naturally is essential. Readers on the Internet are often looking for specific information, so formatting your post with subheadings, bullet points, and numbered lists (where it makes sense) can go a long way in helping your reader appreciate the information you're conveying. Using italics, underlining, bold, and breakout information boxes, where appropriate, are all great ways to highlight important information.

There's a search benefit to intentional formatting, too! Formatting helps search engines identify key pieces of information, so use SEO best practices for every piece of content. For example, format your subheadings with H2, H3, H4 (and so on) tags appropriately, maintaining a sense of consistency as much as possible. Highlight, embolden, italicize, or break out definitions; these might be picked up in Google's Featured Snippets section. Utilize your exact keyword phrases where it's natural and organic. You can always look at similar posts online for ideas about how to format your content. Remember, both search engines and users love information that's easy to read and consume!

#5: Call-to-Action (CTA)

Your content should be engaging, informative, and valuable to your readers while also supporting your business goals. We recommend having some sort of call-to-action within or around every piece of content you create. These don't have to be obnoxious, flashy advertisements; in fact, it's better if they're not. But let's say a user is so convinced by the quality of your content that they want to learn more about your services—you should definitely give them the option!

A CTA can be as simple as embedding a newsletter sign-up form in the footer of your website or cross-linking to a core page. If it makes sense, it can be a direct offer, coupon, or another traditional CTA, but be careful not to appear gimmicky. There are ways to include CTAs in a natural, organic way within or around every post. Don't forget that the business reason for content marketing is to drive leads or sales, so always allow an option for further engagement.

Visit ContentShift.com/Resources for more in-depth tutorials on crafting CTAs.

#6: Images

Most users prefer images to text and tend to read longer posts if they're broken up by images. Posts that include images produce 650% higher engagement than text-only posts, according to WebDAM.[11] It makes sense: Humans are visual creatures and it's much easier to view an image than read a paragraph.

Here's the general rule of thumb: *Always include images.* Basically, consider optimizing all your written posts with images to make them more appealing. Images should break up text and connect to the information. This helps skimmers better understand subsections more easily.

An SEO note for optimizing images: Always name your image files. Don't leave it a generic name like IMG-123.jpg, not just because it's ugly but because images are searchable, too. Giving your image files unique, relevant, and optimized names (using keywords and hyphens between words) increases the chances it will appear in Google's Image results, usually with a link to the page that's hosting it. You don't need to think too much about it; just use common sense to describe the image in a few words. For example, brown-teddy-bear.jpg is much better than IMG-567.jpg. It's easy and worthwhile to make optimizing images a regular habit.

POINTS OF DISCOVERY

Now that you have a pretty good idea of some options to produce different content types, consider what you have to offer and in what format your audience might want to encounter your content:

1. Consider which types of content would be best for your audience. Do some research to test your theories. When you're ready, go back and fill in the "Content Types" section of your content strategy template (found in Chapter 17, Figure 17.1).
2. Consider how important optimization is for your content's visibility. How can you make sure you include on-page optimization in your content production process?
3. What are some ways you could improve calls-to-action across your website?

Chapter 19

STREAMLINING YOUR CONTENT PRODUCTION PROCESS

Great content meets users' needs and supports key business objectives. It engages and informs. It's well-written and intuitively organized. It keeps people coming back for more.

—Kristina Halvorson and Melissa Rach,
Content Strategy for the Web

If you and your content marketing team want your content to be *purposeful* for your company (aligned with your strategic vision and goals) and *valuable* for your audience (offering a benefit to them), you'll need a process to execute it efficiently. Your content should be a gourmet meal, and not fast food. Understandably, it takes more skill to prepare an eight-course meal than it does to flip a hamburger. Likewise, content that excels online will have a team of talented writers and producers behind it. Even if this "team" is just you at first—or if your team is newly learning content marketing—getting a process down helps to cut out the frustration, set expectations, and keep tasks on track.

In this chapter, we'll be looking specifically at the most important things to consider when it comes time to actually sit down and produce content. Ideally, your team has spent time researching, planning, and strategizing. At this point, everyone knows who your audience is, and you've produced a good amount of keyword research and search analysis.

Your content strategy has been documented. Now you're ready to use all this raw intellectual energy to start *producing*. Finally, right?

Because your content marketing team has invested in developing a strategy, the actual execution should be less confusing, less frustrating, and far more effective than if you had bypassed that work and jumped straight into the driver's seat. Doing your prep work is like taking your driver's test before being given a license—the entire purpose is to prevent accidents and prepare you for long-term success on the open road.

As you begin the process of creating content, you'll learn which specific tools, resources, documents, software, and habits work best for you and your team. We've provided as many tools and recommendations as we can, and in addition to our preferences, there are plenty of automated tools, platforms, and different types of software you may consider integrating into your production process. But first, we want to share some of the most important considerations that we've discovered from producing content for companies over the last decade.

TO HIRE OR NOT TO HIRE? IN-HOUSE VS. OUTSOURCING

Previously, we talked about the importance of thinking like a publisher. Of course, there are many types of publishers—online publications, print periodicals, tabloids, book publishers, news publishers, etc. While the scope of each publishing venture may vary, what do they all have in common? A team of skilled writers, editors, and producers. Similarly, the best content marketing success stories also have a group of extremely talented people behind the scenes. But who are these people, and where do you find them?

You may be wondering whether it's better to hire an in-house content production team or to outsource the work. There are pros and cons to each, and we'll go over them here. See Figure 19.1 for a quick snapshot.

In-House Advantages	In-House Considerations
Strong interpersonal relationships. Team members know the brand well, are aligned with company goals, and can easily hit the mark.	Requires a large commitment of time, money, and resources for content management. Not every company can afford the large budget necessary for a complete content team.
A dedicated team supports a steady and consistent output of content.	In-house writers may run the risk of topic fatigue or burnout if only focusing on a narrow range of subjects.
Employees can grow with your brand and contribute their ideas for innovation.	More employees require more management.

Figure 19.1: In-House Advantages and Considerations

Hiring an in-house team can be a surefire way to invest in your content marketing efforts and ensure quality control. An in-house team may consist of some or all of the following roles:

- Content Strategist
- Content Manager
- Managing Editor
- Writer
- Copyeditor
- Proofreader
- Graphic Artist
- Videographer
- Web Designer and/or Developer
- Subject Matter Experts
- SEO Specialist

Your team will consist of the people and roles that are right for your business, but it's essential to have at least some kind of central organizational role, such as a content strategist, manager, or editor who essentially directs the flow of content traffic, assigns tasks, delegates, reports, and innovates.[1]

Outsourcing content production, on the other hand, can also be a good way to get a solid hold on your content output, especially for companies that want to start small and scale up later. See Figure 19.2 for a brief overview. Ideally, at least one in-house person will be responsible for managing and directing the flow of content using outsourced talent. This person would wear a lot of hats and would likely fill multiple roles—such as manager, editor, and proofreader—while managing a team of content producers from afar.

Outsourcing Advantages	Outsourcing Considerations
Relatively easy, inexpensive, and efficient to grow your content output without needing to hire an entire publishing team.	You may need to try out a few different online platforms to find one that best suits your needs to hire freelance writers.
You can utilize a wide variety of writers and content producers with different perspectives to infuse your content with originality and freshness. You may find subject matter experts who deliver consistent quality.	Some initial time up front doing research and screening is usually necessary. A bit of trial and error might be necessary as you try out different writers to find the right fit. This process may need to be repeated regularly.
You can swiftly scale up or down depending on your needs. Outsourcing offers flexibility and the option to produce more or less content without a full commitment to a dedicated team.	You'll need a dedicated person to manage the outsourcing process and workflow. A content manager ensures quality and consistency.

Figure 19.2: Outsourcing Advantages and Considerations

Whether outsourcing or training an in-house team, all the moving pieces should be held together by a documented content strategy and at least one person directing the flow of work.

PRIORITIZE AND SCHEDULE CONTENT TOPICS

> "Selecting topics isn't about brainstorming a list of interesting subjects. It's about narrowing the field—finding the right topic areas to meet your specific set of business requirements and user needs."
>
> —Kristina Halvorson and Melissa Rach,
> *Content Strategy for the Web*

As we noted earlier in the book, once your team gets the hang of search research, you shouldn't have to face the problem of "What do I write about?" ever again. Going forward, whenever you encounter this question, simply conduct some search research to help you uncover relevant content ideas. Once you have the bulk of your research squared away, you can hone in on the topics that will best help you to reach your goals. (From here on out, we'll be referring primarily to written content, but you can also adapt this for video, podcasting, webinars, or other forms of media.)

While it may seem counterintuitive at first (we tend to want bigger, better, and broader), the more specific and nuanced your content can be, the more effectively you can establish your company as an authority in the field. Everyone's brand—and therefore, angle—is different. In order to become truly confident in content marketing, it's important to establish *what* you have to offer specifically and uniquely and *why* your company and your content exists in the first place. Now return to some of the questions you've identified in your keyword research. Which ones are your priority topics?

We encourage you to prioritize evergreen topics that relate closely to your core products and services, or the core pages of your website. All content should support your business objectives, and the closer your questions and keywords are to those, the higher their priority. Create content around those topics.

Hopefully, by now, you've discovered some promising evergreen topics to write about. If not, return to Chapter 14 to conduct some search research and start identifying topics. Once you have a solid handful of evergreen topics to choose from (however many you want to start with), let's dive into those ideas and estimate what it will take to produce them. Consider the following:

- What will it take to make each post better than what's already out there? In other words, what will it take to make your content robust rather than easily forgettable? Return to your competitor research.
- What's the easiest starting point? Different topics will have varying degrees of complexity, so one strategy would be to start with the shorter, more accessible topics to build forward momentum.
- How long will an identified topic or piece of content take to produce? Consider the amount of investment for the level of return. Would you rather produce a greater number of less-intensive pieces or a smaller number of high-intensive pieces? Consider the types of content that serve your audience best.
- And, of course, put everything in the content tracker and/or editorial calendar.

We've found the most efficient way to tackle your content goals is to do this strategic work up front for a batch of different content pieces all at once, generating a whole bunch of titles or topics. This could mean sitting down with your content team once a month to document your plan for the next four weeks, or you could plan ahead every quarter. Then, you can schedule out some ideal dates for completion and publication. For example, if you're producing four blog posts per month, consider planning ahead for three months, for a total of 12 topic titles.

If you're working with an in-house team, you might have regular meetings to generate topics and schedule forward. An in-house team would naturally have more investment and involvement in the process, while an outsourced content team would typically be less hands-on. The bulk of responsibility would fall to the content manager to assign tasks and deadlines, give direction and feedback, and apply the finishing touches to every piece of content in the pipeline.

PREPARING YOUR CONTENT BLUEPRINT

Creating an outline for each piece of content keeps you and your team moving in the right direction. Whether you're writing the content, you've hired an in-house writer, or you're outsourcing to content producers, you can use your content strategy, keyword research, and style guide (which we'll discuss in Chapter 20) to create a blueprint for production. In most cases, the more direction you give a writer, the better the results will be. In-house writers would already be close enough to the company that they might not need much more than an overview of the topic and focus. Outsourced writers may need more direction to stay aligned with your goals and your brand, and your content manager would typically handle this type of direction.

Whichever team structure you have, your writers should want to do a good job, and they can hit the mark better if you know what you're aiming for. The more focused direction you can give, the better the content will turn out. Not everyone knows the best practices for SEO optimization, so you'll want to provide as much information as you can for your writers to ensure your content comes back well-optimized, well-written, and consistent with your company's style.

Using Search Research to Create a Simple Outline

A simple and streamlined way to create a content outline is to use your search research as the skeleton of your written piece of content. Titles and subheadings, as discussed earlier, are not only great ways to break up information for the reader, but they're also useful in flagging content topics for search engines.

We can grab the keywords that we've found to be relevant and build a content outline around them. This will guide production, which accomplishes two things: 1) It helps the writer know what subjects to write about, and 2) it does a lot of the work for you so you (or the writer) can spend more time writing a great piece and less time trying to figure out how to structure it.

Use keyword and search research to inform titles and subheadings. Use related keywords to broaden, narrow, or define the scope of your article. Not every title and subheading needs to contain keywords, but you should always be looking for opportunities to do so naturally.

To illustrate, we'll use the search research we've already done for The Nursing School, using the core keyword "nursing school" to flesh out an outline. (Although the following example is for a written medium—a blog post—you can adapt this idea to craft a content outline for other types of media as well.)

Returning to our keyword research from the subject discovery template (illustrated in Chapter 15, Figure 15.1), we've chosen topics that are relevant, highly searched, and evergreen. Scanning the list, we've decided to start with the following two keyword topics:

- Question: How long is nursing school?
- Question: How much is nursing school?

We chose these topics for a few reasons: 1) The search volume is high, 2) the questions are relevant to the business and to the audience, 3) the questions appear in the information gathering stage of the Search Cycle, and 4) the topics are relatively evergreen. The information may need to be updated every few years, but the question will likely remain the same.

Now, to fill out the rest of your outline for this topic, you have a few options. If you already have some related questions identified in your keyword research, definitely find which ones would make sense to include in this outline. A title is the highest-level topic. From there, look for subtopics that would logically continue answering the question. Not every subtopic needs to be search-researched, but it's always better if it is. If your search-volume results identify a clear need to answer a subquestion, and if that subquestion makes sense within the logic of the outline, include it.

If there are no clear contenders for subheadings within the main topic, narrow in on your topic by performing a little more search research. For example, take your main topic—such as, "how long is nursing school"—and use that as a new starting point. Type that query into SEMrush, Google, or your preferred keyword software, and see what *related topics* come up. This strategy is sometimes referred to as a "content tree." The main topic is the trunk of the tree, and the related topics are the branches (which become your subheadings). Using the content tree approach can help you make a list of related topics for your title.

Once you have your list of related topics, it's time to think about the logical order of ideas and how to satisfy both your audience's curiosity about the topic while also relating the copy to your business objectives. If a subheading doesn't seem relevant to either your audience or your business goals, think twice before including it. (Remember: The business goals we determined for The Nursing School included *increasing leads*, and the content goals included *informing prospective students about their options*).

Next, consider how to convert your visitors into leads. If there's an opportunity in the copy to include a call-to-action naturally and organically, great. If not, we might expect there to be a sign-up form in the footer or some other type of CTA toward the bottom.

Using our two keyword examples, we've created some sample outlines using just the other keywords from our research. Keep in mind, it might not always work out this way; sometimes you may need to dive a bit deeper to find related topics. But, if it does work out like this, it's always a wonderful synchronicity because most of the research has already been done. Now, it's just a matter of putting things in order.

In the following example outlines, shown in Figure 19.3, we've maintained the bold from the original template to signify the top-priority topics. Remember, search volume is a search research metric signifying how many people are searching for that exact phrase every month.

> **Outline Example #1:**
>
> H1: How long is nursing school (Search Volume: 4,400)
>   H2: How many years is nursing school (Search Volume: 1,000)
>   H2: Is nursing school worth it (Search Volume: 210)
>   H2: When do you apply for nursing school (Search Volume: 40)
>
> **Outline Example #2:**
>
> H1: How much is nursing school (Search Volume: 880)
>   H2: How to pay for nursing school (Search Volume: 260)
>   H3: How to get scholarships for nursing school (Search Volume: 70)
>   H3: Who gives nursing school loans (Search Volume: 0)
>   H3: Is it possible to work and go to nursing school (Search Volume: 90)
>   H2: Where can I go to nursing school for free (Search Volume: 30)
>   H2: Is nursing school worth it (Search Volume: 210)

Figure 19.3: Outline Examples

Refining Your Outline and Directing Your Writer

It can be helpful for the writer to identify a few bullet points of direction within each section, as well as keywords that would ideally fit well within that section. We haven't done that here, just to keep it simple, but you can get as detailed as you need to with each outline before giving it to a writer.

Don't forget to check out your competitors and see if there are any holes or gaps you can fill in to create content that stands above the crowd. You may include some keyword direction for the writer, too. Don't try too hard to stuff the post with keywords, but if you already have a list of potential keywords, use that to discover opportunities to direct the content. Don't forget about those head terms and mid-tail keywords that might naturally, organically occur in discussion about the topic. Direct the writer to work those in where they fit.

This outlining process shouldn't take very long if you've already documented your search research, audience research, and content strategy. It's really just a matter of putting all the pieces into an organized outline that your writer can use as a compass for their production. It's a win-win: The writer is given the tools they need to produce exactly what you want, and you can be confident that you'll receive exactly what you want! This is the entire goal of defining a content strategy: It makes smooth sailing of the actual content production process.

Another way to help this process along is to have some boilerplate guidelines ready to go—either as a checklist for an in-house writer or as an introduction to an outsourced writer. This might be a condensed version of your company's style, goals, audience, and tone—as well as any other details about your general expectations. These guidelines should be written up in a boilerplate format and given to your writers as a baseline expectation. You may have a word count expectation for each section, or for the article as a whole. Likewise, you may have company-specific information to include where relevant.

Here's a quick summary of the most common considerations for outlining a piece of written content:

- Title direction (keywords to use)
- Subheadings (keywords to use)
- Keywords to use naturally and organically within the body of the article
- Sources to use (or avoid), if applicable, and how to cite them
- Topics to cover
- Persona or audience group to address (if applicable)
- The business goals of the piece
- A reminder to write a conclusion
- A reminder to add a call-to-action (where appropriate)
- Notes for image direction (where and what types of images to include)
- Any other helpful information (such as style and formatting)
- Related content within your website you want to cross-link to

EXECUTE, REFINE, DESIGN, AND PUBLISH

Once the piece of content is produced, it can be tempting to rush ahead to the finish line and *just publish the thing already*. However, it's worth the extra time to give each piece of content a thorough copyedit and proofread so you don't turn off any potential customers with a glaring typo or funky sentence. If you have an in-house content manager, this person may also act as the editor, or you could have a role entirely designated for editorial management.

Conversely, if you don't have a developed content team, and if you don't feel equipped to act as editor yourself, don't just skip this step! There are plenty of editing tools out there that can do this step for you, or you can hire a freelance editor from afar. In the next chapter, we'll talk more about ensuring quality and style.

> "The value of an editor cannot be understated. The editor is the proxy for the audience."
>
> **—Ann Handley**

Presentation is important, and web users have a low tolerance for bad user experience, so make sure that, in addition to an editor, your marketing department has a skilled graphic or web designer on hand whenever needed. Visually appealing content is more effective, more interesting, and more shareable, so you'll want to package your content in a way that does it justice.

Finally, it's important to document workflow in some way—whether that's in a company-wide content manual or a simple one-page guideline. Consider how the team's workflow relates to the content tracker; for example, putting in deadlines, the author's name, the project's status, etc. (You may have noticed a pattern by now: Document Everything!)

As you're getting started, keep in mind that getting *your* content marketing process down will be unique to your company. In the next chapter, we'll go through the final piece of content production: ensuring you have some guidelines in place—*before you publish anything*—to ensure the highest quality production of everything you do.

POINTS OF DISCOVERY

Are you ready to start producing? Consider the following notes to help you during this process:

1. Take stock of your team if you already have one. If you don't, use this exercise to imagine your ideal content production team. Make a list of all the roles needed to execute your content production strategy on a regular basis. (If you need help, check out the list of roles we noted at the start of this chapter.) For example, if you decide to focus on producing a podcast, you'll need different skillsets than if you were producing a series of infographics. Also, consider the type of content production team that fits your company best right now. Is it in-house, outsourcing, or a combination?
2. Review your list of green-lighted content topics—the ones you identified in Chapter 14. Start prioritizing your topics using the guiding questions we shared earlier in this chapter in the section "Prioritize and Schedule Content Topics." From there, begin planning and scheduling the content pieces you want to produce.
3. Choose the green-lighted content topic that you've determined to be your top priority. Using your keyword research, craft a general outline for the piece. Remember to think about what will set this piece of content apart from the competition. Now's the time to start bringing those elements into planning and production.

Chapter 20

CREATING QUALITY AND STYLE GUIDELINES FOR YOUR BRAND

In our world, quality content means content that is packed with clear utility and is brimming with inspiration, and it has relentless empathy for the audience.

—Ann Handley

Your content speaks for you—and about you. What is yours saying to your audience and your peers? Does it say you're meticulous and astute when it comes to creating valuable information online? Does it say that you consider your customers' concerns and have a unique brand identity that people can't get enough of?

Your answer should be *yes*. Throughout the content production process, you'll need to be focused on producing consistent, quality content that highlights your company's style, expresses your brand identity, and invites your audience to engage. If we haven't already made it abundantly clear (though, we expect we have by now!), higher-quality content will perform *better* in search results than low-quality content, allowing you to reach more of your potential customers.

MAINTAIN A HIGH STANDARD OF QUALITY

One of the biggest misconceptions we run into with clients is that doing content marketing should be fast, cheap, and hyper-efficient—like churning out products on an assembly line. While we all want to increase efficiency and lower our costs, there needs to be some form of quality control in place to ensure high standards.

What do we mean by "high standards?" The entire point of content marketing is to get people to interact with your content and your brand—and it's pretty simple when you think about it: They're not going to do that if your content sucks! At the very least, you want to create content that doesn't deter people from visiting your website or leave a negative impression. Even with all the best research in the world, it's still possible to fall short on the actual *execution*.

That is to say, put as much thought and energy into creating the content as you did preparing for it. A lot of people don't realize the time and energy that goes into creating a well-written piece of content. They think, "If it's easy to *read*, then it must have been easy to *write*." But the opposite is true.

Let's get specific with an example. In this hypothetical scenario, let's say you're an online textbook retailer and you want to increase your influence in this space. You outsource some content to post on your blog because you don't have a large budget, yet you want to expand your reach online. If you're doing this, it's essential to check your sources and manage the content's style, quality, and readability. You don't want to publish just anything you receive. Let's see what a "bargain bin" piece of content might look like that hasn't been fact-checked, edited, or checked for quality:

American History Textbooks

America has a long history of events. Civil war to womens voting, the United States people are a very rich people with a long history. In 1776, the declaration of Independence started the country off on the right foot. Today, American people are valuing their freedom that started from this long history. But who knows the constitutional amendments? It's important to know your history, American people don't know as much as they could. But where to find that information? Sure, the Internet has a lot but what about American History Textbooks? American History Textbooks are the only way to learn about American History...

While this is not an argument against outsourcing content, the point is that this paragraph is an example of flat, thin content that doesn't prioritize the audience or offer value, and, therefore, it doesn't succeed in accomplishing any of your business objectives. It's unlikely that this piece of content would perform well in search or in readers' minds, no matter how much search research you've done.

Even with the best technical SEO, anyone who comes across this page probably wouldn't stay long because it offers nothing of substance. Likewise, this content would not create the most favorable impression of the website, which aspires to be a resource for textbooks. Your company can actually suffer from poor content when readers form negative associations in their minds with your company.

On the other hand, consider something like the following:

Why Every College Student Should Take an American History Class

If you're considering taking an American history class in college, you might be wondering what you can expect to learn. You've probably taken some sort of American history class in high school, or been exposed to various elements of the United States' rich and storied past through TV specials on the History Channel. You might also be wondering how learning about the specific dates of Civil War battles from long ago could possibly have any relevance to your life today. How does the Battle of Little Bighorn have anything to do with your interests or your field of study? These are all valid considerations, especially if history isn't your primary concentration in school...

Notice the difference between the two pieces. The first is a generic, unspecific, poorly constructed string of words with an overt emphasis on the website's product: textbooks. It doesn't offer anything of specific value or interest but peppers the paragraph with random dates and obvious examples, and the title would not be likely to grab anyone's attention. The second piece, on the other hand, offers a unique title with an argument that could entice the target audience: college students.

Notice that the second piece doesn't reference textbooks at all. Instead, it begins an argument in a conversational tone that anticipates the reader's concerns. We can expect that the rest of the article would go on to make substantial, convincing arguments for taking an American history class in college. Though textbooks aren't mentioned at all, this piece of content understands the audience, addresses the reader's needs, answers potential questions, and offers insights and analysis in a conversational tone. This method is more likely to create a positive association in the reader's mind, and when it comes time to purchasing textbooks, a reader may already know where to look, especially if the rest of the site contributes to a positive experience.

Content is not a commodity; it is communication. Thinking of content as a commodity is a losing mindset. While you can pay peanuts online to have someone somewhere across the world bust out a generic, mediocre string of written words, what exactly would that accomplish? Sure, it's fast and cheap. But you know what they say, you get to pick two of the three: fast, cheap, or good. The closer your content producers are to your content marketing goals and the more intimate their relationship is with your brand, the better your content will be.

When it comes to content marketing, there's not a lot of value in taking shortcuts. It can actually hurt you to have too much useless content. Google could lower or omit your website, or sections of it. You don't want readers to be overwhelmed by the *quantity* of content on your site yet underwhelmed by its *quality*. Treating content like a valuable conversation rather than a commodity is more likely to achieve authentic engagement, positive impressions, and sustained interest.

What NOT To Do

It's often better to create no content than to create bad content. As Google's quality guidelines imply, the search engine rewards high-quality, relevant, and useful content—which also indicates that it does *not* reward, and sometimes even penalizes, websites if it's clear that a majority of the pages are low quality. Anything Google considers spam or junk will not return favorable results for your company. Most bad content arises from a lack of planning, a lack of understanding, or carelessness. Don't let your brand get caught in the mire of junk content.

Here are some of the red flags that Google uses to identify low-quality content:

- **Spun content:** This is content that is automatically generated; i.e., constructed by computer programs and not written by humans. For example, some computer programs can take an original piece of writing and rewrite it so that it's uniquely worded but not uniquely produced. This sort of content will not connect with readers since it lacks the emotional and psychological depth of authentic human connection. Remember, you're writing for humans, not search engines.
- **Thin content:** This refers to pages with little or no original content. Often, you'll see very thin pages that are only a few sentences long. These pages are usually considered low quality because they add little to no value to the conversation. They can be viewed as "clickbait" or page traps. For example, a headline may seem to indicate an interesting article, but, when landing on the page, the thin content shows a serious lack of thought. It's a lazy way to publish content. The page probably either shouldn't exist at all if it adds nothing of substance or it should be significantly reworked to contribute value. (A caveat: not all short-form content is bad, and there are some scenarios where it makes sense, but think it through carefully. Consider: if the bulk of a website is short-form, low-quality content, that's not a great sign.)
- **Scraped content:** Sometimes webmasters will make the mistake of

simply republishing good content from another site without asking permission or adding any unique insight. Not only is this plagiarizing, but it's also copyright infringement. So, avoid scraping content unless you're excited by the prospect of legal action and potentially having your site shut down. It's a common misconception that the more pages you have, the better; however, it adds no value to your website to essentially "steal," or copy, someone else's content and publish it as your own. Even if you quote a source correctly, it's bad practice to fill an entire page with someone else's material (and, likely, a violation of fair use). Make sure to add your own insight, analysis, or point of view so that the content is a conversation and not regurgitation.

- **Keyword stuffing:** While keywords are an essential part of any SEO strategy, you should never sacrifice a thoughtful and well-crafted message for the sake of loading the copy with irrelevant or excessively redundant keywords. Use keywords naturally and organically, and don't allow too many keywords to distract you from the main purpose of your content and the message you wish to convey.

Here are some other features of weak content that will hinder your growth rather than improve your content marketing:

- **Offensive:** Be sure not to use language that is sexist, racist, prejudiced, or in any way clearly offensive to a particular group of people. It's not just common sense, either. Google allows users to flag content for various reasons, including content that "promotes hate or violence against a group of people," contains "racial slurs or extremely offensive terminology," "graphic violence," and "explicit how-to information about harmful activities."[1] We hope this would be obvious.
- **Boring:** This one may be harder to define, but a good rule of thumb is to ask yourself whether you can actually remain engaged in the content yourself. If you can't, it's a good indicator your readers won't either. (Exceptions can be made for technical writing that might be dry by nature, but if you can jazz it up, do!)

- **Lacks personality:** Even if your subject is solid, a reader may lose interest if the content doesn't feel authentic. Users want to feel connected, and honing your brand voice can help achieve this. It helps to think about writing like you're having a conversation with the reader.
- **Overly promotional:** Users shy away from overt promotion because it often comes across as too salesy or inauthentic. If you have a call-to-action or a selling point, make sure it is conveyed in a genuine manner and that the rest of your content provides value.
- **Redundant:** Content that says the same thing over and over again in slightly different ways isn't likely to retain a reader's interest. Economy of language and uniqueness keep a reader engaged.
- **Hard to read:** If your content is a huge block of text, or filled with typos, it will be easy to overwhelm a reader and lose their attention. Make sure your text is as accessible as possible by incorporating visuals, utilizing whitespace and formatting best practices, and proofreading everything before it goes out the door.
- **Trendy without substance:** Riding the wave of popular topics is great as long as you have something interesting and unique to add. Just touching on a trendy item without adding anything new or relevant fosters distrust in users, which leads us to our next point.
- **Untrustworthy:** With the massive amount of data available on the Internet, false claims are too often perpetuated and passed off as fact. Cite your sources and do the work to make sure that what you're putting out is trustworthy information.

Using Style to Tell a Better Story

Alright, now that we've beaten you over the head with a reminder that quality is essential (don't produce content that sucks), we can move ahead and talk about style. Style is specific to purpose. If your purpose is to produce YouTube videos that are so quirky and funny that you get millions of views and lots of ad revenue, "style" is going to look different for you than for the company whose purpose is to provide the most affordable sheet metal for large-scale construction projects. In every scenario, it's important to understand your purpose and then align your content with audience interests, *using style as a tool for connection.*

> **QUALITY ASSURANCE CHECKLIST**
>
> We've talked about it already, but let's do a quick refresher. Google has four basic principles in their quality guidelines:[2]
>
> - Make pages primarily for users, not for search engines.
> - Don't deceive your users.
> - Avoid tricks intended to improve search engine rankings. A useful test is to ask, "Does this help my users? Would I produce this content if search engines didn't exist?"
> - Think about what makes your website unique, valuable, or engaging. Make your website stand out from others in your field.
>
> You may have your own internal quality assurance checklist, but every content marketing plan should incorporate these elements into their content production process:
>
> - ☐ Double-check any facts cited.
> - ☐ Run content through plagiarism software to make sure it's unique.
> - ☐ Make sure you properly cite your sources with footnotes, links, or other appropriate attribution.
> - ☐ Copyedit your content for formatting, sense, and flow.
> - ☐ Proofread for spelling and grammar.

Every piece of content you create should aim to meaningfully contribute to your customers' lives. The content shift directs the focus of your content toward your audience. Every person who finds your content online has limited time—and an abundance of options—so they won't tolerate low-value content. They want something that means something to them. Offering value to your customers' lives means understanding them.

Your voice, tone, and aesthetic should directly reflect the messages you want to send to meaningfully connect with your audience.

THINK LIKE A PUBLISHER: REFER TO YOUR STYLE GUIDE

If you're creating content to bolster your brand, a style guide can keep your voice, tone, message, and visual style consistent and coherent for a better user experience. No matter the size of your company, a style guide can save you time on every piece of content by outlining certain parameters that need to be implemented during the content production process.

As you can probably see by now, a "documented content strategy" consists of many written guidelines that are designed to keep your content flow steady and productive. And a style guide is one of them. You don't need to have a 50-page manual; your style guide could be as simple as a one-page document, outlining the elements of style that will guide your content production.

Like most of the documents you're creating, your style guide can and should be a living, breathing document that is updated whenever a new consideration arises.

Your style guide may include any of the following, and more:

- **Color palette:** Defining a few key colors to use across your content will go a long way in creating a consistent look and feel.
- **Logo and usage guidelines:** Having a logo is a no-brainer. But do you have specific guidelines for how to use the logo in different scenarios, such as resizing or sharing? If not, sit down and make sure your logo won't get distorted.
- **Voice:** Voice describes how you choose to use language to communicate as a brand, and this is a huge part of creating a brand identity.
- **Graphics:** Visual imagery is an obviously important factor, and your company can decide what types of images best fit the brand's style and purpose.

- **Typography:** Fonts say a lot! Don't overlook the importance of appropriate and consistent font usage.
- **Punctuation, syntax, and formatting guidelines:** It's helpful to have a documented process when it comes to editing and publishing content.
- **Brand personality/story:** Your mission, vision, and origin story are the foundation of your brand identity and your company's purpose.

You may find that you can inform your content marketing style guide with other department's guidelines, and it might be useful for your entire marketing division. Find out what differentiates you, highlight that in your content, and deliver that unique spark consistently.

> Be the magazine on the porch that people want and not the unwanted flyers taped to your door.

Your Company's Voice Shines through Your Content

Defining your voice clears the channel of communication between you and your potential customers, giving you the best chance of being identified and heard. Voice is your company's distinct personality. A strong and consistent brand voice differentiates your content from your competitors', and it serves to align your message and products with your content across all the materials you produce.

For example, Tony Robbins, world-renowned life coach and motivational speaker, has created an entire brand around his unique voice. His content tends to be inspiring, uplifting, encouraging, and passionate. You'll see throughout all his podcasts, videos, lectures, and blog posts that his voice stays true to his message—that positive intention can empower great change. He utilizes bold, accessible language to embody this voice of motivation. His voice sounds like this:

- **From a blog post:**
  "There are many ways to empower. But at its core the formula is simple: Serve, enjoy, work and live with passion!"

- **From a pop-up ad:**
  "Ready to take the initiative & join our newsletter?"

- **From a byline:**
  "Team Tony cultivates, curates and shares Tony Robbins' stories and core principles to help others achieve an extraordinary life."

You can see that throughout his entire site, the voice is consistent, strong, and on message. People know what to expect from Tony Robbins.

Understandably, you may start to think that your particular product or service doesn't easily possess a unique voice. Let's say you're a helmet manufacturing company. Your voice doesn't have to be over-the-top. In fact, the goal is to be streamlined—*the **way** you communicate is perfectly in alignment with **what** you are communicating.* In this example, a helmet manufacturing company is likely out to communicate the importance of safety, and so a strong company voice could be focused around that value. You could be the "voice of reason," or your voice could aim to "make safety cool," or maybe your voice strives to "warn of the dangers." Your voice, at the heart of it, tells the story of who you are and what you offer.

Your voice should be authentic. Pardot's research reveals that 80% of consumers believe "authenticity of content" is the primary factor that influences their decision to follow a brand.[3] The more defined your brand identity, and the more you are able to consistently produce content that captures your message in a way that's specific to your company, the better aligned your content will feel to the people consuming it. Style can encompass a lot of different brand elements, both in written and visual form.

Here are some questions to consider when thinking about your company voice:[4]

1. What do you want your content to communicate to readers?
2. If your readers were to choose a few adjectives to describe your brand's voice, what words would you want them to use?
3. Consider the purpose of your content. Is it primarily to inform, entertain, or motivate to action? What elements of voice would best achieve this goal?
4. Think about your target audience. What kind of voice would you imagine resonating with them? Is it authoritative, friendly, fact-driven, etc.?
5. What elements do you want to avoid in your voice? For example, you may want to avoid coming across as arrogant, ignorant, sloppy, elitist, etc.
6. Imagine a conversation with your target customer, or listen to one of your sales reps as they talk to a customer. Take note of how messages are conveyed, what seems to resonate and what doesn't.

Consider how The Nursing School is more than a business trying to enroll students. Going to nursing school is also a turning point in many people's lives. As such, the company might aim for a voice that's encouraging, reassuring, and empathetic. Each piece of content you create will be unique, but a consistent voice throughout all your written materials gives your brand a strong sense of identification to better connect with the audience in mind.

Discovering an Overarching Vision Statement

Finally, what about the one-sentence vision statement at the bottom of our content strategy template? This should be a simple statement directing the big vision of your content marketing efforts. It should encompass your highest goals, what you hope to achieve, and what your ideal content marketing results would look like.

Consider what your content would achieve in an ideal world, for both you and your audience. Let's pretend you have all the money for content marketing that you could possibly want, no limits and no restraints. You also have exactly the type of talented team members you could ever hope for, all the tools and resources you could possibly need, and all the time you need to execute your ideas perfectly. Think about your highest aspirations for your company and the best, most ideal type of content you want to be creating. If you already have a mission or vision statement for your company, let your content marketing vision naturally be informed by your business vision.

Perhaps a vision statement for The Nursing School would read:

Become the top online resource for prospective and current nursing students by producing exemplary informational content that helps nurses achieve the career of their dreams.

From this, you can spin off into various types of guiding statements. For example, perhaps a tagline speaking directly to the audience could read: "Embrace your passion, fulfill your dreams, move forward into a job you love . . . *Let us help you heal the world.*"

To go above and beyond, give your readers and customers content that resonates with them, moves them, connects with them, and inspires them. Storytelling is another way of thinking about creating *content that connects.* We all have stories, and the more you can tell your customer's story back to them so they feel understood, heard, validated, and inspired, the stronger and more authentic a bond you create.

Your entire brand should be cohesive and on message, using content to show your audience that you're walking the walk, not just talking the talk. Your vision statement, voice, style guide, and content creation process all work together. For example, you could think about how The Nursing School positively impacts people's lives and write moving blog posts, show captivating photos and videos, feature alumni on social media, etc.

For a closer look at the elements of a one-sentence guiding statement, check out Kristina Halvorson and Melissa Rach's book *Content Strategy for the Web*.

A NOTE ABOUT "BORING" INDUSTRIES

Even if you think your field isn't fun, cool, or exciting (and sure, maybe you're no Red Bull performing outrageous stunts), any industry can create content that speaks rather than sells. If you're focused on the specific needs of your audience, and if your product or service can help them, you can create compelling content. Don't try to be more exciting than you are because that could easily work against you. Consider a car insurance company. Maybe filling out forms is a drag, but consider the drama of getting into a car accident. If you can make your car insurance business a positive part of your customer's story when they need it the most, consider how impactful that is.

Rather than focus on what you think are the unsavory parts of your business, redirect your energies to find the emotional core. It's scary, painful, and frustrating to be in a car accident, no matter what. Provide the emotional support, financial security, and intellectual understanding that someone in a car accident would need—before the accident, during the accident, and after the accident—and put that in your content, in your newsletters, on your social media, etc. Speak in a voice that resonates with your audience and aligns with your company's values. Discover how you can become meaningful in your customers' lives, and take that wherever it leads. If you are providing a product or service that you believe people want, communicate why your company is a necessary addition to their lives.

If you believe your industry is boring, then it will come across that way. If, on the other hand, you believe you can relieve a pain point or provide an opportunity for your customers, then your customers are more likely to believe it, too.

Always Create Outstanding Content

There are endless ways to make sure your content shines and connects. Here are some tips to keep in mind:

- **Make sure your content is well-written, well-produced, and as good as you can possibly make it.** This means proofreading and editing to ensure correct grammar and sentence structure. The extra time spent shining up your material conveys a level of professionalism to your audience.
- **Match your audience's reading level and knowledge base.** If your audience is primarily engineers, don't speak to them on a rudimentary level. Communicate on their high level of mathematical understanding. If your audience is primarily teenagers, on the other hand, speak to them colloquially in terms they'll understand.
- **Use formatting to your advantage.** Internet content is specific and unique to each platform, and visually formatting your content goes a long way in retaining a user's attention. Internet users generally have a short attention span, so use this knowledge to break up your content into smaller chunks, such as creating shorter videos or a series of smaller online articles. The same goes for visually formatting the material. Make sure you're incorporating enough white space and breaking up long blocks of text by utilizing bullet points, subheadings, and short paragraphs—maybe even just one or two sentences long. (This makes it easier to read on mobile, which is a bonus.) This allows users to easily scan for what they're looking for. Intelligent formatting is a seemingly small element that can either amplify or reduce frustration.
- **Use visuals strategically.** Photos, videos, infographics, images—these all have the potential to be eye-catching. Considering that people form an impression in 50 milliseconds, your visual presence online is important. Furthermore, demand for visual content like infographics and videos is increasing among Internet users overall.[5]

- **Provide a positive user experience.** More and more, savvy modern customers are invested in the entire experience of a brand, and not just the product. This is a huge shift from decades ago, arising from the age of interaction and interconnectivity. There are a lot of elements that go into user experience—everything from the ease of navigation on the page, to the quality of images, to the shopping cart experience. It also includes how text is formatted and displayed on different devices. Consider all the details that will help a visitor to your site feel like they enjoyed their stay.

- **Write memorably.** This is often easier said than done, but it's a solid goal to have. You want to be producing content that people eat up, can't get enough of, want to share with friends—content that changes their lives somehow. Every writer strives to write memorably, and every brand would do well to add this goal to their marketing checklist. If people remember something you said, they're likely to view you as an authority worth returning to and sharing. This helps build brand authority. You can't force this. You actually have to know what you're talking about and offer insight in your industry.

- **Foster an emotional connection.** If you think about what gets shared online, there's always an element of real feeling behind it, whether it's a cute baby video or an inspiring blog post. Think about what emotional spark you want to create in a reader or viewer.

- **Be unique.** If you're the first one to put forward a new recipe, a new way of thinking, an easier how-to guide, a never-before-seen angle on a popular topic in your industry, your content is set to shine. This, again, is not always easy. But when you look to what makes your brand different from all the others, you may begin to notice areas where you can offer your unique position or perspective to your audience.

- **Put yourself in your user's shoes.** All too often, companies produce content with a one-way mentality in mind: publish post, sell products. We want to understand our customers' mindsets so that our content is more likely to actually solve their problems. Practice taking a step back to really think about what someone might be feeling or thinking when they type a search phrase into Google, and use this to build empathy into your content. In the editing and polishing stage of content production, practice reading your content as if you were a prospective customer who found it online. What would your reaction be? What could be improved? What sustains your interest and makes you feel understood, engaged, or inspired? Aim towards these elements, and make this part of your regular content mindset.

To hammer home one of the main concepts of this book, content is not like a hose, spraying out word gunk to water a lawn. Content is a conversation. The questions your audience is asking online could be considered the beginning of the conversation, and your content is the response. Your digital content is your virtual face to the world—a representation of your company's products, values, story, and integrity. This means ensuring quality at every step.

Your content should strive to be purposeful, intentional, valuable, relevant, and accessible. Put the reader first. Put your audience first. And write from there. Content shouldn't be separate from what you do; it should be an intelligent extension of your business. Every time. Otherwise, why do it at all? Respect your audience by taking the time and care to make sure your content meets the highest quality guidelines.

And then, voila! You're published. That's the magical moment this entire book has been leading to. It will happen over and over again, regularly and consistently, with quality and purpose. All the hard work you put into identifying your audience, conducting search research, and documenting your content strategy pays off when you hit that publish button.

Over time, the fruits of your labor will become apparent: growing organic traffic, increased audience engagement, greater leads and conversions, consistently growing brand identity, outranking competitors, and burgeoning subject-matter authority in your field.

> **MAKE YOUR CONTENT SPARKLE**
>
> - Do more of what your audience wants.
> - Do what you do best.
> - Prioritize quality over quantity.
> - Don't write just to write.
> - Find the emotional core.
> - Listen to your audience.
> - Provide value, always.
> - Give before you ask.
> - Evolve your strategy.
> - Think outside the box!

POINTS OF DISCOVERY

How are you making sure your quality and style are the best they can be? Take a moment to think about the following:

1. How can your content meaningfully contribute to your customers' lives?
2. If you don't have one already, create a company style guide to direct your content flow.
3. Answer the questions listed earlier in the section "Your Company's Voice Shines through Your Content." What are 3–5 words that describe your company's voice.

Chapter 21

MEASURING SUCCESS WITH KEY METRICS

When evaluating website metrics, there is no difficulty in finding the data you want to measure [...] The level of difficulty increases when deciding what to measure rather than determining how to measure.

—**Lee Odden**, *Optimize*

Once you've created your content strategy and put it into action, how do you know if it's working? After all this talk about crafting a strategy, doing your research, and implementing a content marketing plan, you need a way to gauge the results. Content marketing is about growing your brand online through search. So, naturally, you'll want to check in at specific intervals to measure that growth and adjust course if necessary.

There is an almost-endless array of tools out there, allowing you to uncover any kind of data you could possibly want. Google Analytics alone has 10,000 different metrics available for you to track.[1] But you don't need to be overwhelmed by all the data that's available to you. You can pick and choose which metrics to look at—intentionally. Out of those 10,000 metrics, you likely just need to pay attention to a select few on a regular basis.

Choosing which metrics to use will depend on what your goals are and what you're trying to learn about any given content marketing campaign. Learning *what* to interpret and *how* to interpret it can save you a lot of headaches when it comes to measuring the success of your content marketing efforts. You really don't need to look at every single metric. In fact, we advise against it. You don't want to overload yourself with unnecessary data points; more is not necessarily better. Strategically choose which measurements are the most essential for determining whether you're moving closer to your business goals—and how. In this chapter, we'll cover the metrics that will be the most relevant to nearly any business.

Avoid paralysis by analysis.

HOW TO ENSURE YOUR CONTENT STRATEGY IS WORKING

We all know the big question that business owners, executives, and marketing directors are asking: "How can I guarantee I'm getting a return on my investment?" If you're putting out content that addresses the needs of your audience, is search-focused, and has clear goals, you can rest assured your content strategy will be bringing more traffic to your website overall.

But how do you *know* that you're increasing conversions and growing your business *because* of content marketing? The conversion journey (or, in this case, the Search Cycle, specifically) doesn't always have a clear linear progression because, as we mentioned before, modern humans are busy people using *many* devices across *multiple* locations with an *endless* array of emotions, questions, habits, distractions, and concerns.

But what is easy to understand is this: In order to increase online conversions, you first need to increase traffic to your website. Want more leads or sales? Bring more people in the door. Content is what brings people in the door. Content generates traffic. Relevant, focused traffic leads to conversions. At the highest level, it really is that simple.

Let's remember our nursing school example. If our business goal is to increase student enrollment to 90% over one year using content marketing to drive leads, we can pretty easily determine whether the campaign was successful, and here's how: Simply track whether there is any difference in the enrollment rate from organic traffic since the beginning of the content marketing campaign when enrollment capacity stood at 75%. If enrollment increases by around 15%, we can consider our goal met. We can also compare the percentage of enrollment with a few metrics on the back end of The Nursing School's website to see how well content was performing, how much organic traffic increased, and what the rate of conversion was (in this case, driving leads). In the case of your own company, you can put all this data together for a pretty good insight into how content marketing is driving your business.

Once you're increasing your organic traffic, the next logical metric to evaluate is whether that increased traffic is leading to more conversions. Organic traffic converts at about 2–3%, generally speaking. That means if you receive 100 visitors to your website, you could expect around 2 or 3 to engage in a conversion activity.

You get to define what types of conversions you're seeking. If you're primarily focused on lead generation, your conversions may include signing up on a form, making a call, or expressing interest by leaving contact information. If you're running an e-commerce business, your conversions may be primarily focused on purchase completion.

It's the job of your content to not only get relevant potential customers to your website but also into the top of the conversion funnel. Certain types of content should even have the power to get people all the way *through* the conversion funnel. You may want to know which pieces of content are really connecting, what kind of traffic you're getting, and how effectively that content is achieving your business goals.

We asked a few metrics experts what *they* thought were the most important metrics to track. Our friend Dave Rohrer is the founder of Northside Metrics, co-host of *The Business of Digital* podcast, and a prolific public speaker. The goals for a specific project should determine what kind of metrics to employ. As Rohrer put it, the goals are usually either focused around 1) driving conversions or 2) raising brand awareness.[2]

If the clearly defined goal of a content marketing campaign is to increase conversions, then Rohrer's top metrics are email signups, webinar signups, MQL (marketing qualified lead), SQL (sales qualified lead), and form fills. If the goal is to raise awareness and increase brand visibility, his top metrics are links, traffic, and rankings.

It's important to be flexible, too. Some pieces designed for conversions may end up becoming pure awareness pieces, and that's okay. Rohrer said, "You might really want content to do X, but as you put it in the game, you may realize it is better suited to Y. Don't be afraid to pivot your goals and figure out where some content best fits."[3]

Different metrics are relevant to different goals. Always tie your analysis back to what your content marketing is trying to achieve with a certain project, and consider it a snapshot that can help you move forward. The aim is to make your data interpretable and actionable. Content marketing is about being less wrong over time and allowing space within your documented strategy for innovation and feedback.

Here are our top 4 key performance indicators (KPIs) based on what we've taught you so far about content marketing using audience research and search-focused topics. Again, your primary metrics may vary based on your content marketing goals and projects, but we think these 4 KPIs can be suitable for almost any business to track.

QUANTITATIVE ANALYSIS: 4 KEY PERFORMANCE INDICATORS (KPIS) TO TRACK

With 10,000 different ways of looking at data in Google Analytics, you've got to pare it down and get specific. In other words, you've got to know what you're looking for. There are an endless number of ways of looking at your data for different purposes, so we don't want to limit you. However, more than that, we don't want to overwhelm you. So, in the spirit of condensing over a decade of knowledge into a helpful, actionable chapter, we've chosen the four KPIs we think will help anyone check their progress against their business goals.

These are:

1. Organic traffic growth over time
2. Growth of conversions over time
3. Keyword performance
4. Audience engagement

Your overall content marketing goals may involve a number of things—increasing online presence, growing authority over time, reaching your audience, and achieving business growth goals (such as sales, leads, live chats, subscriptions, or other actions). Use your best judgment to determine what metrics to track based on your situation.

A Quick Note About Using Metrics Tools

Before we look at KPIs, we need to talk about which tools we're using to track this data. While there are plenty of amazing free and low-cost tools out there that'll help you achieve different goals, the main tool we suggest is Google Analytics. We can reasonably expect that 95% of the people reading this book have some familiarity with Google Analytics since it's free and available to anyone. You can supplement your Google Analytics data with lots of other software (for example, SEMrush, which we used earlier for search research), but Google Analytics is the foundational data-collection tool for website analytics. Using Google Analytics data, you can see how visitors find your website, what channel they came through, and other ways they interact with your content.

Google Search Console (GSC) is a separate yet related free tool that we also suggest. Using GSC, you can analyze your website's indexing status in Google, identify potential technical issues, and also see your organic search performance in Google. Inputting a URL can show you which queries are sending traffic to that page, what average ranking position the page had, and how many impressions the page is receiving (the number of times the web page shows up for a query in search).

If you haven't already, make sure to set up a Google Analytics and GSC account because we'll be referencing both of these tools from here on out. Analytics is fairly complex to use and has a bit of a learning curve, but once you get it down, it's immensely useful. Luckily, Google offers free video tutorials, and you'll find the URL for their Google Analytics tutorial in the footnotes.* Each platform is a little different, so you'll want to spend some time familiarizing yourself with the features of each. With that out of the way, let's gear up and dive into Google Analytics to start tracking our data.

METRIC #1: IS YOUR ORGANIC TRAFFIC FROM SEARCH GROWING?

While your goals may be nuanced, all this content marketing work generally leads to the same place for everyone: You want your content, your website, and your business to be seen more frequently, more favorably, and more consistently online by the people you're trying to reach. The simplest indicator of whether you're achieving these goals is to track how much organic search traffic is coming into your site over time.

The simple idea is that, yes, your organic traffic should be growing. If you're putting in consistent effort to publish content on your website that utilizes relevant search terms, insightfully addresses topics of interest to your readers, and skillfully links your content to your business objectives, then you can reasonably expect to enjoy more visitors to your website. Simply put, more search-focused content creates more organic search traffic. So, the highest, broadest level of measurement is to see if this is actually the case. (It should be.)

---

* Check out this URL for a video tutorial on Google Analytics: https://analytics.google.com/analytics/academy/course/6

Evaluating Organic Traffic Growth

It's helpful to think about organic traffic on a site-wide, section, and page level. You can get the broadest view by checking in on your site-wide traffic growth. Over time, you can segment traffic growth across different sections of your website and then check in on individual pages. If you've been producing search-focused content for many months, or even years, you will likely see growth in your organic traffic across your entire site and/or in specific sections and pages of your site.

Site-Level Growth

Because content marketing is a marathon and not a sprint, looking at your site-wide organic traffic on a quarterly, biannual, or yearly basis will usually paint the best picture. Furthermore, looking at traffic year over year eliminates seasonal traffic trends that may change from month to month. Aggregate data over time shows patterns, and these high-level indicators are what give us information about trends in site traffic. So, it's really important to take the long view when it comes to evaluating site-wide search traffic growth.

Section-Level Growth

Using the tools in Google Analytics, you can view incoming traffic trends across different sections of your website. A *section* can be any portion of your website that has multiple pages underneath it. These might be "Categories" in your blog or a section of the site that includes multiple sub-pages, such as a "Folder." For example, in the site hierarchy of The Nursing School's website, they would theoretically have a section called "Programs" at the URL domain.com/programs. Underneath this folder, you would find their individual program pages, like RN Training and LPN Training. At the folder level in Google Analytics, you can choose to see traffic growth across all pages within that folder category.

Page-Level Growth

You can also filter traffic data by individual page. Blog posts are considered pages, so we are including both site pages and blog posts in this category. This means you can see, at a granular level, how much traffic each individual page on your site is bringing in. This is great data to have, as it shows you which posts are performing well and which aren't. You'll probably want to pay special attention to your core pages (those that directly promote or sell your products/services). Insight into traffic on these pages can help you determine how well your content marketing is driving people to the places where conversions are possible.

Looking at organic traffic on a page level can help you fine-tune your content strategy. This information can provide feedback to your content strategy and production team, and it has the most ground-level influence over the types of content you ultimately decide to produce.

Not every piece of content will be equivalent to a strike in bowling, but you'll want to notice which ones are driving traffic and take lessons from those successes. Similarly, there may be some things you can learn from the pages that aren't driving traffic in the way you expected. As Rohrer had mentioned earlier, sometimes we need to "pivot" a piece of content that isn't working the way we expected. We'll go into repurposing content in the next chapter.

> "Ahh, you know, strikes and gutters, ups and downs."
>
> —The Dude

METRIC #2: ARE YOU WINNING MORE CONVERSIONS?

Conversion journeys can be simple—like typing an e-mail address into a subscription box and hitting submit—or they can be complex, extravagant adventures. There are entire agencies devoted to conversion rate optimization (CRO). While we won't be wading too far into the weeds, suffice it to say, conversions are complex processes that just about every business owner should want to understand and improve.

TRACKING IMPRESSIONS

Another valuable metric to keep an eye on is *impressions*. An impression is not website traffic, but it may still be useful to consider from a search performance perspective. When a user conducts a search for any query and then sees a SERP (the search engine results page that appears after you perform a search in Google) and your web link appears in the results *but your link is not clicked*, that's called an impression. Google will populate a SERP with various different kinds of results, such as a featured snippet, a knowledge panel, a carousel of images, or a map pack. Sometimes, Google is able to answer a user's question right there on the SERP, and the user may not feel the need to click any further. We can track these impressions as another measure of content performance, if we wish, using Google Search Console.

The value of collecting any data is always to provide insight on how our content is performing. We can use data about impressions to understand how our content is being seen on the SERP. Google Search Console can show the clicks and impressions for any of your website's sections or pages. You can see how clicks and impressions compare to each other over time and consider what that might mean. If your website is considered valuable enough by Google to be presented in a featured snippet, the user may not even need to click over to your website. If there's a clear answer that can be given from your page, that's a strong sign that your content is robust and valuable.

> Why does this matter if it's not even driving traffic? Even impressions without clicks are valuable for raising brand awareness. As Google continues to refine their method of delivering answers on the SERP, we expect impressions to be an important metric for measuring the relevancy of brand visibility in search.

Using Google Analytics, you can set up different parameters to track different conversion metrics. You can track how often users fill out a form or navigate through an e-commerce funnel—from adding an item to a cart, to setting up billing, to checking out. This information can be useful for understanding how users engage with your sales funnel and identifying any roadblocks or opportunities for improvement.

It may not seem like it, but increasing a conversion rate by just half a percentage point is huge. If you're dealing with traffic in large numbers—let's say 5,000 visitors per day—and you raise your conversion rate from 2% to 2.5%, that means you've increased conversions from 100 per day to 125 per day. If you look at that monthly, you're increasing conversions from 3,000 to 3,750. That's 750 more conversions per month, or 9,000 more conversions per year! For half a percentage point, that's not just chump change. Even a fractional increase in your conversation rate could mean more business.

This book is focused on understanding the importance of search-focused content marketing and how to think about doing it strategically, but after you start bringing in more traffic, you might want to invest in CRO for your company. Just know that CRO comes later, after you've built significant traffic to your website. You can think of CRO as a way of squeezing more conversions out of the traffic you're already attracting. With that in mind, here are eight tips to consider when doing your regular content audit if you want to improve your conversion rate:

1. **Target a specific audience.** Theoretically, the rate of conversions will increase (more conversions per visitors) if you fine-tune your audience research and make sure you're reaching the people who want what you have to offer. Maybe it's time to focus content toward some personas. A more specific audience translates into a more qualified lead.

2. **Track conversions directly generated from the content you produce.** You can use the Google Analytics Landing Pages report to observe the specific conversion rate of any blog post, web page, or piece of online content. Noticing and comparing which posts are bringing traffic into your website and leading directly to conversions can provide insight on what's working and what's not.

3. **Follow the conversion funnel.** You can track the various steps a visitor makes when they enter a conversion funnel on your website; for instance, the steps to make a purchase on an e-commerce website. Setting up Funnels in Google Analytics can be helpful to know what digital steps your visitors are taking, where they stop, and where they continue. Are there any roadblocks on the journey to conversion you can fix?

4. **Revisit the Search Cycle.** If you feel like you're producing a lot of content and not seeing the types of conversions you want, consider revisiting the types of content you're producing along the Search Cycle. If you're in a position where your primary goal is to have potential customers take a purchasing action, you may want to adjust your strategy to produce more content for the evaluation and commitment stages, where a user is farther along in the Search Cycle. To focus on sales, try prioritizing more conversion-friendly types of content for a while.

5. **Check your calls-to-action.** Do you have an appropriate call-to-action on every piece of content? Does the call-to-action match the type of content? Every stage of the Search Cycle can be driving engagement when the

call-to-action is aligned with the content. For example, for content in the awareness and information gathering stages, you may offer additional free info by request, while the evaluation and commitment stage content may encourage the user to take a stronger action, like purchasing, signing up, or calling. Your calls-to-action will vary depending on whether you're working a lead generation or sales strategy. Either way, they should make sense considering the type of content presented.

6. Check user experience (UX) and technical aspects. User experience, while more on the technical end of things, is massively important. UX basically refers to how easy and pleasant it is to use your website. Make sure to check that all your links are working, your e-commerce platform is simple and fast, and your forms are functioning as they should be. Don't forget to check the user experience of your website and pages on multiple devices since users will visit on various devices and platforms. Check your content for overlooked errors or egregious mistakes that could be turning people off. It's definitely not ideal to lose a potential customer in the last 10% of the journey because of a misdirected link, broken form, or serious misinformation.

Here's a short list of UX elements to check on the page level:

- **Visuals.** Are your images high resolution and relevant?
- **Button Colors.** Are your button colors cohesive and intentional?
- **Font Sizes.** Are your fonts large enough to read but not so large as to be obnoxious?
- **Content Structure.** Is the content visually easy to read, scan, and understand?
- **Mobile.** Does your content transition seamlessly to mobile devices?

7. Check your page speed. Considering the short attention spans of Internet users, if your content takes a long time to load on a visitor's screen, you may lose visitors before they even get to interact with your content. Google has a free tool called PageSpeed Insights (PSI) that's super easy to use.

Just input your URL and Google will analyze your page speed, then give improvement suggestions.

8. Perform A/B testing. Once you've ramped up your organic traffic and you're ready to tackle increasing conversions, the next step is to go into full-on testing mode. A/B testing allows you to compare two different elements (it can be nearly anything—pages, images, headlines, subheadings, button colors, etc.) and see which is more likely to deliver the results you want.

METRIC #3: ARE YOUR TARGETED KEYWORDS GAINING TRACTION?

One of the ways to track your *visibility* (how many people encounter your content online) and *ranking* (proximity to Google's first page of search results) is to measure *keyword performance.* When you create content with targeted keywords, as you've already done using your keyword research, you want to know whether those keywords are actually performing well in search.

In other words, you want to know if by targeting certain keywords, Google starts delivering your content in search results more frequently to the people searching with those keywords. The more often your content appears in the SERP, the more *visible* your brand becomes. The more relevant your keywords are to the content you've produced, the higher your *ranking* should be. All the work you've done to find relevant keywords to boost your brand exposure can be measured for effectiveness.

Here are two simple and effective ways to monitor keyword performance:

1. GSC Performance Report: This is a free report that you can create using Google Search Console (GSC). It's easy and straightforward to use GSC for generating reports at any time to see a snapshot of how your content is performing. For most businesses, using this free tool should serve you well. You won't necessarily need anything else because the data here is reliably from Google and it's all very user-friendly.

Here's how you track performance in GSC on a single piece of content: Choose the URL of a piece of content you want to measure for keyword performance. In the GSC "Performance on Search Results" report page, filter the report using that URL. In the resulting report, you can see which search queries your content is showing up for and how well your content is performing for those queries by tracking impressions, clicks, CTR, and average ranking position. You can do this for any URL and see results on up to 1,000 keywords. You can configure your settings to see up to 16 months of historic data, and you can check this report at any given time within that 16-month time frame for a snapshot of keyword performance for any URL. You could export the report and link it to a third party tool if you're working with one, or simply retrieve the report whenever you're ready to measure your content results.

So what do you do with this GSC keyword performance report? Whether you're using an external tracking process or exporting the report automatically, you can determine which keywords are performing better over time. You can see the *average ranking position* and *impressions* for the search queries in that piece of content. (There are plenty of other variables you can check, such as clicks and click-through rate [CTR], but we'll focus on average ranking position and impressions.)

- ❏ **Average Ranking Position: Are the targeted keywords that appear increasing in ranking over time?** Since ranking position changes all the time, average ranking position is the average spot that your URL occupies in Google search results. We are looking for lower numbers when it comes to ranking position. The lower the ranking position, the closer that keyword is to appearing on the first page of Google. You may see keyword positions very far out, such as in position fifty or farther, which is normal. What we want to see happening is the progression of keywords toward the first page over time. If you view results in a three-month time frame, for example, which keywords have a better ranking position at the end of the three months than at the beginning? In general, we want to see which keywords are moving closer to the first page of Google. We can expect incremental organic search traffic to start increasing as a keyword moves toward positions on the first page, but we still might not see any significant traffic growth until page one.

- **Impressions: Are impressions growing?** If impressions are trending upwards, that's a good sign. Impressions are a metric to track visibility. Impressions are the number of times the URL has appeared in a search result for a specific keyword, regardless of whether it is "in view," which means it may not actually be *seen* by a user, but it has appeared on the SERP nonetheless. You might see impressions for a keyword, but not necessarily an average ranking, near a page-one position, especially at first. We want to see a higher number of impressions over time, which could indicate the keyword is appearing more often in SERPs. (The caveat: If impressions drop for any reason for a particular search query—for example, due to seasonal trends or other external influences—this may not be the case.)

You can generate a GSC Performance Report for any URL, including specific blog posts and page posts. You can also input the URL of a subfolder if you want to measure an entire section of the site—for example, www.domain.com/folder/. Then you will see a report for all the pages within that folder. One downside: Google will show results for your report on a national or global basis, depending on how you filter your report, so there's no way to track results for a specific region at this point, unfortunately.

The goal overall with this organic search keyword performance report is to see if you are in fact moving toward the goals of increasing visibility and ranking toward Google's front page for any given piece of content. The report is entirely free, so taking the time to check in on keyword performance every quarter (or however often you prefer) will help you track and measure performance.

Bonus: As targeted keywords in a page URL approach the more desirable ranking positions, you may also begin to see other related keywords ranking for that page, which is a great sign. (In the next chapter, we'll give you some ways to use this information to expand your content even further.)

2. Keyword Ranking Report: Another type of valuable keyword performance report is a *keyword ranking report* that can be generated by any of your preferred keyword research platforms. Our favorite, of course, is SEMrush. These reports will be more in-depth and detailed, as they are usually part of a paid subscription package. If your budget allows for this type of tracking, you can get another perspective on keyword performance with this type of paid tool.

How it works: If you know which primary keywords you want to target for an entire domain (essentially, your entire website), you can preselect these keywords ahead of time and set your keyword ranking tool to automatically track these keywords. For example, let's say you identify 50 core keywords you want to measure across your website. You would create a "project" in your platform, input the domain and the 50 keywords, and the platform will track their ranking positions automatically. You can see a snapshot of how those keywords are performing at any given moment in time and even which content pieces (URLs) are ranking with those keywords. This can be really helpful if you have a select basket of keywords you really want to monitor.

Why You Might Opt for a Paid Keyword Report Tool:

You might benefit from the additional keyword performance metrics in a paid keyword report tool. We recommend using both, GSC and your preferred paid tool, rather than discarding GSC altogether, since these two types of reports can complement each other well.

We use SEMrush, but most third-party tools should offer similar features. Here's what we find valuable with a keyword ranking report:

- **You can set geo-location:** In SEMrush, you can select a regional focus to monitor keyword ranking in a specific geographic area—by city, state, or country. This is a great tool for local companies that are most concerned about attracting customers in a specific geographical area only. If you're a multi-national company, it may be helpful to see traffic from Google's search engines in different countries.

- **You can track rankings by device:** You can get an idea of how your website ranks for the keywords tracked by device, such as mobile or desktop. It can be helpful to know if your rankings are skewed more heavily towards one so you can address any possible causes.
- **You can track rankings by search engine:** Because these third-party tools run independently, you can set up tracking for other search engines outside of Google, if you wish. This can provide a larger picture than just using GSC.
- **You can see greater clarity of keyword rankings:** When a keyword is ranking on page one, a paid tool will also show what type of ranking it is. You'll be able to see whether that keyword is showing up as a featured snippet, as part of a map pack, in a knowledge panel, and more. SEMrush even provides screenshots of the type of ranking.
- **You can track competitors:** It can be helpful to see where your competitors are ranking for the keywords you're tracking.
- **You can track visibility:** Visibility is a metric loosely defined as how often your website is found in search. If visibility is at 100%, it means that the domain is ranking #1 for all keywords in the project. Knowing your visibility can be helpful in understanding where your website stands among competitors and uncovering opportunities to increase rankings. Think of visibility as your market share of search for keywords that you're monitoring.

The keyword ranking report runs every day automatically, and you can check it anytime. However, the number of keywords you can track in this way across your entire domain is not unlimited. And it can get costly, depending on how many keywords you track. If you do use this tool, we suggest focusing your energy on your content production and checking in on your keyword rankings at the same time you run a GSC search performance report. Then you can evaluate these metrics at the same time.

We prefer monitoring keyword performance using both methods;

however, you absolutely don't need to use the paid tool to get the most out of this process. Essentially, you just want to see whether the keywords you've targeted are in fact helping to move your content needle—increasing visibility, improving average ranking positions, and heading toward organic search traffic growth. Using the free tools available through GSC will tell you a lot about how your keywords are performing over time in Google!

METRIC #4: HOW WELL DOES YOUR CONTENT MEET AUDIENCE NEEDS?

Another way to see how well your content is working for the people it's designed for is to track certain audience-engagement indicators. You may be getting more traffic, but how can you tell if people are actually consuming and enjoying the content you've worked so hard to produce? Of course, you hope your audience and search research are translating into effective relationships with customers, potential customers, and industry influencers.

Different types of user data, such as how long users are staying on individual pages, whether they're returning, and whether they're engaging (buying, subscribing, chatting, inquiring, etc.) can show you different pictures of what's going on. This is the type of evidence that can help you determine which efforts are successful and which can be improved. You can use some of the following metrics to gain insight into whether your relationship with your audience is engaging, valuable, and relevant.

> A **session** in Google Analytics is defined as "a group of user interactions within a given time frame." By default, a session on Google is contained to 30 minutes. For example, if a visitor stopped engaging after 30 minutes and then started engaging again, this would signal a new session. One session can include multiple types of interactions, such as page views and transactions. However, session settings can be adjusted.[4]

Here are our top 10 audience engagement metrics:

1. **Average Time on Page:** This metric in Google Analytics tells you how long, on average, visitors are staying on individual pages before clicking to another page. This can sometimes be an indicator of engagement. For example, if you're producing long-form content, the more time spent on the page, the more likely it is a visitor enjoyed what they were reading. The caveat is that some types of content don't require visitors to spend much time on the page, such as a short-form article, a brief video, or a contact page.
2. **Pageviews:** This tells you how many times someone requested a page on your site and it loaded (or reloaded). You could have multiple pageviews in a session, for example, if someone reloaded a page or clicked away and then returned to the original page. What you're looking for: Are pageviews overall increasing?
3. **Entrances:** An entrance is when a visitor enters your website on a specific page. We can expect that most visitors will arrive to your website on the home page or core pages, but if another page, such as a blog post, has a high entrance rate, that's helpful to notice. Entrances show you which content is driving visitors to your website.
4. **Exits:** An exit is when a visitor exits your website. Like entrances, you can track which pages have a high exit rate. A high exit rate is not always a bad thing. For example, we can expect that a contact page or a thank you page would have a high exit rate because the user found what they needed or performed the expected action (like filling out a form) and then left the website. In this case, the high exit rate shows that the content fulfilled the intent. If, however, you are noticing high exit rates on pages that are designed to lead visitors to another page, it could be a sign that the content is not performing the way you had hoped.
5. **Bounce Rate:** The bounce rate in Google Analytics can tell you what percentage of visitors exit your website after only a single page visit. If you're producing content that's meant to lead to other

pages or next steps, a high bounce rate may indicate a problem (or disconnect), which means you'll want to investigate.

6. **Pages Per Session:** This is "the average number of pages viewed per session." In other words, you can track the number of pages a site visitor viewed within a single session or time frame. In general, we can expect that the more pages visited, the more likely it is a visitor liked what they saw and wanted to discover more of what your site has to offer. On the other hand, it's not an absolute metric. Someone might have quickly found exactly what they were looking for on a single page and had no need to continue perusing your website.

7. **Return Visitors:** When people decide to come back to your site, this is a good indicator they want more of what you have to offer, and it's a positive step in the direction of building customer loyalty and a strong audience base.

8. **New Users:** Similarly, you can see how many new users visit your site via Google Analytics. If there's a lot and the number's growing, this is a good sign your content is being discovered through search and attracting a wider audience base.

9. **Subscribers:** If you have a subscription system, tracking subscribers via goal tracking in Google Analytics is a good way to see how many people sign up to receive more of whatever you've got.

10. **Locations of Visitors:** Depending on your business focus, tracking where people are geographically when they visit your site could be valuable information.

Other Advanced Metrics:

Depending on your goals, you might find that other metrics are useful. Here are just a few more:

1. **Backlinks:** When people link to your site, this is a good sign they like and trust your information enough to want to direct other

people to you. It shows that other people on the Internet endorse your content. You can track backlinks in Google Search Console and SEMrush. Another great tool for this is Majestic.com.
2. **Previous Page Path/Next Page Path:** This metric is a little more complicated, but it can be useful. You can see the "page path" of visitors as they browse your website. For example, you can see that someone enters the site on Page A, then goes to Page B, and then Page C, and so on. This is a little more complicated because it's not an aggregate measurement like many of the others but dependent on analyzing individual pages. If you have the time and interest, it can give you insight on how people are navigating around your site.
3. **Opt-Ins:** If you have a contact page, e-mail opt-ins, or other forms that you want visitors to fill out, you can track these as well.

QUALITATIVE ANALYSIS: LISTEN TO FEEDBACK FROM YOUR CUSTOMERS

The metrics we've just mentioned analyze aggregated data and not individual or personal responses. However, you can supplement quantitative data with qualitative feedback as well. This might mean having the content marketing department meet regularly with the sales department to discover the specific concerns customers are sharing. It could also mean regularly reviewing comments posted to your website, blog posts, or social platforms and taking a bird's-eye view to notice patterns, concerns, or questions that seem to be common among your audience. If you have a Yelp page or a Facebook page, regularly check and see what the reviews are like, both good and bad. Good reviews are obviously awesome, but bad reviews are helpful, too. A local business with a Google My Business account can view the "Questions & Answers" section for commonly asked questions. Remember that content marketing is a game with a constantly shifting target, and it's important to listen to your customers.

The Internet is such a gift for businesses, as it allows us to hear firsthand from customers what they like and don't like, what resonates and what doesn't. Though these types of qualitative metrics may be less trackable and percentage-driven, this doesn't mean they're any less valuable. Some might argue that metrics like direct conversations and reviews are even *more* valuable because you're able to receive more specific information straight from the mouths of your customers. What do your customers *really* want? Everything in data analysis is up for interpretation, so it can be extremely valuable to hear direct comments from customers and users.

If you can let both quantitative and qualitative metrics talk to each other, this is the most ideal scenario. Numbers can tell us a lot. People can tell us even more. Don't be afraid to ask questions about why content isn't performing or what your audience wants. Don't just assume you're doing everything correctly. You might be, but you might also be missing something obvious that you could uncover from user surveys or other ways of listening in. Content is about communication. Remember to communicate within your company to investigate and understand the problems your customers are having so you can create content to *meet their needs and solve their problems.*

Basically, once you've started bringing in more traffic to your site and interacting with more people, don't neglect to listen to what these people are saying to you—and about you!

A Note about Social Media

Because this is a content marketing book specifically geared towards helping businesses of all types and sizes increase their organic traffic online, social media is not included in our list of primary metrics. For some businesses and situations, social media can be a huge generator of traffic and sales, but other businesses benefit more from driving traffic through organic search.

The type of search-focused content we've been talking about is not necessarily always accessible and shareable on social media. Think about a video or article called "Nursing Assistant vs. Medical Assistant Career."

This may be highly relevant to the person looking for it and related to our prospective nursing students, but we don't expect it to be a socially popular post, necessarily. Someone surely might share it in the comments section of a friend asking about that topic, and that's awesome. But that might be about it.

Search behavior and intent differs in meaningful ways from social behavior and intent. Search behavior is more focused on asking a question and finding specific information, while social behavior may involve other aims, such as bonding, communicating, and discovering.[5] Therefore, a separate, focused approach for social media marketing would yield the best results.

We want to be clear: Social media can be a great tool. And social media is obviously a form of content creation and sharing. There are entire books, webinars, classes, and other resources out there specifically designed to help businesses improve their social media strategy. We encourage you to seek out social media resources and work with your content team to integrate your search-focused content marketing with your social outreach plans.

CONDUCT REGULAR CONTENT AUDITS

In order to track your metrics data, you will need to conduct a regular content audit. A content audit is essentially a progress report, providing key information to help you determine your next steps. You can measure any of the KPIs we've laid out here, or others.

How often should you do a content audit? It's really up to you, your goals, your resources, your capacity, or even what stage of content marketing you're at (early, mid, late), but we recommend plotting out and scheduling time for a content audit ahead of time. When you can plan audits in advance, you and your team will already be expecting to complete the task, so you can make sure it doesn't go overlooked. This might be once or twice a year or every quarter, depending on your situation. This is the time to check in on your goals, observe your progress, make any necessary reports, and apply your findings to your current content plan. Decide what works for you and plug it into your content strategy template. Adjust over time if needed, but make sure to revisit the audit step regularly.

As you plan ahead, you can also determine which metrics you'll review when it comes time for the audit. You can even decide this *as you set your goals*. For example, let's say The Nursing School wanted to check in on their specific enrollment goal for the previous year. So, when each enrollment season ends, their content marketers will logically be checking to see whether their content strategy is contributing to this goal, and how. We can logically assume that their primary internal metric will be enrollment statistics. Has their enrollment gone up? In addition to this, they should be checking related metrics using Google Analytics to see how the content is performing.

Also, consider that new content is a bit like a fine wine; it can take a while to age and produce results, so give each piece of content enough lead time. Time frames also depend on the competition of the search phrases you're targeting. Really, though, how long does it take to see results? Rohrer summed it up perfectly for us when he said, "Not to sound like an SEO, but it really depends."[6]

In general, content marketing can take around three months minimum to start showing results if you're an already-established website. It can take more like 6–12 months if you're brand new. But Rohrer is right; it really does depend on so many factors.

We also asked Sujan Patel, co-founder of Mailshake and author of *100 Days of Growth*, how long people can generally expect to see results from content marketing. He said it usually takes around 5–6 months to see large traffic increases, 8–9 months to start seeing meaningful email opt-ins, and 12–24 months to start seeing revenue impact.[7] Speaking of Patel, here are his top 3 KPIs (key performance indicators) for content marketing: traffic, e-mail opt-ins, and leads/conversions/revenue.[8]

At an even more foundational level, checking in periodically with the data can uncover hidden roadblocks you may have missed that are negatively affecting your bottom line, such as a broken link, outdated information, a confusing call-to-action, or even a broken form. Similarly, you might be able to glean insight from pieces of content that are driving a lot of traffic and continue building on what's working well. We'll discuss how to use this data to repurpose content in the next chapter.

POINTS OF DISCOVERY

Now that you know some valuable KPIs to track, consider the following questions:

1. Which metrics will be the *most* helpful for you to track? Make a list of these, and be sure to pay attention to these metrics when measuring analytics.
2. Set some goals for growth, then check back in at your pre-determined intervals to take stock of your metrics and analytics. Each time you do this, come up with 3–5 recommendations to evolve your content strategy forward.
3. How often do you plan on conducting a content audit? Schedule due dates and assign this task.

Chapter 22

REPURPOSING CONTENT TO MAXIMIZE RESULTS

"Content repurposing is about getting the maximum return from every single piece of content you create. Content repurposing can take many forms, and there are lots of different and creative ways that you can repurpose your content, but every content creator must repurpose."

—**Amy Woods**

So, what do you do with all these data points and measurements you've collected? Use them to improve and adjust your content strategy. You conduct your regular content audits, use your tools for teasing out the data from your metrics, and use what you find to inform your future content strategy. If your content is performing well, learn from it. If it's not performing well, learn from that as well.

What does it mean for content to "perform well"? As we mentioned in the previous chapter, this may vary depending on the metrics you're looking at and what your criteria for success is. So, take your specific content strategy into account, but, generally speaking, content that drives organic traffic and/or conversions is thought to be "performing well." Those are the main goals after all, right? If something is performing well, you'll be able to see traffic from it.

You can get a very useful report from Google Analytics in the "content performance" section. From there, you can sort and filter results to view your top-performing posts. You can also sort/filter by type of post or by section of the site. The great thing about this function is you can generate a list to see which pages are driving the most and the least traffic. Whether you check this frequently or at regularly scheduled intervals, you should definitely stay apprised of what's at the top and bottom of this list.

Keep in mind, depending on your goals and strategy, you may consider organic search traffic your main indicator of success, or you may be more concerned with conversion rate. For example, let's say one post only drives 100 page views per month, but 50% of those views result in immediate sales. You might consider that pretty successful. In another instance, perhaps having a low bounce rate is the most important indicator for a certain campaign. Just be sure you know what you're looking for when you're analyzing the numbers, and keep an open perspective to really understand what's going on and why.

Right now, the simplest way for us to get a generalized view of what's working and what's not is by looking at organic search traffic and conversions. Content pieces that drive a lot of traffic and/or conversions show you what's working well. Content pieces at the bottom of the list show you what's not working. So, what should you do in each of these cases? In this chapter, we'll walk you through some of the key elements to consider with content that's doing well—and content that's not doing so hot. The bottom line: Once you invent the wheel, keep it turning. (You don't need to reinvent it every time.)

WHAT YOU CAN LEARN FROM STRONG CONTENT

Your super-strong top posts are clearly driving traffic, creating conversions, engaging your audience, and building your brand. Good job! You can put your feet up, pat yourself on the back, and relax with a nice whiskey (Mark's recommendation).

And then you can dive back in and see what you can learn from this success. What's great is that once you identify pieces of content that are really working for you, you can potentially repurpose or even expand on those content topics to keep the momentum going, maximizing your efforts and getting more "bang for your buck." Why not keep the winning streak going?

Ideas for Repurposing Existing Content

If you have a good idea that's working, see if you can get the most out of that success by repurposing this content idea into different formats. For example, let's say a blog post called "How to Become a Nurse" is really doing well. You're getting lots of organic search traffic and the topic is generating conversions. You're even noticing people sharing it on social media. The blog post is solid, well-written, informative, and engaging. Your audience loves it, and, even more importantly, some of them are on the path to enrolling as students. You're seeing a good number of users navigate from the blog post to content that's linked in the post, like the RN program page, which is one of your core pages and designed to capture conversions. Sure enough, you can follow the data and see that new leads are coming in; there is an uptick in requests for enrollment information.

Now that you have a clear winner, consider creating different types of content assets using the same topic and information. If this were a blog post, for example, you might consider creating a YouTube video on the topic to reach people on that particular platform. You wouldn't need to reinvent the wheel here because you'd basically have all the content already compiled; you'd just be repurposing it for a different medium. Of course, you'd optimize the content for search within YouTube, just as you would on any platform, all the while building your brand, reaching new audiences, and pointing people back to your website. It is important to note that repurposed content still needs to be unique—as in, not plagiarized or replicated verbatim.

You may also consider writing a similar blog post on the topic to publish on another high-quality website, like an industry news source or a partner blog. This is called *guest posting*, and it can help expand your audience and drive more traffic through backlinks. Guest posting can be part of your content strategy once you have a strong internal base built.

It's a bit more advanced, but we definitely wanted to let you know that posting relevant, quality content on other platforms is a great way to expand your website's reach and referral traffic once you reach this point. You contribute free content to them, and they let you use their platform. It's a win/win.

In other words, you can take a content topic that's performing well and repurpose it, publishing it in different formats for different channels. This is an advanced way of reaching more of your relevant audience on other well-trafficked platforms by reusing the content topics you already know hit home. The more you can position yourself across the Internet as a trustworthy and quality brand, the more you will build online authority to keep expanding your visibility and reach.

Ideas for Expanding Content Topics

Another way to get more mileage out of your top-performing posts is to actually create more content around certain topics or keywords. For example, let's say the blog post "How to Become a Nurse" is your #1 trafficked post. In addition to repurposing the content and creating a video or another type of content piece for another platform, you can also dive into the post and expand on one or more of the subtopics. For instance, perhaps within this post one of your subheadings is "What Does a Nurse Do?"—and it's only a paragraph long. At the same time, you find *search evidence* to support your belief that it could be a good idea to expand that topic—either expanding that paragraph into a few more paragraphs or creating an entirely separate post dedicated to the topic.

So, what kind of evidence can help you decide this? Keywords. You can actually determine which keywords are specifically driving traffic from within that individual post by using SEO software. We use SEMrush, but there are others out there that can give you similar information. Basically, you just grab the URL of the post you want to look at and generate a *keywords ranking report* (which we discussed in Chapter 21). If there is data, you can see which keywords are ranking for that page URL. You may be surprised to see a very long list, including keywords you *weren't* specifically targeting. For example, let's say you targeted 20 keywords in this post, but you see that your post is ranking for 500 queries. Not all of these will be meaningful to you, but you will be able to see this information clearly. You can filter the keywords in the report by "position" to see which keywords are in the top positions for a particular search query—meaning, nearest to page 1 of Google. You can also do this in Google Search Console for a URL.

To continue our example, let's say the post "How to Become a Nurse" shows you that the keyword "what does a nurse do" is a highly searched term, and this term is actually driving traffic to your article. The keyword shows up as one of the top-ten keywords in your keywords ranking report. The report shows you that *this post* is ranking on page 2 of Google *for that term*. Page 1 of Google is where everyone wants to get. If you have a strong keyword showing up around position 10, which is equivalent to somewhere around page 2, that's a strong enough gravitational pull to warrant more energy. It's like, you're almost there, and your post is orbiting the target.

The keyword itself is ranking well as just a subheading, so this would be the *evidence* that you could probably justify expanding on this content topic. The reasoning goes: If you've only put in a minimal amount of effort producing content for this particular keyword (just a basic paragraph within the whole post) and the topic is showing up strong in terms of search ranking, then this is a great indication that pouring more energy into this topic would likely generate decent results. This may become a new, high-priority content topic, all based around what you learned from your keywords ranking report.

Just to provide some comparison, let's say you see another keyword in your keywords ranking report—"is nursing a good job"—further out in the search results, around position 30. In your article, you wrote just a few sentences about this. What this information tells you is you're not really getting traffic from that keyword in that position. However, you see that the keyword itself has pretty good search volume of around 5,000. For this reason, you could consider adding it to your list of content topics to flesh out later.

You may also find keywords ranking that you didn't expect. If they're relevant to your audience and your business, what a bonus! Perhaps you didn't target the topic of "nursing salary" in your "How to Become a Nurse" post, but you're noticing these types of keywords have pretty good search volume, too. You might consider adding a bit more to the salary discussion in that post, or you might create an entirely new post on the topic.

You may have noticed that the process of repurposing content essentially brings us back to keyword research again—this time, using your published posts as the starting point. Essentially, you can identify the keywords or topics that are ranking on a particular page. This means they may be worth targeting.

You may be thinking, "Isn't there a way to do this without manually inputting every single URL individually?" My friend, we wish there were. At the time of this writing, this is a fully manual process. But maybe by the time you read this book, there will be easier options. Keep in mind, you don't need to check keyword performance for every single piece of content. But it's definitely worth using this manual method for your top-performing posts to discover opportunities for content expansion.

> **Savvy Tip:** Whenever you create additional content inspired by a topic you've already covered, don't forget to cross-link between relevant pages! This is a simple and easy way to make sure that new content gets internal link love, but unfortunately this step is too often overlooked.

WHAT YOU CAN DO WITH WEAK CONTENT

Okay, so we've talked about your top performers, but what about the duds? If you've been producing content for a while and not quite seeing the results you want, what's your best course of action? Once you start producing content, it's a sizeable resource, so you don't want to just let your old content wither and die. While you're continuing to produce new content, don't forget about what you've already produced. Not every piece can be a huge hit, but going back and improving content that isn't performing well is part of a holistic content strategy.

Ideas for Revitalizing Low-Performing Content

For content that's not working, you have a few options. But, as we've said throughout the book, we're always making educated guesses to keep us improving over time. Not every piece can be a winner, and that's just part of the content marketing game. Use your best judgment to determine which content pieces are worth trying to resuscitate, and don't worry about saving every one. There will always be posts at the bottom of the list. Sometimes, you can take note of what you think may not have been successful and use that information to improve going forward—and that's enough. Otherwise, if there is reason to, you can go back and edit the post to try to revitalize it.

If a piece of evergreen content isn't bringing in the traffic you want, why is that? Does it need more information? Is it thin content compared to your competitors'? Does it need better optimization? You always have the option to go back into a page and revitalize it. Content marketing is not static. You can change, update, or rearrange content whenever it seems appropriate. Sometimes, you might need to expand the information. Other times, you might decide to scrap the content altogether and use those ideas to create something new that's even better. As a part of your content auditing process, be sure to spend at least a little bit of time returning to old pages and updating or improving them. If you notice an opportunity to improve a page and it won't take too much effort, what's there to lose?

The caveat: Simply being unable to outrank your competition may not be fixable with a small content tweak. So, take the bigger picture into consideration. Use your best judgment to discern whether it's an external or internal problem. If it's internal and you notice a few pieces that you think should be performing better, consider what might be happening.

With that in mind, here are some ways you can freshen up your old content:

- **Check your competitors' content.** If you're not ranking, go ahead and see what your search competitors are up to. These competitors might be your actual business competitors, but they could also be *search competitors* or entirely unrelated businesses that appear for the same keywords you're targeting. For example, Wikipedia is everyone's search competitor. The website isn't competing for your business, but it usually appears at the top of the SERP, so you can consider it competing for those coveted spots in search. A search competitor isn't stealing *business* opportunities but rather *traffic* opportunities. That being said, just type your content title into Google and see what results pop up first. What are they doing that you're not? How do they approach the subject matter? What can you learn about their success that you can apply to your own content? A little bit of competitor research can go a long way to see what *is* ranking for your topic. Notice any opportunities for improvement?
- **Check for related topics.** While you're at it, also notice what shows up for "People Also Ask" and "Related Results" on the SERP for a content title. What you're looking for are *related topics*. Are you missing out on covering related ideas in your post? Are other articles on the same topic more robust with more subtopics? This could be an indicator you've found some blank spots in your content. Maybe you need to include some more subheadings and subtopics to offer a more well-rounded approach. Is your focus too narrow? If you have reason to believe your topic would benefit from additional related content, consider beefing it up a little with related topics.
- **Check that the information is relevant and current.** Does anything need to be updated or edited? Perhaps new information has surfaced

since publishing, like a major study, piece of news, or popular trend. Would it make the content more robust to update it with these new findings? If you're adding new information, can you link out to new posts that you've since published? You'll want to make sure that, if you add new information, the topic is still streamlined, comprehensive, and clear (not like you've just "Frankenstein-ed" it).

- **Check the title.** Is it targeted for search? Is it relevant to the body of the content? Inaccurate titles can be a reason for a high bounce rate. You definitely want to make sure the title is not a "bait and switch." Similarly, topics and trends change over time. The way people use language changes, so maybe people are searching for this topic differently now. Maybe do some search research. Would updating the title with different language while keeping the rest of the content the same be a possible adjustment you could make?
- **Check semantic keyword usage overall.** Sometimes, you might discover that the language you're using isn't the language your audience is searching for. If you notice any opportunities to vary up the language, go back to your keyword research to see if you missed anything previously. For example, if you're optimizing for "automobile repair" but you find your audience is searching far more heavily for "car repair," this is a great sign you can make some small, easy adjustments to your language to better communicate with the people searching for you.
- **Check subheadings and keyword usage.** Can you update the subheadings to be more search-focused? Again, check what else is out there for ideas. You can also do another round of keyword research for your subheadings to see if there are any slight changes in phrasing that might be more search-friendly. In addition, ask yourself, "Is the content too unnaturally stuffed with keywords?" If it's not easy to read and obviously gimmicky, you might have a poor-quality situation. In that case, try writing in a more natural way. On the other hand, are you lacking keywords that might bring in more traffic? Can you do a little keyword research to work in more search-related questions to the body of the post?

- **Check internal linking.** Make sure other pages and posts on your site are cross-linking internally to your post when relevant. You can check your content tracker to see if there are other similar posts you can cross-link to each other. When you're creating new content, always look for opportunities to reference back to previous posts where it makes sense. Google views internal linking as a signal of value, so it's good to do it.
- **Check your quality in general.** Maybe when you published the piece you thought it was the best it could be. Or maybe you decided to publish even though there were still some areas for improvement. If a piece of content isn't performing, you can always look for ways to increase its quality—whether that's adding substance, improving the writing, changing perspective, or finding new sources.
- **Check your images and formatting.** Would adding more images or section breaks to the content make it easier to read? Is the actual content itself great, but it's one huge block of text that hurts the eyes? Perhaps the problem isn't quality but accessibility. Maybe a simple fix like adding more paragraph breaks or bullet points could help.
- **Check your calls-to-action.** If you're actually seeing high traffic but low conversions for a page that you think *should* be converting better, check all your calls-to-action, making sure they're clear, concise, and compelling. Do they sound too salesy? Not urgent enough? Are they disconnected from the subject? Consider what might not be working. Also, check your placement of these calls-to-action on the page. Are they too far down where people don't see them, or too loud too soon? Is everything working technically as it should?
- **Check your page speed.** There are a few different ways of looking at page speed, but there's no hard-and-fast method for checking it. PageSpeed Insights is a free tool from Google that offers back-end recommendations to help your page load more quickly. Page speed isn't really going to affect how much traffic you get, but it can impact how well you keep that traffic on the page. If your pages load too slowly, users can get easily frustrated and bail more quickly than you'd like. This

really has nothing to do with how Google serves the page, but it's a user experience factor to pay attention to. You'll want to make sure your content loads quickly, especially images and text first.
- **Technical issues.** Other issues for your developer may include crawl issues, dead pages, redirect issues, mobile usability issues, site map errors, canonical issues, or blocked/no index tags. This shortlist just means something may have happened on the technical end that prevents Google from finding and indexing your pages. You can pinpoint specific issues by inputting a URL into Google Search Console's URL section. It will ID issues there. Don't overlook these back-end problems that may be affecting your results.

You can use this checklist, or add ideas of your own, to regularly check back on your content and revitalize any old pieces that aren't performing as well as you think they should. There are certainly a million ways to make positive changes to your strategy, depending on your unique needs. But, to sum it all up, you can always do three things:

1. Revitalize and improve old content that's not performing well.
2. Repurpose content ideas, publishing them in new mediums for different platforms.
3. Expand content topics into even more nuanced, in-depth content pieces.

Make repurposing content a regular part of your content process, and be sure to track your results to see what makes a difference. You can also use these methods to refresh your well of content ideas in general when you feel stuck. Once you've been producing content for a long time, you may begin to feel like you're running out of topics, but, as we've mentioned before, this is rarely ever true. You can always return to the well and discover new opportunities at every turn.

Likewise, you can also go back and review your search research to find new opportunities. There are some great tools out there to help give you new ideas, like Answer the Public, which creates topic clusters using one initial key phrase. What else does your audience want to know about? What other topics are related to your main subjects? How can you explore a subject in a new or different way? Don't forget, you can use personas to slice and dice a popular topic into even more specific themes for a particular audience. You can use any of these tools to find related topics within posts you've already done.

Trust us, there is an endless amount of content out there that you could produce, sometimes overwhelmingly so. If or when you reach a point where you think you are out of ideas, try a different tool or a different approach. Sometimes even going back and revisiting the basics can provide a fresh perspective.

Remember that your goal is to be less wrong over time, and Rome wasn't built in a day. Keep your content efforts steady, strong, and informed by search research, and you *will* expand your brand, drive traffic, and connect with your customers online.

And that's it. We've covered a lot of ground, and we've almost reached the end of the book. In the final chapter ahead, we'll summarize our findings and tie everything together.

POINTS OF DISCOVERY

When is content marketing ever done? Consider how you can return to content pieces you've already produced:

1. Take a look at your content audit for a given period of time. What differences do you notice between your top-performing posts and your lower-performing posts? Name some concrete qualities you notice in your top-performing posts. Let this inform your content production going forward.
2. Are there any top-performing posts you could expand upon? Perhaps combine a few posts into a long-form e-guide, or take a sub-

topic in one of your posts and expand upon it as a new piece of content.

3. Choose a few lower-performing posts that you think have potential to be improved. Add these to your next content cycle. You may add content, edit content, change a title, add images, reformat, or otherwise optimize the piece. Consider it a "second draft" and send it back out into the world.

Conclusion

ALL BOATS RISE WITH THE TIDE

> Marketing is an ongoing communications exchange with customers in a way that educates, informs and builds a relationship over time. The over time part is important because only over time can trust be created.
>
> —**Renee Blodgett, Founder and CEO, Magic Sauce Media**

Imagine: You wake up to an alarm set by your digital personal assistant based on your schedule, with coffee brewed specifically to your taste and a queue of news articles already lined up for you to read. Your digital assistant reminds you of your meetings for the day, and you browse online for some shoes you're interested in before heading out.

Your GPS directs you to a meeting location based on email correspondence, and it also notifies you that the shoes you were looking at earlier are available in-store a few blocks away. A video pops up on your device featuring a celebrity wearing those shoes, engaging in activities you enjoy, like hiking and biking.

On your lunch break, you are directed to a nearby Thai restaurant because your digital assistant already knows what type of food you might be looking for in a new area. While at lunch, you snap a photo of your lunch and one of your favorite apps automatically calculates the number of calories in the meal, adding it to your fitness plan. In between meetings, you leisurely browse more curated articles and videos tailored to your interests and habits, and your digital assistant notifies you of a podcast just released on a topic in your field. After your workday, you come home to a queue of your favorite shows already lined up on your streaming device. (In between all of this, you are having real-time, face-to-face interactions with colleagues, friends, and family members.)

What does this scenario show us? Digital content is woven into the daily fabric of our lives, and we can expect this trend to continue. As acclaimed futurist Daniel Burrus predicts, rapid transformation in the next few years will change everything about the way we do business, including increased personalization and more integrated technology with even greater capabilities.[1] As his predecessor Alvin Toffler predicted in his 1970 book *Future Shock*, the convergence of capital, science, and communications has created a giant shift in our society.[2] We're still right in the middle of this exponential process.

Technology will certainly advance over the next five, ten, and fifteen years in ways some experts are predicting, but how that will play out exactly is not, as of yet, fully known. We may search for information by look, gesture, image, and voice, or use virtual reality to participate in real-time transactions with others, and more.[3] Rather than letting the possibilities overwhelm us, we recommend acknowledging the shift and working to create content that transcends these changes—content that is focused on the user, no matter the device, medium, or platform.

This is the essence of the content shift: Understand your audience and how they search for information online to create a content strategy that's tailored to answering their questions.

No matter how technology evolves, humans are always going to be curious. From the time that *homo sapiens* first quested for fire, to the advent of the printing press, and all the way forward to virtual reality, people have always—and will always—search for information. It's essential for the survival of our species to communicate and use language to pass on knowledge. The Internet breaks open the barriers to knowledge; no longer is education reserved for the elite.

Today, the Internet serves as an endless library, and every person and company has the opportunity to share a particular subset of knowledge with the specific group of people searching for it. Searching for information is a very human way of problem-solving. Understanding this principle will help keep you focused on what people want. The content shift asks you to focus on what your audience is searching for so you can provide those answers and win their business.

Human behavior isn't going to change. What's going to change is how we consume content and how we get information. It's virtually impossible to know which new tech trends will stay and become a regular part of our lives and which ones will streak brightly across the sky before burning out (like Myspace, Plurk, and any other number of platforms or apps). Instead, understand that things will change beyond your control, and your company's content marketing duty is to provide the answers your customers are searching for.

The difference between a master and a novice is that the master knows which realm he can control—his own. Let the tide come to you and be as absolutely prepared as you can be for every transformation. It's almost paradoxical what we're proposing: Acknowledge the changes in tech, use them to your advantage, but don't chase the tide. The content shift can help "future proof" your company and its marketing initiatives, keeping you relevant long into the future by reminding you to provide your customers with the information they're searching for.

Effective content marketing is like a tsunami—the results are easy to see, but the powerful build-up occurs beneath the surface over a long period of time. While strategic content marketing requires a large initial expenditure of energy to get going, and generally needs a substantial time frame, there is certainly a tipping point. And once you begin to build momentum and authority, the strength of your brand increases in an amazing way. You start seeing traffic, conversions, and results that you may not have ever expected or imagined.

When you put effort into optimizing one area of your website—then another and another—eventually, your entire website becomes more visible to search engines, more highly trafficked, and more available to your ideal audience and potential customers. This can reasonably lead to increased user engagement across all your marketing channels and campaigns, growth in brand awareness, and more consistent sales—not to mention recognition, success, and increased energy for forward movement. In this sense, *all boats rise with the tide.* The more content you strategically produce, the more that content will work for you over time.

In our experience, watching organic traffic grow over time is extremely rewarding. Knowing that consistent effort produces tangible results (visible in graphs and tables from your reporting) helps take the guesswork out of an otherwise nebulous process. We've found that once clients are able to make it past the initial strategy planning and implementation phases, and once they clearly see how their traffic is growing, the value of content marketing really becomes apparent. It's a positive feedback loop that requires an understanding of the process, but the results are inarguable!

FINDING YOUR PLACE ONLINE

As we approach the end of this book, you'll notice we haven't told you *what* your strategy should be or given you a formula for guaranteed success. We wish we could just tell you to produce ten 500-word blog posts each month and you'll be on your merry way, but it doesn't quite work that way. Content marketing relies on your specific vision and resources.

There's no one-size-fits-all formula, but your efforts can be enhanced by implementing a tried and true strategy. You'll have found no formula for overnight success in these pages; from years of experience, we know that's simply not how long-term success is reliably achieved. Consider the millions of users that coalesce to create the digital environment—kind of like how traffic moves. There are rules and roads well traveled, but we still have to navigate through a sea of other people directing their own intentions.

While a *formula* asks you to simply recreate something that has worked before, a *strategy* provides deeper insight, helping you to achieve results based on principles and guidelines. Your strategy will be based on *who* you are as a brand, *what* you uniquely have to offer, and *why* you are creating content for your specific audience in the first place. A strategy is flexible and can change with your business and audience needs.

If you only remember one thing from this book, remember this: Content marketing is about the connection between you and your audience. A content strategy intelligently uses your resources to connect with real people: your customers. Customers don't care about you; they care about how you can help them solve their problems. We want to give people what they want rather than pushing out messages they don't want. Listen to your customers, find out their needs and desires, and give them something they can use. Focusing on your audience's needs rather than your company's overt agenda makes all the difference. Talk less about yourself and more about what's important to your audience. Find out what's important to them by learning how they search online, then create content toward those topics. How you relate to your audience plays a big role in shaping your brand—and you can relate to your audience through content.

That being said, the window to infinite digital possibilities is open. Remember what your business is about and why you're doing what you're doing, as specifically as possible. A unique and reasonable content marketing vision often develops after lots of ideas are thrown on the table—even ideas from all departments. Then, keep the best ones. From there, think about balancing your time and energy costs with your goals and strategy so you're confident that what you're producing is in alignment with your company's best interests. This is the benefit of applying a strategy to all your efforts—minimal wasted time and effort; maximum output and returns.

And don't forget to check in—regularly. The Internet, your business, and your customers are constantly evolving entities, so your content strategy should constantly be evolving. You don't just create a content strategy and expect it to age like a fossil. This doesn't mean you need to rewrite your content strategy every month, but it does mean that, as you periodically conduct content audits, you'll want to use all the data and feedback you have and consider how you might innovate, adjust course, or try something new.

While planning and strategy are essential for content marketing success, don't forget that creativity and innovation are welcome partners to organization and analysis. While success is 99% perspiration, it's also 1% inspiration. Don't forget to leave room in your content strategy to think outside the box and consider creative ideas that require a bit more risk to implement. Find the balance that works for your particular company. If you have 90% of your content plan focused on research and results, perhaps allow 10% to explore what might be a huge failure or a wild success. If all these pieces are functioning properly and working together, you might find an outstanding idea or two that really sets you apart from the rest.

And try to enjoy the little things along the way. Remember from the beginning of the book, we said that content marketing shouldn't be an endless list of to-do items? Enjoy the beautiful moments of connecting with your audience. Celebrate each improvement to your strategy, lessons learned, and milestones achieved on the path to your goals. Take some time to slow down and allow yourself to feel proud, happy, and successful. These moments are essential to keeping the journey light-hearted, productive, and positive, wherever you happen to be in relationship to any destination.

As you move forward with your content marketing, keep the following questions in mind:

- How can your content be different or better than your competitors'?
- What will inspire your audience to trust you?
- What areas or topics related to your brand can you really focus on to become an authority in the field?
- What kind of content can help people better understand your product, service, or offering?
- What questions are your potential customers asking that you can reasonably answer?

With the endless reach of the Internet and ever-expanding innovations in technology, the sky's the limit when it comes to creating effective, successful content for your customers. Because there's so much freedom, it's the **practice of content marketing** that leads you to develop and hone your specific strategy. And it's the **consistent application of your strategy** that leads to long-lasting results.

Now, go forth and *communicate meaningfully with your customers.*

CONGRATULATIONS, AND GODSPEED!

Well, that's it! Congratulations! You've made it through the book. We truly appreciate the time you've taken to read through these pages. Like any topic, there's always more to be said, but we hope we've been able to provide you with both inspiration and a strong practical foundation for developing your own content strategy. You're pretty much set up to apply all these concepts and tools to your own unique content marketing strategy.

You can visit ContentShift.com for even more resources, templates, blog posts, and tutorials. Find what works for you, and do what you do best. Give the world the best you have to offer, and you'll inevitably be contributing to the conversation.

You can reach Jon or Mark at www.contentshift.com/contact/.

> "Now go produce great content and change the world!"
>
> **—Jon Heinl (ironically)**

> "Now go crack a beer."
>
> **—Mark Hawks (unironically)**

Glossary

Audience grouping: Also called "segmentation." The process of subdividing a general audience into distinct subsets of customers who occupy similar demographics, behave similarly, or have similar needs.

Audience mindset: The perspective that your company or brand's audience should be at the center of your marketing strategies, which includes doing audience research and becoming "audience to your audience."

Audience research: The process of collecting data about your target audience to learn about their interests and motivations for the purposes of forming audience groups and personas.

Brand awareness: The extent to which people recognize the existence of a company's product or service.

Brand identity: The image constructed by a company about itself.

Brand voice: Your company's distinct personality across online and offline marketing materials.

Buyer personas: Fictional characters designed from customer interactions and insights to represent a type of customer.

Competitor analysis: The process of researching the content produced by your online search competitors to identify opportunities and weaknesses in your own content production.

Consumer psychology: The field of study that researches, investigates, and explores how thoughts, feelings, beliefs, and perceptions may influence purchasing decisions.

Content: Any material produced that can be viewed, read, heard, consumed intellectually, or shared.

Content audit: A type of progress report for a content marketing strategy that should be conducted regularly to help identify what is working well and could be improved.

Content marketing: The act of producing relevant materials for a targeted audience group in order to provide value to the customer, inspire trust, and cultivate brand loyalty.

Content optimization: Strategic practices designed to make content more easily discoverable and readable across the web.

Content shift: The process of evolving a marketing mindset from product- or company-centered thinking toward audience- and search-focused strategies tailored to answering customer questions with high-quality, relevant content.

Content strategy: A written document that outlines how your content marketing will achieve your business goals.

Content strategist: A manager or editor on a content marketing team who is responsible for overseeing and directing overall content production, from defining goals and assigning tasks to measuring success and innovating.

Content tracker: May also be called a "content planner" or "editorial calendar." A working document that keeps track of all relevant content production details, such as deadlines, publication dates, and other status information.

Core keywords: The queries or phrases determined through search research to be the most relevant and valuable to your business, usually closely related to your core pages and often reflective of the business's primary services or products.

Core pages: The revenue-producing pages on a company's website, often product or service pages, usually landing pages.

Core questions: Keyword-researched customer search queries that are closely related to what your business does or sells.

GLOSSARY

Cross-linking: A key element of on-page optimization that connects relevant anchor text to another page on-site using a hyperlink.

Cumulative advantage: The business phenomenon that occurs when a customer continues to stay with a service or goods provider because of the convenience and ease that has built over time, in other words, the effort that would be required to switch providers would be more painful than continuing with the current provider.

Evergreen content: Naturally helpful and organically robust topics that stay relevant and fresh to search engines and users long after the material has been published because of their popularity among your audience and relatively timeless nature.

Google Analytics: A free online data-collection tool for tracking website metrics.

Head terms: Extremely popular and heavily searched terms online that have very high search volume, often general or vague phrases that are only one or two words long.

Keyword: In digital marketing, a word or phrase used by customers to perform a search, often linked to the content of a Search Engines Results Page (SERP).

Keyword modifiers: Additional words added onto a core keyword that increases the specificity of the search, such as adjectives, verbs, slang, locations, shopping terms, or parts of a question.

Keyword research: The process of gathering data about the search terms people use to find information related to your business online.

Long tail: The "mile wide and inch deep" part of the search curve that contains the longer, more specific, more detailed, and less popular search queries, including multiple iterations and modifications of any given keyword.

Organic traffic: Web traffic directed to your website through a search engine, and not paid advertisements.

Processing fluency: The ability of our brains to recognize repeated experiences.

Query: A phrase typed into a search engine.

Related keyword: A word or phrase that is closely linked to another keyword, semantically or conceptually.

Sales cycle: The series of marketing events that occur during the pre-purchase discovery phase of a product being sold.

Search Cycle: An online model of the buyer's path to purchase, which specifically details five stages of customer interactions on search engines, including: Awareness, Information Gathering, Evaluation, Commitment, and Support.

Search Engine Optimization (SEO): Also called "organic search marketing." An arm of digital marketing focused on growing web traffic organically through non-paid advertising.

Search Engine Results Page (SERP): The page that appears after a search query is typed into a search engine.

Search metrics: Website indicators that can be measured to track and improve web page performance.

Search mindset: The perspective that centers search engines as a valuable tool for connecting customers with companies in the online marketplace.

Search volume: The average number of searches for a keyword during a set time frame, usually measured monthly.

Semantic search: A search engine's ability to consider the context, intent, relationship, location, and history of a searcher in order to deliver relevant results.

Subheading: An additional heading or title that appears after the main title or headline of an article.

Target audience: A group of people who buy your products or consume your content.

User experience (UX): The practice of making web pages easier and more pleasant to read and navigate.

Please visit contentshift.com/resources for more glossary resources.

Acknowledgments

We would like to thank the extraordinary team behind the scenes who helped make this book possible. Grateful acknowledgement is made to the SEO Savvy editorial team Nancy Woo and Auroriele Hans, who write, edit and research like nobody's business. Thank you for helping us develop our content strategies over the years and for your contributions to this book. Thank you, as well, to our long-time web developer and graphic designer Alex Kater, who developed some of the initial search cycle models with us and who has been an integral part of the Savvy team. Sending thanks also to Sarah Cisco, our fantastic copyeditor, who helped us shape the raw material into the final product.

We are very grateful for the many, many people in the content marketing and SEO industry who have influenced and inspired us throughout our careers, including all of our partners, collaborators, and friends over the years.

Finally, we'd like to thank all of our current and past clients for trusting us with their business, working alongside us, and helping us refine the strategies and methods we've outlined here in *The Content Shift*.

And thank you, reader, for taking the time to read this book and consider your own content marketing strategies. We sincerely hope that we've conveyed ideas that inspire you in your marketing journey.

Notes

Introduction

1. SEO Savvy, "Content Marketing of Yore: The Jell-O Story," Seosavvy.com, September 18, 2014, accessed December 2019, http://www.seosavvy.com/blog/content-marketing-yore-jell-o-story/.
2. "The Woodward Family," Woodward Memorial Library, accessed March 2020, http://www.woodwardmemoriallibrary.org/family.php.
3. Matt Buzz, "The Fascinating, Untold History of Jell-O," Gizmodo.com, last modified January 24, 2014, accessed April 2020, https://gizmodo.com/the-fascinating-untold-history-of-jell-o-1508125288.
4. Neil Patel, "38 Content Marketing Stats That Every Marketer Needs to Know," Neil Patel, accessed January 2020, https://neilpatel.com/blog/38-content-marketing-stats-that-every-marketer-needs-to-know/.
5. Mitchell Hall, "Content Marketing Statistics: The Ultimate List," Curata.com, last modified July 17, 2017, accessed December 2019, http://www.curata.com/blog/content-marketing-statistics-the-ultimate-list/.
6. Heidi Cohen, "72 Marketing Definitions," HeidiCohen.com, March 29, 2011, accessed December 2019, https://heidicohen.com/marketing-definition/.
7. Dave Walters, *Behavioral Marketing: Delivering Personalized Experiences at Scale* (Hoboken, NJ: Wiley, 2015), 67.

Chapter 1: Let's Talk About Content

1. "What Is Content Marketing?" Content Marketing Institute, accessed January 2020, http://contentmarketinginstitute.com/what-is-content-marketing/.
2. A. Guttmann, "Ad Blocking User Penetration Rate in the United States from 2014 to 2021," Statista, September 25, 2020, accessed December 2020, https://www.statista.com/statistics/804008/ad-blocking-reach-usage-us/.
3. "The Ultimate List of Marketing Statistics for 2020," HubSpot, accessed December 2020, https://www.hubspot.com/marketing-statistics.
4. Kyle Byers, "What 3.25 Billion Site Visits Tell Us About Google, Facebook, and Where Different Niches Get Their Traffic," GrowthBadger, October 3, 2019, accessed December 2020, https://growthbadger.com/traffic-study/.

5. Mimi An, "What's the Deal with Ad Blocking? 11 Stats You Need to Know," HubSpot Blog, last modified August, 27, 2017, accessed January 2020, https://blog.hubspot.com/marketing/ad-blocking-stats#sm.000ebvhcl19vifqnuld2ae3mrfgw4.
6. Tanya Robertson, "Difference Between Push & Pull Marketing," Smallbusiness.chron.com, last modified March 1, 2019, accessed January 2020, http://smallbusiness.chron.com/difference-between-push-pull-marketing-31806.html.

Chapter 2: Great Content Builds Trust

1. Rani Molla, "Tech Companies Tried to Help Us Spend Less Time on Our Phones. It Didn't Work." Vox, last modified January 6, 2020, accessed February 2020, https://www.vox.com/recode/2020/1/6/21048116/tech-companies-time-well-spent-mobile-phone-usage-data.
2. Mark Dolliver, "US Time Spent with Media 2019," eMarketer, last modified May 30, 2019, accessed February 2020, https://www.emarketer.com/content/us-time-spent-with-media-2019.
3. Gary Small, M.D. and Gigi Vorgan, *iBrain: Surviving the Technological Alteration of the Modern Mind* (New York: HarperCollins, 2008), 16.
4. Pat Ahern, "25 Mind-Bottling SEO Stats for 2019 (and Beyond)," Junto, last modified June 5, 2019, accessed January 2020, https://junto.digital/blog/seo-stats/.
5. Ibid.
6. Kate Gardiner, "The Story Behind 'The Furrow,' the World's Oldest Content Marketing," Contently, last modified October 3, 2013, accessed February 2020, https://contently.com/2013/10/03/the-story-behind-the-furrow-2/.
7. Limor David, "Help Influence and Understand How Your Products Appear on Google," Google, last modified January 7, 2019, accessed January 2020, https://blog.google/products/ads/help-influence-and-understand-how-your-products-appear-google/.
8. B2B Content Marketing 2020, PDF, accessed December 2020, https://contentmarketinginstitute.com/wp-content/uploads/2019/10/2020_B2B_Research_Final.pdf.
9. B2C Content Marketing 2020, PDF, accessed December 2020, https://contentmarketinginstitute.com/wp-content/uploads/2019/12/2020_B2C_Research_Final.pdf.

Chapter 3: Strategy Starts at the Search Cycle

1. PYMNTS, "Study Finds Consumers Research Before They Buy," PYMNTS.com, January 9, 2018, accessed January 2020, https://www.pymnts.com/news/retail/2018/omichannel-ecommerce-consumer-habits/.
2. Tom Ryan, "How Long Is the Customer Journey?" Retail Wire, July 23, 2019, accessed December 2020, https://retailwire.com/discussion/how-long-is-the-customer-journey/.
3. "The Modern Consumer Decision-Making Journey," Deloitte, PDF, accessed December 2020, https://www2.deloitte.com/content/dam/Deloitte/us/Documents/CMO/us-modern-consumer-decision-making-journey.pdf.
4. Tom Anthony, "Revisiting 'Navigational,' 'Informational,' & 'Transactional' Searches

in a Post-PageRank World," last modified January 18, 2016, accessed February 2020, https://moz.com/blog/revisiting-navigational-informational-transactional-search-post-pagerank.
5. Ibid.

Chapter 4: Achieving Online Authority

1. Megan Marrs, "18 Sneaky Ways to Build Brand Awareness," The WordStream Blog, last modified June 9, 2019, accessed January 2020, https://www.wordstream.com/blog/ws/2015/07/10/brand-awareness.
2. Erik Sherman, "20 Years of Amazon's Expansive Evolution," CBSnews.com, July 15, 2015, accessed January 2020, https://www.cbsnews.com/news/20-years-of-amazons-expansive-evolution/.
3. Robert Rose and Carla Johnson, *Experiences: The 7th Era of Marketing* (Cleveland: Content Marketing Institute, 2015), 25.
4. Chris Kelly, "Coca-Cola Kicks off Massive Agency Review to 'Fundamentally Transform' Its Marketing," *Marketing Dive*, December 10, 2020, accessed December 2020, https://www.marketingdive.com/news/coca-cola-kicks-off-massive-agency-review-to-fundamentally-transform-its/591932/.
5. Ibid.
6. Marc de Swaan Arons, "How Brands Were Born: A Brief History of Modern Marketing," *The Atlantic*, October 3, 2011, accessed January 2020, https://www.theatlantic.com/business/archive/2011/10/how-brands-were-born-a-brief-history-of-modern-marketing/246012/.

Chapter 5: Why Consistency Matters

1. A.G. Lafley and Roger L. Martin, "Customer Loyalty Is Overrated," Harvard Business Review, January–February 2017, accessed January 2020, https://hbr.org/2017/01/customer-loyalty-is-overrated.
2. Thomas A. DiPerete and Gregory M. Eirich, "Cumulative Advantage as a Mechanism for Inequality: A Review of Theoretical and Empirical Developments." *Annual Review of Sociology* 32, no. 1 (January 2008), http://citeseerx.ist.psu.edu/viewdoc/download?doi=10.1.1.529.6139&rep=rep1&type=pdf.

Chapter 6: Making the Content Shift

1. Rick Levine, Christopher Locke, et al., *The Cluetrain Manifesto: The End of Business as Usual* (Cambridge, MA: Basic Books, 2011), chap. 4, http://www.searls.com/cluetrain/markets.html.
2. "Total Number of Websites," InternetLiveStats.com, accessed December 2020, https://www.internetlivestats.com/total-number-of-websites/.
3. Mary Wallace, "How to Market Successfully in a Digital World? Put Customers' Needs First," Marketing Land, March 1, 2016, accessed January 2020, https://marketingland.com/technology-took-customers-away-brought-back-166455.
4. Ann Handley and Lisa Murton Beets, "11th Annual B2B Content Marketing: Benchmarks, Budgets, and Trends—Insights for 2021," PDF. https://contentmarketing

institute.com/wp-content/uploads/2020/09/b2b-2021-research-final.pdf#page=32.
5. Julia McCoy, "How to Explain Content Marketing ROI to Win (or Keep) Buy-In," Content Marketing Institute, June 7, 2018, accessed January 2020, https://contentmarketinginstitute.com/2018/06/explain-content-marketing-roi/.
6. Ibid.
7. Danny Goodwin, "60+ Mind-Blowing Search Engine Optimization Stats—SEO 101," Search Engine Journal, December 29, 2017, accessed January 2020, https://www.searchenginejournal.com/seo-101/seo-statistics/.
8. "The Ultimate List of Marketing Statistics for 2020," HubSpot, accessed December 2020, https://www.hubspot.com/marketing-statistics.
9. "Content Marketing Infographic," DemandMetric.com, accessed January 2020, https://www.demandmetric.com/content/content-marketing-infographic.

Chapter 7: Building Relationships through Content

1. "Definitions Of Marketing," American Marketing Association, last modified 2017, accessed January 2020, https://www.ama.org/the-definition-of-marketing-what-is-marketing/.
2. Theodore Levitt, *Marketing Myopia*, ebook (Boston: Harvard Business Press, 2008), accessed January 2020, https://books.google.com/books?id=-HP_BgAAQBAJ.
3. Heidi Cohen, "72 Marketing Definitions," HeidiCohen.com, March 29, 2011, accessed January 2020, https://heidicohen.com/marketing-definition/.
4. CopyPress, "The Difference Between Your Target Market and Target Audience," CopyPress.com, February 3, 2014, accessed January 2020, https://www.copypress.com/blog/how-to-resonate-with-your-target-market/.

Chapter 8: Audience Grouping

1. Eric Siu, "We Break Down B2B vs. B2C Marketing," HubSpot, September 7, 2015, last modified October 29, 2019, accessed January 2020, http://blog.hubspot.com/marketing/b2b-b2c-content-marketing#sm.00001mo9w1shu9f5gt6scf901i67j.
2. Rick Levine, Christopher Locke, et al., The Cluetrain Manifesto: The End of Business as Usual (Cambridge, MA: Basic Books, 2000), 1.
3. Maximilian Claessens, "Requirements for Profitable Segments – Select Attractive Market Segments," Marketing-Insider, June 27, 2016, accessed March 2020, https://marketing-insider.eu/requirements-for-profitable-segments/.
4. "Criteria for Effective Market Segmentation," SegmentationStudyGuide.com, accessed January 2020, http://www.segmentationstudyguide.com/understanding-market-segmentation/criteria-for-effective-market-segmentation/.

Chapter 9: Emotional and Psychological Needs

1. FireflySixtySeven, Pyramid Showing Maslow's Hierarchy of Needs, November 2, 2014, Wikimedia Commons, accessed March 11, 2020, https://commons.wikimedia.org/wiki/File:MaslowsHierarchyOfNeeds.svg.

2. Courtney Seitner, "The Science of Emotion in Marketing: How to Leverage Our Feelings," Buffer.com, March 4, 2014, last modified April 26, 2016, accessed January 2020, https://blog.bufferapp.com/science-of-emotion-in-marketing.
3. Ibid.
4. Ibid.
5. Ibid.
6. Andrew Draughon, "Four Email Marketing Lessons from the Greatest Advertising Campaign of the 20th Century," Elite Marketing Pro, accessed January 18, 2020, https://elitemarketingpro.com/blog/four-email-marketing-lessons-greatest-advertising-campaign-20th-century/.
7. Kit Yarrow, Decoding the New Consumer Mind: How and Why We Shop and Buy (San Francisco: Jossey-Bass, 2014), 106.
8. Ibid.

Chapter 10: Using Personas

1. Adele Revella, *Buyer Personas: How to Gain Insight into Your Customer's Expectations, Align Your Marketing Strategies, and Win More Business* (Hoboken, NJ: Wiley, 2015), 184.
2. *Buyer Personas*, 10.

Chapter 12: Understanding Search Engines

1. David Zheng, "The 15 Second Rule: 3 Reasons Why Users Leave a Website," The Daily Egg, last modified February 26, 2019, accessed January 2020, https://www.crazyegg.com/blog/why-users-leave-a-website/.
2. StatCounter, "Search Engine Market Share Worldwide, May 2019-May2020," GlobalStats, accessed June 2020, https://gs.statcounter.com/search-engine-market-share.
3. Google, "About," About.google, accessed January 2020, https://about.google/.
4. Google, "Webmaster Guidelines – Search Console Help," Support.google.com, accessed January 2020, https://support.google.com/webmasters/answer/35769?hl=en.
5. Ibid.
6. Wikipedia, "Wikipedia: About," En.wikipedia.org, last modified January 20, 2020, accessed January 2020, https://en.wikipedia.org/wiki/Wikipedia:About#Strengths.2C_weaknesses.2C_and_article_quality_in_Wikipedia.

Chapter 13: Speaking the Language of Search

1. Aleh Barysevich, "Semantic Search: What It Is & Why It Matters for SEO Today," Search Engine Journal, September 6, 2018, accessed January 2020, https://www.searchenginejournal.com/semantic-search-seo/264037/#close.
2. "What Is a Keyword? – Definition & Information," MarketingTerms.com, accessed January 2020, http://www.marketingterms.com/dictionary/keyword/.
3. Barry Schwartz, "Google Reaffirms 15% of Searches Are New, Never Been Searched Before," Search Engine Land, April 25, 2017, accessed January 2020,

https://searchengineland.com/google-reaffirms-15-searches-new-never-searched-273786.
4. "Head Term: What Is a Head Term?," WordStream.com, accessed January 2020, https://www.wordstream.com/head-term.
5. "'Why?' Dominated the 2020 Google Year in Search," ThinkwithGoogle.com, accessed December 2020, https://www.thinkwithgoogle.com/consumer-insights/consumer-trends/2020-year-in-search/.
6. SEO Glossary—Mid-Tail Keyword," InternetMarketingNinjas.com, accessed January 2020, https://www.internetmarketingninjas.com/glossary/mid-tail-keyword.htm.

Chapter 14: Keyword Research to Discover Content Topics

1. Greg Satell, "Why Our Numbers Are Always Wrong," DigitalTonto.com, October 28, 2012, accessed January 2020, http://www.digitaltonto.com/2012/why-our-numbers-are-always-wrong/.
2. Josh Freedman, "Definition of Anchor Text," Web 1 Consulting LLC, November 8, 2019, accessed January 2020, http://www.web1marketing.com/glossary.php?term=Keyword+Research.
3. "About Us | SEMrush," SEMrush.com, accessed January 2020, .
4. "Search Volume Definition | Ryte Wiki," En.ryte.com, accessed January 2020, https://en.ryte.com/wiki/Search_Volume.
5. "How Google Search Works | Maximize Access to Information," Google.com, accessed January 2020, https://www.google.com/search/howsearchworks/mission/open-web/.

Chapter 15: Evaluating Keyword Questions

1. Kathi Kruse, "Rule of 7: How Social Media Crushes Old School Marketing," Kruse Control Inc, March 29, 2018, accessed January 2020, https://www.krusecontrolinc.com/rule-of-7-how-social-media-crushes-old-school-marketing/.
2. John Lynch, "Mapping Search Strategy to the Buy Cycle," Search Engine Watch, February 23, 2011, accessed January 2020, https://www.searchenginewatch.com/2011/02/23/mapping-search-strategy-to-the-buy-cycle/.

Chapter 16: Taking Search Research Even Deeper

1. Kristine Schachinger, "4 Reasons Organic Search Is Better," Search Engine Land, September 9, 2015, accessed January 2020, http://searchengineland.com/4-reasons-organic-better-230003.
2. Rand Fishkin, "Google CTR in 2018: Paid, Organic, & No-Click Searches," SparkToro, October 30, 2018, accessed January 2020, https://sparktoro.com/blog/google-ctr-in-2018-paid-organic-no-click-searches/.

Chapter 17: Documenting Your Content Strategy

1. Lee Odden, Optimize: How to Attract and Engage More Customers by Integrating SEO, Social Media, and Content Marketing (Hoboken, NJ: Wiley, 2012), 115.

Chapter 18: Content Types and Optimization

1. Michael Kwan, "From Where Did the Word Blog Come?," LoveToKnow, accessed February 2020, https://socialnetworking.lovetoknow.com/From_Where_Did_the_Word_Blog_Come.
2. Adam Hayes, "The State of Video Marketing in 2020 [New Data]," HubSpot, December 23, 2019, last modified January 2, 2020, accessed February 2020, https://blog.hubspot.com/marketing/state-of-video-marketing-new-data.
3. Brian Dean, "104 Content Marketing Stats Every Marketer Needs to Know," Backlinko, September 12, 2019, accessed March 2020, https://backlinko.com/content-marketing-stats.
4. Ying Lin, "10 Powerful Podcast Statistics You Need to Know in 2020 [Infographic]," Oberlo, January 7, 2020, accessed June 2020, https://www.oberlo.com/blog/podcast-statistics.
5. "11th Annual B2B Content Marketing Benchmarks, Budgets, and Trends: Insights for 2021," Content Marketing Institute, September 25, 2020, https://www.slideshare.net/CMI/11th-annual-b2b-content-marketing-benchmarks-budgets-and-trends-insights-for-2021-238645831/1, (slides 25 and 35).
6. Jeremy Moser, "The Top 101 Blogging Statistics for 2019," Codeless, June 24, 2019, accessed February 2020, https://getcodeless.com/blogging-statistics/#1.
7. "Quote by Dr. Seuss," Goodreads, accessed June 2020, https://www.goodreads.com/quotes/176857-so-the-writer-who-breeds-more-words-than-he-needs.
8. Andy Crestodina, "[New Research] How Has Blogging Changed? 5 Years of Blogging Statistics, Data and Trends," Orbit Media Studios, January 16, 2020, accessed February 2020, https://www.orbitmedia.com/blog/blogging-statistics/#Q5.
9. Ibid.
10. Moser, "Blogging Statistics."
11. Larry Kim, "16 Visual Content Marketing Statistics That Will Wake You Up," Medium.com, March 9, 2018, accessed February 2020, https://medium.com/marketing-and-entrepreneurship/16-visual-content-marketing-statistics-that-will-wake-you-up-59c4c0b80465.

Chapter 19: Streamlining Your Content Production Process

1. Kristina Halvorson and Melissa Rach, Content Strategy for the Web, 2nd Edition (Berkeley, CA: New Riders, 2012), 129–157.

Chapter 20: Creating Quality and Style Guidelines for Your Brand

1. Danny Sullivan, "Google Launches New Effort to Flag Upsetting or Offensive Content in Search," Search Engine Land, March 14, 2017, accessed February 2020, https://searchengineland.com/google-flag-upsetting-offensive-content-271119.

2. Google, "Webmaster Guidelines—Search Console Help," Support.google.com, accessed February 2020, https://support.google.com/webmasters/answer/35769?hl=en.
3. Sasha Laferte, "Style Guide: How to Write One for Your Brand," Content Marketing Institute, May 10, 2017, accessed February 2020, http://contentmarketinginstitute.com/2017/05/write-style-guide-brand/.
4. Julie Wildhaber, "Understanding Voice and Tone in Writing," Quick and Dirty Tips, July 1, 2010, accessed February 2020, http://www.quickanddirtytips.com/education/grammar/understanding-voice-and-tone-in-writing?page=1.
5. Larry Kim, "16 Visual Content Marketing Statistics That Will Wake You Up," Medium, March 9, 2018, accessed February 2020, https://medium.com/marketing-and-entrepreneurship/16-visual-content-marketing-statistics-that-will-wake-you-up-59c4c0b80465.

Chapter 21: Measuring Success with Key Metrics

1. Paige Jones, "What's the Difference between Google Analytics and Google Search Console?," Twenty Over Ten, January 23, 2019, accessed February 2020, https://blog.twentyoverten.com/whats-the-difference-between-google-analytics-and-google-search-console/.
2. Dave Rohrer, email conversation with Mark Hawks, November 2020.
3. Ibid.
4. Google, "How a Web Session Is Defined in Universal Analytics—Analytics Help," Support.google.com, accessed February 2021, https://support.google.com/analytics/answer/2731565.
5. Mimi An, "Rethinking Social Media Marketing: How to Use a Behavior Based Approach for Content on Social Media," HubSpot, December 19, 2018, last modified April 25, 2019, accessed December 2020, https://blog.hubspot.com/marketing/rethinking-social-media-marketing-how-to-use-a-behavior-based-approach-for-content-on-social-media.
6. Conversation with Dave Rohrer.
7. Sujan Patel, email conversation with Mark Hawks, November 2020.
8. Ibid.

Conclusion: All Boats Rise with the Tide

1. Burrus, Daniel, "Daniel Burrus' Top 20 Technology-Driven Hard Trends," Burrus Research, January 4, 2018, accessed March 2021, https://www.burrus.com/2018/01/daniel-burrus-top-20-technology-driven-hard-trends-shaping-2018-beyond/.
2. Ryan, Kevin J. "4 Things Futurist Alvin Toffler Predicted About Work Back in 1970." Inc. June 30, 2016. https://www.inc.com/kevin-j-ryan/4-things-futurist-alvin-toffler-predicted-about-work-in-1970.html.
3. Edwin van Bommel, David Edelman, and Kelly Ungerman, "Digitizing the Consumer Decision Journey," McKinsey & Company, June 2014, accessed February 2020, http://www.mckinsey.com/business-functions/marketing-and-sales/our-insights/digitizing-the-consumer-decision-journey.

Works Cited

"11th Annual B2B Content Marketing Benchmarks, Budgets, and Trends: Insights for 2021." Content Marketing Institute. September 25, 2020. https://www.slideshare.net/CMI/11th-annual-b2b-content-marketing-benchmarks-budgets-and-trends-insights-for-2021-238645831/1. (Slides 25 and 35).

"About Us | SEMrush." SEMrush.com. Accessed January 2020. https://www.semrush.com/company/.

Ahern, Pat. "25 Mind-Bottling SEO Stats for 2019 (and Beyond)." Junto. Last modified June 5, 2019. Accessed January 2020. https://junto.digital/blog/seo-stats/.

An, Mimi. "Rethinking Social Media Marketing: How to Use a Behavior-Based Approach for Content on Social Media." HubSpot. December 19, 2018. Last modified April 25, 2019. Accessed December 2020. https://blog.hubspot.com/marketing/rethinking-social-media-marketing-how-to-use-a-behavior-based-approach-for-content-on-social-media.

An, Mimi. "What's the Deal with Ad Blocking? 11 Stats You Need to Know." HubSpot Blog. Last modified August, 27, 2017. Accessed January 2020. https://blog.hubspot.com/marketing/ad-blocking-stats#sm.000ebvhcl19vifqnuld2ae3mrfgw4.

Anthony, Tom. "Revisiting 'Navigational,' 'Informational,' & 'Transactional' Searches in a Post-PageRank World." Last modified January 18, 2016. Accessed February 2020. https://moz.com/blog/revisiting-navigational-informational-transactional-search-post-pagerank.

B2B Content Marketing 2020. PDF. Accessed December 2020. https://contentmarketinginstitute.com/wp-content/uploads/2019/10/2020_B2B_Research_Final.pdf.

B2C Content Marketing 2020. PDF. Accessed December 2020. https://contentmarketinginstitute.com/wp-content/uploads/2019/12/2020_B2C_Research_Final.pdf.

Barysevich, Aleh. "Semantic Search: What It Is & Why It Matters for SEO Today." Search Engine Journal. September 6, 2018. Accessed January 2020. https://www.searchenginejournal.com/semantic-search-seo/264037/#close.

Burrus, Daniel. "Daniel Burrus' Top 20 Technology-Driven Hard Trends." Burrus Research. January 4, 2018. Accessed March 2021. https://www.burrus.com/2018/01/daniel-burrus-top-20-technology-driven-hard-trends-shaping-2018-beyond/.

Buzz, Matt. "The Fascinating, Untold History of Jell-O." Gizmodo.com. Last modified January 24, 2014. Accessed April 2020. https://gizmodo.com/the-fascinating-untold-history-of-jell-o-1508125288.

WORKS CITED

Byers, Kyle. "What 3.25 Billion Site Visits Tell Us About Google, Facebook, and Where Different Niches Get Their Traffic." GrowthBadger. October 3, 2019. Accessed December 2020. https://growthbadger.com/traffic-study/.

Claessens, Maximilian. "Requirements for Profitable Segments—Select Attractive Market Segments." Marketing-Insider. June 27, 2016. Accessed March 2020. https://marketing-insider.eu/requirements-for-profitable-segments/.

Cohen, Heidi. "72 Marketing Definitions." HeidiCohen.com. March 29, 2011. Accessed December 2019. https://heidicohen.com/marketing-definition/.

"Content Marketing Infographic." DemandMetric.com. Accessed January 2020. https://www.demandmetric.com/content/content-marketing-infographic.

CopyPress. "The Difference Between Your Target Market and Target Audience." CopyPress.com. February 3, 2014. Accessed January 2020. https://www.copypress.com/blog/how-to-resonate-with-your-target-market/.

Crestodina, Andy. "[New Research] How Has Blogging Changed? 5 Years of Blogging Statistics, Data and Trends." Orbit Media Studios. January 16, 2020. Accessed February 2020. https://www.orbitmedia.com/blog/blogging-statistics/#Q5.

"Criteria for Effective Market Segmentation." SegmentationStudyGuide.com. Accessed January 2020. http://www.segmentationstudyguide.com/understanding-market-segmentation/criteria-for-effective-market-segmentation/.

David, Limor. "Help Influence and Understand How Your Products Appear on Google." Google. Last modified January 7, 2019. Accessed January 2020. https://blog.google/products/ads/help-influence-and-understand-how-your-products-appear-google/.

de Swaan Arons, Marc. "How Brands Were Born: A Brief History of Modern Marketing." *The Atlantic*. October 3, 2011. Accessed January 2020. https://www.theatlantic.com/business/archive/2011/10/how-brands-were-born-a-brief-history-of-modern-marketing/246012/.

Dean, Brian. "104 Content Marketing Stats Every Marketer Needs to Know." Backlinko. September 12, 2019. Accessed March 2020. https://backlinko.com/content-marketing-stats.

"Definitions of Marketing." American Marketing Association. Last modified 2017. Accessed January 2020. https://www.ama.org/the-definition-of-marketing-what-is-marketing/.

DiPerete, Thomas A. and Gregory M. Eirich. "Cumulative Advantage as a Mechanism for Inequality: A Review of Theoretical and Empirical Developments." *Annual Review of Sociology* 32, no. 1 (January 2008). http://citeseerx.ist.psu.edu/viewdoc/download?doi=10.1.1.529.6139&rep=rep1&type=pdf.

Dolliver, Mark. "US Time Spent with Media 2019." eMarketer. Last modified May 30, 2019. Accessed February 2020. https://www.emarketer.com/content/us-time-spent-with-media-2019.

Draughon, Andrew. "Four Email Marketing Lessons from the Greatest Advertising Campaign of the 20th Century." Elite Marketing Pro. Accessed January 18, 2020. https://elitemarketingpro.com/blog/four-email-marketing-lessons-greatest-advertising-campaign-20th-century/.

FireflySixtySeven. *Pyramid Showing Maslow's Hierarchy of Needs*. November 2, 2014. Wikimedia Commons. Accessed March 11, 2020. https://commons.wikimedia.org/wiki/File:MaslowsHierarchyOfNeeds.svg.

WORKS CITED

Fishkin, Rand. "Google CTR in 2018: Paid, Organic, & No-Click Searches." SparkToro. October 30, 2018. Accessed January 2020. https://sparktoro.com/blog/google-ctr-in-2018-paid-organic-no-click-searches/.

Freedman, Josh. "Definition of Anchor Text." Web 1 Consulting LLC. November 8, 2019. Accessed January 2020. https://www.web1consulting.com/?term=Keyword+Research.

Gardiner, Kate. "The Story Behind 'The Furrow,' the World's Oldest Content Marketing." Contently. Last modified October 3, 2013. Accessed February 2020. https://contently.com/2013/10/03/the-story-behind-the-furrow-2/.

Goodwin, Danny. "60+ Mind-Blowing Search Engine Optimization Stats—SEO 101." Search Engine Journal. December 29, 2017. Accessed January 2020. https://www.searchenginejournal.com/seo-101/seo-statistics/.

Google. "About." About.google. Accessed January 2020. https://about.google/.

Google. "How a Web Session Is Defined in Universal Analytics – Analytics Help." Support.google.com. Accessed February 2021. https://support.google.com/analytics/answer/2731565.

Google. "Webmaster Guidelines – Search Console Help." Support.google.com. Accessed January 2020. https://support.google.com/webmasters/answer/35769?hl=en.

Guttmann, A. "Ad Blocking User Penetration Rate in the United States from 2014 to 2021." Statista. September 25, 2020. Accessed December 2020. https://www.statista.com/statistics/804008/ad-blocking-reach-usage-us/.

Hall, Mitchell. "Content Marketing Statistics: The Ultimate List." Curata.com. Last modified July 17, 2017. Accessed December 2019. http://www.curata.com/blog/content-marketing-statistics-the-ultimate-list/.

Halvorson, Kristina and Melissa Rach. *Content Strategy for the Web, 2nd Edition* (Berkeley, CA: New Riders, 2012). 129–157.

Handley, Ann and Lisa Murton Beets. "11th Annual B2B Content Marketing: Benchmarks, Budgets, and Trends—Insights for 2021." PDF. https://contentmarketinginstitute.com/wp-content/uploads/2020/09/b2b-2021-research-final.pdf#page=32.

"Head Term: What Is a Head Term?" WordStream.com. Accessed January 2020. https://www.wordstream.com/head-term.

"How Google Search Works | Maximize Access to Information." Google.com. Accessed January 2020. https://www.google.com/search/howsearchworks/mission/open-web/.

Jones, Paige. "What's the Difference between Google Analytics and Google Search Console?" Twenty Over Ten. January 23, 2019. Accessed February 2020. https://blog.twentyoverten.com/whats-the-difference-between-google-analytics-and-google-search-console/.

Kelly, Chris. "Coca-Cola Kicks off Massive Agency Review to 'Fundamentally Transform' Its Marketing." *Marketing Dive*. December 10, 2020. Accessed December 2020. https://www.marketingdive.com/news/coca-cola-kicks-off-massive-agency-review-to-fundamentally-transform-its/591932/.

Kim, Larry. "16 Visual Content Marketing Statistics That Will Wake You Up." Medium.com. March 9, 2018. Accessed February 2020. https://medium.com/marketing-and-entrepreneurship/16-visual-content-marketing-statistics-that-will-wake-you-up-59c4c0b80465.

Kruse, Kathi. "Rule of 7: How Social Media Crushes Old School Marketing." Kruse Control Inc. March 29, 2018. Accessed January 2020. https://www.krusecontrolinc.com/rule-of-7-how-social-media-crushes-old-school-marketing/.

Kwan, Michael. "From Where Did the Word Blog Come?" LoveToKnow. Accessed February 2020. https://socialnetworking.lovetoknow.com/From_Where_Did_the_Word_Blog_Come.

Laferte, Sasha. "Style Guide: How to Write One for Your Brand." Content Marketing Institute. May 10, 2017. Accessed February 2020. https://contentmarketinginstitute.com/2017/05/write-style-guide-brand/.

Lafley, A.G. and Roger L. Martin. "Customer Loyalty Is Overrated." Harvard Business Review. January–February 2017. Accessed January 2020. https://hbr.org/2017/01/customer-loyalty-is-overrated.

Levine, Rick, Christopher Locke, et al. *The Cluetrain Manifesto: The End of Business as Usual* (Cambridge, MA: Basic Books, 2011). Chap. 4. http://www.searls.com/cluetrain/markets.html.

Levine, Rick, Christopher Locke, et al. *The Cluetrain Manifesto: The End of Business as Usual* (Cambridge, MA: Basic Books, 2000). 1.

Levitt, Theodore. *Marketing Myopia*. ebook (Boston: Harvard Business Press, 2008). Accessed January 2020. https://books.google.com/books?id=-HP_BgAAQBAJ.

Lin, Ying. "10 Powerful Podcast Statistics You Need to Know in 2020 [Infographic]." Oberlo. January 7, 2020. Accessed June 2020. https://www.oberlo.com/blog/podcast-statistics.

Lynch, John. "Mapping Search Strategy to the Buy Cycle." Search Engine Watch. February 23, 2011. Accessed January 2020. https://www.searchenginewatch.com/2011/02/23/mapping-search-strategy-to-the-buy-cycle/.

Marrs, Megan. "18 Sneaky Ways to Build Brand Awareness." The WordStream Blog. Last modified June 9, 2019. Accessed January 2020. https://www.wordstream.com/blog/ws/2015/07/10/brand-awareness.

McCoy, Julia. "How to Explain Content Marketing ROI to Win (or Keep) Buy-In." Content Marketing Institute. June 7, 2018. Accessed January 2020. https://contentmarketinginstitute.com/2018/06/explain-content-marketing-roi/.

"The Modern Consumer Decision-Making Journey." Deloitte. PDF. Accessed December 2020. https://www2.deloitte.com/content/dam/Deloitte/us/Documents/CMO/us-modern-consumer-decision-making-journey.pdf.

Molla, Rani. "Tech Companies Tried to Help Us Spend Less Time on Our Phones. It Didn't Work." Vox. Last modified January 6, 2020. Accessed February 2020. https://www.vox.com/recode/2020/1/6/21048116/tech-companies-time-well-spent-mobile-phone-usage-data.

Moser, Jeremy. "The Top 101 Blogging Statistics for 2019." Codeless. June 24, 2019. Accessed February 2020. https://getcodeless.com/blogging-statistics/#1.

Odden, Lee. *Optimize: How to Attract and Engage More Customers by Integrating SEO, Social Media, and Content Marketing* (Hoboken, NJ: Wiley, 2012). 115.

Patel, Neil. "38 Content Marketing Stats That Every Marketer Needs to Know." Neil Patel. Accessed January 2020. https://neilpatel.com/blog/38-content-marketing-stats-that-every-marketer-needs-to-know/.

Patel, Sujan. Email conversation with Mark Hawks. November 2020.

PYMNTS. "Study Finds Consumers Research Before They Buy." PYMNTS.com. January 9, 2018. Accessed January 2020. https://www.pymnts.com/news/retail/2018/omichannel-ecommerce-consumer-habits/.

"Quote by Dr. Seuss." Goodreads. Accessed June 2020. https://www.goodreads.com

/quotes/176857-so-the-writer-who-breeds-more-words-than-he-needs.

Revella, Adele. *Buyer Personas: How to Gain Insight into Your Customer's Expectations, Align Your Marketing Strategies, and Win More Business* (Hoboken, NJ: Wiley, 2015). 184.

Riley, Tonya. "The Minty Fresh Psychology Behind America's Toothpaste Obsession." Heleo.com. November 25, 2015. Accessed January 2020. https://heleo.com/the-minty-fresh-psychology-behind-americas-toothpaste-obsession/1196/.

Robertson, Tanya. "Difference Between Push & Pull Marketing." Smallbusiness.chron. Last modified March 1, 2019. Accessed January 2020. http://smallbusiness.chron.com/difference-between-push-pull-marketing-31806.html.

Rose, Robert and Carla Johnson. *Experiences: The 7th Era of Marketing* (Cleveland: Content Marketing Institute, 2015). 25.

Ryan, Kevin J. "4 Things Futurist Alvin Toffler Predicted About Work Back in 1970." Inc. June 30, 2016. https://www.inc.com/kevin-j-ryan/4-things-futurist-alvin-toffler-predicted-about-work-in-1970.html.

Ryan, Tom. "How Long Is the Customer Journey?" Retail Wire. July 23, 2019. Accessed December 2020. https://retailwire.com/discussion/how-long-is-the-customer-journey/.

Satell, Greg. "Why Our Numbers Are Always Wrong." DigitalTonto.com. October 28, 2012. Accessed January 2020. https://www.digitaltonto.com/2012/why-our-numbers-are-always-wrong/.

Schachinger, Kristine. "4 Reasons Organic Search Is Better." Search Engine Land. September 9, 2015. Accessed January 2020. https://searchengineland.com/4-reasons-organic-better-230003.

Schwartz, Barry. "Google Reaffirms 15% of Searches Are New, Never Been Searched Before." Search Engine Land. April 25, 2017. Accessed January 2020. https://searchengineland.com/google-reaffirms-15-searches-new-never-searched-273786.

"Search Volume Definition | Ryte Wiki." En.ryte.com. Accessed January 2020. https://en.ryte.com/wiki/Search_Volume.

Seitner, Courtney. "The Science of Emotion in Marketing: How to Leverage Our Feelings." Buffer.com. March 4, 2014. Last modified April 26, 2016. Accessed January 2020. https://blog.bufferapp.com/science-of-emotion-in-marketing.

SEO Glossary – Mid-Tail Keyword." InternetMarketingNinjas.com. Accessed January 2020. https://www.internetmarketingninjas.com/glossary/mid-tail-keyword.htm.

SEO Savvy. "Content Marketing of Yore: The Jell-O Story." Seosavvy.com. September 18, 2014. Accessed December 2019. http://www.seosavvy.com/blog/content-marketing-yore-jell-o-story/.

Sherman, Erik. "20 Years of Amazon's Expansive Evolution." CBSnews.com. July 15, 2015. Accessed January 2020. https://www.cbsnews.com/news/20-years-of-amazons-expansive-evolution/.

Siu, Eric. "We Break Down B2B vs. B2C Marketing." HubSpot. September 7, 2015. Last modified October 29, 2019. Accessed January 2020. http://blog.hubspot.com/marketing/b2b-b2c-content-marketing#sm.00001mo9w1shu9f5gt6scf901i67j.

Small, Gary, M.D. and Gigi Vorgan. *iBrain: Surviving the Technological Alteration of the Modern Mind* (New York: HarperCollins, 2008). 16.

StatCounter. "Search Engine Market Share Worldwide, May 2019-May2020." GlobalStats. Accessed June 2020. https://gs.statcounter.com/search-engine-market

-share.

Sullivan, Danny. "Google Launches New Effort to Flag Upsetting or Offensive Content in Search." Search Engine Land. March 14, 2017. Accessed February 2020. https://searchengineland.com/google-flag-upsetting-offensive-content-271119.

"Total Number of Websites." InternetLiveStats.com. Accessed December 2020. https://www.internetlivestats.com/total-number-of-websites/.

"The Ultimate List of Marketing Statistics for 2020." HubSpot. Accessed December 2020. https://www.hubspot.com/marketing-statistics.

van Bommel, Edwin, David Edelman, and Kelly Ungerman. "Digitizing the Consumer Decision Journey." McKinsey & Company. June 2014. Accessed February 2020. https://www.mckinsey.com/business-functions/marketing-and-sales/our-insights/digitizing-the-consumer-decision-journey.

Wallace, Mary. "How to Market Successfully in a Digital World? Put Customers' Needs First." Marketing Land. March 1, 2016. Accessed January 2020. https://marketingland.com/technology-took-customers-away-brought-back-166455.

Walters, Dave. *Behavioral Marketing: Delivering Personalized Experiences at Scale* (Hoboken, NJ: Wiley, 2015). 67.

"What Is a Keyword? – Definition & Information." MarketingTerms.com. Accessed January 2020. http://www.marketingterms.com/dictionary/keyword/.

"What Is Content Marketing?" Content Marketing Institute. Accessed January 2020. http://contentmarketinginstitute.com/what-is-content-marketing/.

"'Why?' Dominated the 2020 Google Year in Search." ThinkwithGoogle.com. Accessed December 2020. https://www.thinkwithgoogle.com/consumer-insights/consumer-trends/2020-year-in-search/.

Wikipedia. "Wikipedia: About." En.wikipedia.org. Last modified January 20, 2020. Accessed January 2020. https://en.wikipedia.org/wiki/Wikipedia:About#Strengths.2C_weaknesses.2C_and_article_quality_in_Wikipedia.

Wildhaber, Julie. "Understanding Voice and Tone in Writing." Quick and Dirty Tips. July 1, 2010. Accessed February 2020. https://www.quickanddirtytips.com/education/grammar/understanding-voice-and-tone-in-writing?page=1.

"The Woodward Family." Woodward Memorial Library. Accessed March 2020. http://www.woodwardmemoriallibrary.org/family.php.

Yarrow, Kit. *Decoding the New Consumer Mind: How and Why We Shop and Buy* (San Francisco: Jossey-Bass, 2014). 106.

Zheng, David. "The 15 Second Rule: 3 Reasons Why Users Leave a Website." The Daily Egg. Last modified February 26, 2019. Accessed January 2020. https://www.crazyegg.com/blog/why-users-leave-a-website/.

Index

A/B testing, 340–341
accessibility levels (content types), 278–288
   apps, 286–287
   blogs/articles/web pages, 279
   books, 288
   e-guides, 282–283
   graphics, 280
   infographics, 281
   magazines/catalogs, 287
   online classes/webinars, 285–286
   podcasts, 284–285
   videos, 283–284
   whitepapers, 281–282
aggregate research, 107
Amazon, 55
anchor text, 291
Anderson, Chris, 99, 176, 179
answering questions, 189–190
apps, as content type, 286–287
articles, as content type, 279
attracting customers, 36–38, 80
audience. *see also* customer relationships; customers
   emotional needs, 116–121
   psychological needs, 123–125
   top-level, 103–104
audience engagement. *see* user engagement
audience grouping. *see also* personas
   in content strategy development, 99–103, 247–248
   factors in, 107–109
   nursing school example, 109–112
   Search Cycle and, 143–150
audience research
   methods of, 105–107
   nursing school example, 109–112
   for personas, 130–131, 135–136
   Search Cycle and, 142
average ranking position, 342–343
average time on page, 347
awareness stage (Search Cycle), 46
   audience grouping, 143–144
   content strategy for, 223–224

B2B (business to business), 103–104
B2C (business to consumer), 104
backlinks, 349
banner ads, 25
Bayes, Thomas, 187
Blodgett, Renee, 369
blogs, as content type, 279
blueprints for content, 303–307
Blumberg, Matt, 12
books, as content type, 288
boring content, 316
"boring" industries, content for, 324
bounce rate, 348
brain, Internet's effect on, 30
brand authority, 53
brand awareness, 53, 59, 85
brand identity, 53, 58
brand image, 59
brand recognition, 59
brands
   consistency, 65–72
   expanding, 134

brands (*cont.*)
    online authority, building, 61–63
    online experience of, 56–58
    vision statement, 322–323
    voice of, 320–322
Burrus, Daniel, 370
business objectives
    content strategy and, 84–86, 258–260
    defined, 258
    evaluating keywords, 217–220
    in keyword research, 194–195, 212–213
    nursing school example, 194, 212
    personas and, 133–134
buyer's journey. *see* path to purchase

call-to-action (CTA)
    conversions and, 339
    repurposing content, 364
    SEO with, 294
catalogs, as content type, 287
chat logs, for audience research, 107
clickbait, 315
The Cluetrain Manifesto (Levine, et al.), 75–76, 78
Cohen, Heidi, 20
commitment stage (Search Cycle), 46–47
    audience grouping, 148
    content strategy for, 227–228
community, building, 65–66
competitor analysis, 244–246, 362
connections. *see* customer relationships
consistency
    community, building, 65–66
    cumulative advantage, 66–68
    publishing mindset and, 71–72
    repeatable experiences, 68–71
consumer-decision journey.
    see path to purchase
content
    for "boring" industries, 324
    as conversation, 29–31, 314, 327
    defined, 18–20
    Google guidelines for, 163–166, 315–316, 318
    history of SEO, 43
    platforms for, 289
    poor vs. high quality examples, 311–314
    purpose of, 33
    requirements, 159
    strong content, repurposing, 356–360
    style of, 317–319
    tips for, 325–328
    tracking, 270–274
    value provided by, 4, 79, 80
    weak content, repurposing, 360–366
    what to avoid, 315–317
content audits, 351–353
content blueprints, 303–307
content marketing
    as action inspiring, 26–27
    attracting/keeping customers, 36–38
    customer engagement in, 92–93, 373–375
    defined, 20–22, 29
    emotional needs and, 116–118
    history of, 1–3, 31–33
    as investment, 33–35
    keyword research goals, 189
    in long sales cycles, 4, 40–42
    as permission marketing, 22–24
    principles of, 79–81
    psychological needs and, 123–125
    publishing mindset, 71–72
    as pull marketing, 24–26
    quality, importance of, 86–87
    ROI (return on investment), 82–83
    SEO and, 161–162
    value provided by, 21–22, 26–27, 371–372
content marketing goals, 258, 267
Content Marketing Institute, 21
content optimization. *see* SEO (search engine optimization)
content production goals, 258–259
content production process
    editing and presentation, 308–309
    in-house vs. outsourcing, 298–300
    personas in, 132–133
    preparing content blueprint, 303–307
    prioritizing content topics, 301–303
    search research in, 157–160

INDEX 399

content shift
    conversations and, 75–78
    customer needs and, 81–82
    defined, 8–9, 29, 76
    future of technology, 370–371
    types of shifts, 79–81
content strategy. *see also* documented content strategy
    answering questions, 189–190
    audience grouping, 99–103, 247–248
    brand online experience, 56–58
    business objectives and, 84–86, 258–260
    competitor analysis, 244–246
    conversations and, 79–80, 96–97
    criteria for success, 355–356
    customer relationships in developing, 91–92
    evaluating keyword questions, 215–222
    evergreen content, 242–244
    grouping related questions, 248
    importance of, 9–11
    keyword research in, 187–188
    online authority, building, 59–63
    paid ads, 250–251
    planning, 81
    primary vs. secondary topics, 150–152
    prioritizing keyword questions, 231–239
    search and, 31, 39–51
    for Search Cycle, 223–231
    style guide, 319–320
    tips for, 252
    tools for, 249
    vision statement, 322–323
    voice of brand, 320–322
Content Strategy for the Web (Halvorson and Rach), 323
Content Strategy Template, 264–266
    nursing school example, 268–270
content types by accessibility levels, 278–288
    apps, 286–287
    blogs/articles/web pages, 279
    books, 288
    e-guides, 282–283
    graphics, 280
    infographics, 281
    magazines/catalogs, 287
    online classes/webinars, 285–286
    podcasts, 284–285
    videos, 283–284
    whitepapers, 281–282
conversations
    content as, 29–31, 314, 327
    content strategy and, 79–80, 96–97
    in markets, 75–78
conversions
    criteria for success, 356
    metrics for, 331, 336–341
Cooper, Alan, 130
Cooper, Peter, 2
core keywords, 174–175
    defined, 172
    as head terms, 177
    for keyword research, 195–196
    in long-tail keywords, 177–178, 183
    questions related to, 196–203
core pages
    core keywords and, 175
    defined, 172
    nursing school example, 173
CRO (Conversion Rate Optimization), 249
cross-links
    SEO with, 291–292
    when repurposing content, 360, 364
CTA (call-to-action)
    conversions and, 339
    repurposing content, 364
    SEO with, 294
cumulative advantage, 66–68, 125
customer relationships
    community, building, 65–66
    in content strategy development, 91–92
    conversations in, 75–78
    cumulative advantage, 66–68
    engagement in content marketing, 92–93, 373–375
    humanity in, 96–97
    online authority, building, 61–63
    repeatable experiences, 68–71

customer relationships (cont.)
   target audience, 94
   types of, 94–96
   user engagement, 85
customer service feedback, for audience research, 106
customer surveys, for audience research, 106
customers. *see also* audience; customer relationships; personas
   answering questions, 189–190
   attracting/keeping, 36–38, 80
   audience grouping, 99–103
   feedback from, 349–351
   listening to, 79, 81–82

Dame, Nate, 162
Davis, Andrew, 141
Deere, John, 31–33, 287
demographics, personas vs., 139
difficulty score, 249
Digital Immigrants, 30
Digital Natives, 30
DiPerete, Thomas A., 67
Dude, The, 39, 51, 336
documented content strategy
   content marketing goals, identifying, 267
   Content Strategy Template, 264–266
   importance of, 260–262
   tracking content, 270–274
   writing, 262–266

editing, in content production process, 308–309
editorial calendars, 274
e-guides, as content type, 282–283
Eirich, Gregory M., 67
emotional needs
   connection with, 326
   content marketing and, 116–118
   nursing school example, 118–121
engaging relationships, 93
entrances, 347
Epic Content Marketing (Pulizzi), 274, 278
evaluating keyword questions, 215–222
evaluation stage (Search Cycle), 46

audience grouping, 146–148
   content strategy for, 226–227
evergreen content, 242–244, 301–302
exits, 347–348
expanding
   brands, 134
   content topics, 358–360

false content, 317
feedback from customers, 349–351
filtering
   in keyword research, 202
   searching vs., 157
Five Ws, 196–203
Flanigan, Paul, 93
formatting of posts
   repurposing content, 364
   SEO with, 293
   tips for, 325
The Furrow (magazine), 32
future of technology, 370–371
Future Shock (Toffler), 370

Gevelber, Lisa, 1
Gladwell, Malcom, 12
Godin, Seth, 22
Google
   competitor analysis, 245
   in keyword research, 202–203
   quality content and, 163–166, 315–316, 318
   rankings, 158
   sessions, 346–347
Google Analytics, 333–334, 355
graphics
   as content type, 280
   repurposing content, 364
   SEO with, 294–295
   tips for, 325
GSC (Google Search Console), 333–334
GSC Performance Report, 341–344
guest posting, 357–358

Halvorson, Kristina, 75, 260, 297, 301, 323
Handley, Ann, 308, 311
Harmon, Jeffrey, 169

INDEX

Hax, Arnoldo, 241
Hayzlett, Jeffrey, 9
head terms, 177, 179
history
    of content marketing, 1–3, 31–33
    of SEO, 43
Hopkins, Claude, 122
humanity, in customer relationships, 96–97

images
    as content type, 280
    repurposing content, 364
    SEO with, 294–295
    tips for, 325
implied questions, 222
impressions, tracking, 337, 343
inbound marketing, 24
influencers, 95–96
infographics, as content type, 281
information gathering stage (Search Cycle), 46
    audience grouping, 144–146
    content strategy for, 224–225
informational searches, 48, 179
in-house content production, 298–300
intellectual needs, 117
internal cross-linking
    SEO with, 291–292
    when repurposing content, 360, 364
Internet, effect on brain, 30
interruption marketing, 23–24
investment, content marketing as, 33–35

Jell-O, 1–3
Johnson, Carla, 53, 56

Keyword Explorer (Moz), 191–192
Keyword Magic Tool (SEMrush), 200–201
keyword ranking report, 344–346, 358–360
keyword research
    business goals and, 194–195, 212–213
    in content strategy development, 187–188

core keywords, choosing, 195–196
evaluating keyword questions, 215–222
goals of, 189
outlines from, 303–306
prioritizing keyword questions, 231–239
questions related to core keyword, 196–203
Search Cycle applications, 223–231
search volume, identifying, 203–211
steps in, 193–212
Subject Discovery Template, 197–200, 232–238
time allocation for, 252–253
tips for, 252
tools for, 190–193
keyword stuffing, 316
keywords. *see also* core keywords; long-tail keywords; head terms; mid-tail terms
    defined, 171–172
    directing traffic with, 172
    expanding content topics, 358–360
    importance of choosing, 169–171
    performance metrics, 341–346
    semantic usage, 363
    subheadings and, 363
KPIs (key performance indicators), 332–349
    conversion rate, 336–341
    keyword performance, 341–346
    organic traffic growth, 334–336
    user engagement, 346–349

Lafley, A.G., 67
length of posts, SEO with, 292–293
Levine, Rick, 75, 78
Levitt, Theodore, 92
listening to customers, 79, 81–82
locations of visitors, 348
Locke, Christopher, 75, 78
long sales cycles, 4, 40–42, 104–105
long tail, 177
The Long Tail (Anderson), 176
long-tail keywords, 176–184
    defined, 180

long-tail keywords (*cont.*)
   formation of, 177–178
   targeting, 183–184
   user intent and, 180–182
low search volume, 205

MacLeod, Hugh, 29
magazines, as content type, 287
marketing, defined, 92, 93
Marketing Myopia (Levitt), 92
Marketing Rule of 7, 224
markets, conversations in, 75–78
Martin, Roger L., 67
M.A.S.A. (Measurable, Accessible, Substantial, Actionable), 108
Maslow's Hierarchy of Needs, 116
memorable content, 326
metrics
   content audits, 351–353
   criteria for success, 355–356
   Google Analytics, 333–334
   GSC (Google Search Console), 333–334
   qualitative analysis, 349–351
   quantitative analysis, 332–349
   what to track, 329–332
mid-tail terms, 180
modifiers
   defined, 172, 176
   in long-tail keywords, 177–178, 183
Moz, 157
Moz Keyword Explorer, 191–192

navigational searches, 48
new users, 348
next page path, 349
nonlinear search cycle, 49–51
nonrelevant traffic, 82
nursing school example
   audience grouping, 109–112
   business objectives, 133–134, 194, 212
   content blueprint outlines, 304–306
   Content Strategy Template, 268–270
   core keywords, 174–175
   core pages, 173
   emotional needs, 118–121
   evaluating keywords, 218–219
   organic traffic metrics, 330–331
   personas, 128–130, 137–138
   primary vs. secondary topics, 150–151
   prioritizing keywords, 231–239
   Search Cycle, 143–150
   search volume, 206–211

Odden, Lee, 262, 277, 329
offensive content, 316
one-time customer engagement, 95
ongoing customer relationship, 95
online authority, 84–85
   benefits of, 63
   building, 59–63
   defined, 54–56
online classes, as content type, 285–286
online experience of brands, 56–58
online marketing. *see* search marketing
on-page optimization elements, 290–295
   with call-to-action (CTA), 294
   with cross-links, 291–292
   with formatting of posts, 293
   with images, 294–295
   with length of posts, 292–293
   with titles, 291
optimization. *see* SEO (search engine optimization)
opt-ins, 349
organic search marketing. *see* SEO (search engine optimization)
organic traffic
   criteria for success, 356
   directing to core pages, 172
   increasing, 84
   metrics for, 330–331, 334–336
   paid ads vs., 250–251
   relevant vs. nonrelevant, 82
Outliers (Gladwell), 12
outlines from search research, 303–306
outsourcing content production, 298–300

page paths, 349
page speed, 340, 364–365
page-level organic traffic growth, 336

pages per session, 348
pageviews, 347
paid ads, 7, 147, 250–251
Patel, Sujan, 352–353
path to purchase, 17–18, 44. *see also* Search Cycle
Pepsodent, 122
permission marketing, 22–24
personas
    building, 135–138
    business objectives and, 133–134
    in content production process, 132–133
    in content strategy development, 247–248
    defined, 130–131
    importance of, 138–139
    nursing school example, 128–130, 137–138
    purpose of, 131–132
    Search Cycle and, 143–150
physical needs, 118
planning content strategy, 81
platforms for content, 289
podcasts, as content type, 284–285
presentation, in content production process, 308–309
previous page path, 349
primary topics, in content strategy development, 150–152
prioritizing
    content topics, 301–303
    keyword questions, 231–239
processing fluency, 69–71
promotional content, 317
psychological needs, content marketing and, 123–125
publishing mindset, in content marketing, 71–72
Pulido, Alfonso, 65
Pulizzi, Joe, 39, 257, 270, 274, 278
pull marketing, 24–26
push marketing, 24, 76

qualitative analysis, 349–351
quality content
    checklist, 318
    Google guidelines for, 163–166, 315–316, 318
    importance of, 86–87
    poor vs. high quality examples, 311–314
    reviewing, 364
    style and, 317–319
    style guide for, 319–320
    tips for, 325–328
    what to avoid, 315–317
quantitative analysis, 332–349
    conversion rate, 336–341
    keyword performance, 341–346
    organic traffic growth, 334–336
    user engagement, 346–349
queries, 51
questions
    answering, 189–190
    evaluating keywords, 215–222
    grouping related, 248
    implied, 222
    long-tail keywords as, 180–182
    prioritizing keywords, 231–239
    related to core keyword, 196–203

Rach, Melissa, 260, 297, 301, 323
redundant content, 317
related topics, 362
relationships. *see* customer relationships
relevant topics, 362–363
relevant traffic, 82
repeatable experiences, 68–71
repurposing
    strong content, 356–360
    weak content, 360–366
researching
    audience. *see* audience research
    keywords. *see* keyword research
retargeting, 25
return visitors, 348
Revella, Adele, 129–130, 135
reviews
    for audience research, 107
    as customer feedback, 349–351
Robbins, Tony, 320–321

Rohrer, Dave, 331–332
ROI (return on investement), 82–83.
    see also metrics
Rose, Robert, 53, 56
Rutter, Kate, 131

sales funnel, complex loop vs., 49–51
Satell, Greg, 188
scheduling content topics, 301–303
Scott, Samuel, 17
scraped content, 315–316
search. see also keyword research; keywords
    categories of, 48
    content strategy and, 31, 39–51
    filtering vs., 157
    implied questions in, 222
    online authority, building, 61
    queries in, 51
search competitors, 362
Search Cycle, 40, 44–48
    audience research and, 142
    awareness stage, 46, 143–144
    commitment stage, 46–47, 148
    content strategy for, 223–231
    conversions and, 339
    evaluating keywords, 221–222
    evaluation stage, 46, 146–148
    funnel vs. loop, 49–51
    information gathering stage, 46, 144–146
    nursing school example, 143–150
    short vs. long sales cycles, 40–42
    support stage, 47–48, 149–150
Search Demand Curve, 178–179
search engine marketing (SEM), 7
search engine optimization.
    see SEO (search engine optimization)
search engines. see also Google
    history of SEO, 43
    operation of, 160–161
    semantic search, 170
search evidence, 151, 358–359
search marketing
    audience grouping, 99–103
    defined, 7

history of SEO, 43
search mindset, 42–43, 80, 157
search rankings, increasing, 85
search research. see also keyword research
    audience grouping, 247–248
    competitor analysis, 244–246
    in content production process, 157–160
    evergreen content, 242–244
    grouping related questions, 248
    outlines from, 303–306
    time allocation for, 252–253
    tips for, 252
    tools for, 249
search strategy, components of, 166
search volume, 177
    evaluating keywords, 220
    in keyword research, 203–211
    low or zero, 205
    nursing school example, 206–211
Searls, Doc, 75
secondary topics, in content strategy development, 150–152
section-level organic traffic growth, 335
segmentation. see audience grouping
SEM (search engine marketing), 7
semantic keyword usage, 363
semantic search, 170
SEMrush, 172, 191, 193
    competitor analysis, 245
    Keyword Magic Tool, 200–201
    keyword ranking report, 344–346
SEO (search engine optimization), 277
    with call-to-action (CTA), 294
    content marketing and, 161–162
    with cross-links, 291–292
    defined, 7
    with formatting of posts, 293
    history of, 43
    with images, 294–295
    with length of posts, 292–293
    on-page optimization elements, 290–295
    SERP and, 161
    with titles, 291
    tools for, 249

SERP (Search Engine Results Page), 160–161, 337
sessions (Google), 346–347
Shewan, Dan, 215
short sales cycles, 40–42, 104–105
Sinek, Simon, 66
site-level organic traffic growth, 335
Sobchak, Walter, 221
social media
   for audience research, 107
   as customer feedback, 350–351
social needs, 117
Sorofman, Jake, 70
Sparktoro, 250
spun content, 315
Stone, Dorian, 65
Strevel, John, 65
strong content, repurposing, 356–360
style, quality content and, 317–319
style guides, importance of, 319–320
subheadings
   keywords and, 363
   related questions as, 248
Subject Discovery Template, 197–200, 232–238
subscribers, 348
support stage (Search Cycle), 47–48
   audience grouping, 149–150
   content strategy for, 228–231

target audience, 94
   factors in, 107–109
   grouping, 99–103
   nursing school example, 109–112
technical issues, effect on search results, 365
technology, future of, 370–371
teeth brushing campaign, 122
thin content, 315
titles
   repurposing content, 363
   SEO with, 291

Toffler, Alvin, 30, 370
Tom's of Maine, 54–55
tools for keyword research, 190–193
tracking
   content, 270–274
   impressions, 337, 343
traffic. *see* organic traffic
transactional searches, 48, 179
trendy content, 317
trust, building, 33–38

Ubersuggest, 192
user engagement, 85, 346–349
user experience, 326, 340
user intent, 180–182

value
   in content, 4, 79, 80
   content marketing and, 21–22, 26–27
videos, as content type, 283–284
vision statements, 322–323
voice of brand, 320–322

Wait, Pearl and May, 2
Wallace, Mary, 81
Walters, Dave, 13, 91, 187, 188, 252
weak content, repurposing, 360–366
web pages, as content type, 279
webinars, as content type, 285–286
website marketing. *see* search marketing
Weinberger, David, 75
whitepapers, as content type, 281–282
Wikipedia, 165–166
Woods, Amy, 355
Woodward, Frank, 1–3
writing content strategy, 262–266

Xtensio, 136

Yarrow, Kit, 96, 115, 123, 127

zero search volume, 205

About the Authors

Mark Hawks is the co-founder of the digital marketing agency SEO Savvy, started in 2007 with his business partner, Jonathan Heinl. With over fifteen years of experience in SEO and digital marketing, Mark enjoys helping businesses improve their strategic content marketing efforts.

Jonathan Heinl is a veteran digital marketing professional and co-founder of SEO Savvy, an organic search marketing agency. Jon has over fifteen years of hands-on experience helping company owners, startups, and internal marketing teams, from a wide range of industries but with most focus on the postsecondary education and finance industries, grow website traffic and revenue through organic search. Prior to co-founding SEO Savvy, he worked in-house as an SEO & Digital Marketing Manager for a leading student finance company.

Made in the USA
Las Vegas, NV
14 December 2023